Gerald Fitzmaurice (1865–1939),
Chief Dragoman of the British
Embassy in Turkey

History of International Relations, Diplomacy, and Intelligence

VOLUME 1

Gerald Fitzmaurice (1865–1939), Chief Dragoman of the British Embassy in Turkey

By

G. R. Berridge

University of Leicester

LEIDEN • BOSTON
2007

This book is printed on acid-free paper.

A Cataloging-in-Publication record for this book is available from the Library of Congress

ISSN 1874-0294
ISBN 978 90-04-16035-4

PRINTED IN THE NETHERLANDS

For Caroline Mullan

CONTENTS

LIST OF ILLUSTRATIONS

The illustrations can be found between Chapters Four and Five.

ACKNOWLEDGEMENTS

I owe a great many debts for assistance with this study, the first of which is to Caroline Mullan. However, I refer to her in the following Prologue so shall say nothing more about her here. I must also single out for special thanks Keith Hamilton and Thomas Otte, both of whom not only gave me advice as I went along but did me the great service of criticising the manuscript in draft, thereby saving me from more than one ill-considered judgement and error of fact. Any that remain are of course my own responsibility. My wife, Sheila, was also of enormous assistance, especially in helping me to sift through interminable Foreign Office general correspondence files. Among others who helped me to develop the project, some of whom may have done so without realising it, I must mention John W. Young, Esin and Nuri Yurdusev, Sinan Kuneralp, Fr. Seán P. Farragher CSSp, Torsten Riotte, Markus Mösslang, Dietmar Grypa, Alex May, David Barchard, Ömer Tecimer, Heiner Gillmeister, John A. FitzMaurice, Secil Karal Akgun, Spencer Mawby, Derek Aldcroft, Sue Smith, and not least my son, William, currently a post-graduate student in the History Department at the University of Durham. I wish also to thank the staff of the various archives in which I have worked, especially at Churchill College Cambridge, the National Archives at Kew, the Middle East Centre Archives at St. Antony's College Oxford, Somerset County Archives, and Hull University Archives. Mark Maynard was a great help in producing the maps and tweaking some of the illustrations, as was Simon Kear; and Claire Knight gave me excellent advice on copyright permissions. Finally, I must mention Hylke Faber of Martinus Nijhoff, together with his reader, who with amazing speed and efficiency came to my rescue when I. B. Tauris, with whom the book was originally to be published, kindly released me from my contract when it became clear that my early completion of the manuscript made it a practical impossibility for them to bring it out as soon as my revised plans required.

For financial assistance with the research for this book, I would like to thank first of all the Nuffield Foundation, which gave me a generous grant for the pilot stage of my British Embassy in Turkey project, of which this biography is a spin-off. I am also very grateful to the

British Academy, which more recently gave me a grant specifically for this book.

For permission to reproduce material under copyright, I wish to thank Blackrock College, Dublin (the photographs of the young Fitzmaurice and the French College, and the photograph of Fitzmaurice used on the cover); Sir Tatton Sykes (the two cartoons drawn by Sir Mark Sykes, now held by Hull University Archives in DDSY (2), 1/2f/41 and 1/15); and Churchill Archives Centre, Churchill College, Cambridge (the photographs of the young George Lloyd and of Fitzmaurice with the musician, both located in The Papers of Lord Lloyd of Dolobran, GLLD 3/5). The photograph of Sir Nicholas O'Conor was taken by the company of Joseph Elliott (d. 1903) and Clarence Fry (d. 1897). The remaining photographs are by unknown photographers and are in any case similarly presumed to be in the public domain. I must nevertheless acknowledge that, with the exception of the photograph of Hugo Marinitch and his Slave Department (which I discovered in Waugh, *Turkey*), these all appear in Pears, *Forty Years in Constantinople*. (Should any photographs used prove not to be in the public domain I stand ready to make appropriate arrangements at the first opportunity.) For allowing me to quote from the Gertrude Bell papers at www.gerty. ncl.ac.uk/, I wish to express my gratitude to the Special Collections and Archives Librarian, Robinson Library, University of Newcastle upon Tyne. Last but by no means least, for permission to quote from the private correspondence of Gerald Fitzmaurice, other than that in Crown copyright (waived since 1999), I must give a special word of thanks to Mrs Máirín Benson.

G. R. B., Leicester, February 2007

ABBREVIATIONS USED IN THE FOOTNOTES

ABC Diary   Diary of the Aden Boundary Commission
AR   Annual Report of the British Embassy in Turkey [e.g. 'AR 1907']
ASC Dur.   Archives and Special Collections, Durham University
BCA   Blackrock College Archives, Co. Dublin
BD   *British Documents on the Origins of the War 1898–1914*, ed. by G. P. Gooch and Harold Temperley (HMSO: London)
CAC Cam.   Churchill Archives Centre, University of Cambridge
FO   Foreign Office
FO List   *The Foreign Office List and Diplomatic and Consular Year Book*
GBP   The Gertrude Bell Papers, Robinson Library Special Collections, University of Newcastle upon Tyne www.gerty.ncl.ac.uk/
GDD   *German Diplomatic Documents, 1871–1914*, selected and translated by E. T. S. Dugdale, vol. IV, *The Descent to the Abyss, 1911–1914* (Methuen: London, 1931)
HUA   Hull University Archives
IO   India Office
IOL   India Office Library (British Library, London)
MECA Oxf.   Middle East Centre Archives, St. Antony's College, Oxford
ODNB   *Oxford Dictionary of National Biography*, Oxford University Press, online ed., May 2006 [http://www.oxforddnb.com/view/article/…]
Parl. Debs. *The Parliamentary Debates* (Official Report). United Kingdom of Great Britain & Ireland (HMSO: London)
RNVR   Royal Naval Volunteer Reserve
SCA   Somerset County Archives, Taunton
S of S   Secretary of State for India
TNA   The National Archives, London (formerly the 'Public Record Office')

GLOSSARY OF TURKISH WORDS, INCLUDING ABBREVIATIONS USED IN FITZMAURICE'S LETTERS

A.H.	Sultan Abdul Hamid II
Amb.	Ambassador
Bash Tilki	Chief Dragoman or 'Chief Fox'
CUP	Committee of Union and Progress
G.V.	Grand Vizier
Elchi	The ambassador
H.M.E.	His Majesty's Embassy
iradé	a formal decree of the sultan
kaimakam	deputy governor or governor of an Ottoman sub-district
M.F.A.	Minister [not Ministry] of Foreign Affairs
O'C.	Sir Nicholas O'Conor
Porte	The Ottoman administration
tel.	telegram
tilki	fox
vali	provincial governor
vilayet	Ottoman province
yavri	cub

PROLOGUE

At the end of the 1990s I commenced an ambitious project to write a history of the British Embassy in Turkey from its establishment in 1583 until the present day. I did a great deal of work on this but other things came up, including the offer to be the Associate Editor on the *Oxford* [then *New*] *Dictionary of National Biography* (*ODNB*) with responsibility for 20th Century diplomatists. I accepted this and among the essays I sought to commission was one on Gerald Henry Fitzmaurice, whom I had discovered to have the reputation for being the real power in the British Embassy in Constantinople before the First World War. Fitzmaurice had as yet no biographer, as the late Professor Elie Kedourie had lamented in an article in the journal *Middle Eastern Studies* in 1971, so there was no obvious candidate for authorship. Casting around also failed to turn up anyone willing and able to do it.

By this time Fitzmaurice had also started to interest me for another reason. He was a classic example of an important kind of diplomatist that I had come to think was too neglected by scholars, namely, what the *ancien regime* called a 'Minister of the Second Order'. In the late seventeenth century Abraham de Wicquefort had written a short chapter on such ministers in his landmark work *L'Ambassadeur et Ses Fonctions* and, having been one himself, remarked naturally enough that "princes would be more inconvenienced from the want of these ministers than from that of ambassadors". However, despite the prejudice, I found the argument convincing: not having the *'full* representative capacity' relative to his sovereign that was the burden of his ambassador, a minister of the second order could take risks in pursuit of intelligence and influence that his chief could not. But diplomatic historians have been mesmerised by ambassadors, Wicquefort's 'comedians'. Not surprisingly, there is no biography of Wicquefort himself. Moreover, despite the libraries of books that have been written about the great Niccolò Machiavelli, another minister of the second order, relatively little has been written about his diplomatic career. Even his diplomatic despatches—despite the fact that they contain the earliest expression of some of his key ideas, as Quentin Skinner has pointed out—have only once been translated into English and that was in the late nineteenth century by a (very gifted) German-American railroad surveyor and engineer. In short, with these thoughts in my mind, I concluded that a study of Gerald Fitzmaurice might also throw light on a neglected question of more general significance in the history of diplomacy. In the end, therefore, I decided to write the article on him for the *ODNB* myself—and hence eventually the present full-length biography.

I soon discovered, of course, that one of the reasons why there was no biography of Fitzmaurice—as no doubt of the many other shadowy but influential figures in diplomacy—was that he left no collection of his own papers and refused to write his memoirs. Nevertheless, it turned out that he was a great writer of private letters and memoranda, as also drafter of ambassadorial despatches, and many of these I was able to locate without great difficulty at The National Archives in London. However, it was at the Churchill Archives Centre at Cambridge that I gained the most valuable insight into his mind and the ups and downs of his extraordinary career. The papers located there of Sir Nicholas O'Conor, who was British Ambassador in Constantinople from 1898 until his death ten years later, and above all of George Lloyd (later Lord Lloyd of Dolobran), whom Fitzmaurice first met when he arrived at the Embassy as an honorary attaché in late 1905, contain a wealth of Fitzmaurice's private letters. The letters to George Lloyd, which number over 50 and go strong up to 1910, are particularly full and frank. The hand-writing is sometimes difficult but digital photography made it possible for me to understand and transcribe them reasonably easily, and perhaps one day I shall publish them separately. Of course, the fact that Fitzmaurice left no papers of his own means that I was able to locate very few letters written *to* him, and this remains a weakness of this study because obviously it was not always possible to deduce from his own letters what they contained.

I was also lucky to find that Fitzmaurice's old school, originally the French College, now Blackrock College, Co. Dublin, not only has archives going back to the nineteenth century but an archivist—and what an archivist! On being approached for help, Caroline Mullan, despite being unwell at the time, at once showed enormous enthusiasm for my project. On recovering she threw herself into helping me document Fitzmaurice's family history and school and university career with an energy, resourcefulness, and tenacity that was quite exceptional and—in the inroads it made into her private time—well above and beyond the call of professional duty. Tramping through graveyards, queuing at Joyce House in Dublin, making endless phone calls, email-ing all and sundry, surfing the web for sites she thought might interest me, she often left me speechless with gratitude. Fitzmaurice's family background was murky and without her help the first part of Chapter 1 could not have been written. It was also she who discovered the memoir by Bridget Boland on which I lean heavily in the Epilogue, so I owe a good part of that to her as well. It is because of these and other great debts I owe her that I have dedicated this book to Caroline Mullan.

It will soon be apparent to the reader that I have chosen to use the spelling of proper names that was current in the Foreign Office and among British diplomatists and consular officers in the Ottoman Empire at the time of my study. Hence 'Constantinople' rather than 'Istanbul', 'Ortakeui' rather than 'Ortaköy', 'Adrianople' rather than 'Edirne', 'Moslem' rather than 'Muslim', and so on. I make no apologies for this. This is a study of British diplomacy in Turkey and not of Ottoman history, so it would be historically anachronistic to do otherwise.

Gerald Henry Fitzmaurice has long been an elusive character in the pages of British diplomatic history. Fittingly, therefore, we find Dorina Lady Neave referring to him in her memoirs as 'George Fitzmaurice' and, in his *Life of Lord Lloyd*, Colin Forbes Adams describing him as 'R. G. Fitzmaurice'. In his comparatively recent *Aden Under British Rule*, R. J. Gavin introduces him as 'Captain Fitzmaurice'—though he never had even honorary military rank—while in his own memoirs no less an authority at the time than Valentine Chirol gave him another title that he never had: 'Oriental secretary'. Most played safe and referred to him, with the formality of the times, simply as 'Mr. Fitzmaurice'. I hope that this book goes some way to making this man less elusive and to show that he justified the title given to him at the end of his career by those who knew something of what he had done: 'Fitzmaurice of Constantinople'.

MAPS

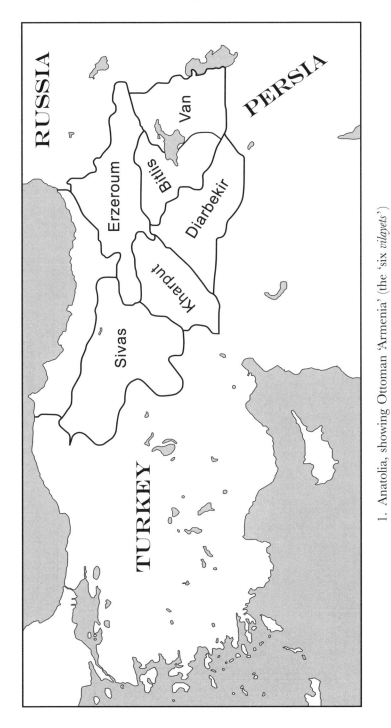

1. Anatolia, showing Ottoman 'Armenia' (the 'six *vilayets*')

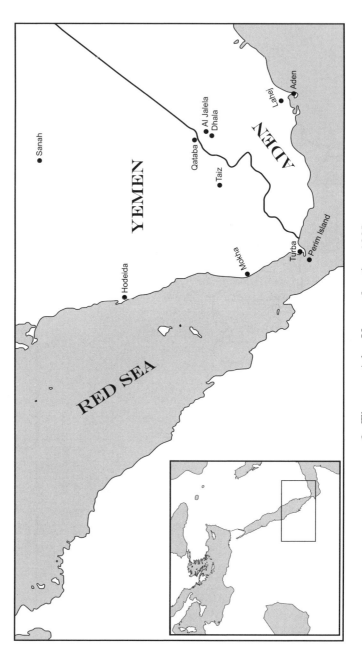

2. The new Aden-Yemen frontier, 1905

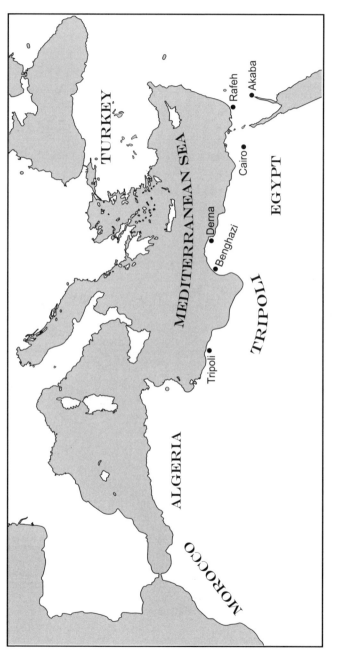

3. Tripoli in Barbary

4. The Balkans, 1915

CHAPTER ONE

NEARLY A PRIEST, 1865–91

Gerald Henry Fitzmaurice was born on 15 July 1865 in Howth Town in Ireland. Located on the north side of the peninsula forming the northern side of Dublin Bay, Howth had a harbour that had been Dublin's chief packet-station earlier in the nineteenth century. However, at the time of Gerald's birth, it was little more than a fishing village, though the isthmus itself was already on its way to becoming the playground of the capital and home to various Dublin magnates.

Gerald's father, Henry Fitzmaurice, was a native of the village of Duagh in County Kerry and a member of the Catholic branch of the vastly wealthier Petty-Fitzmaurice family, the head of which was the Protestant landowner, the Marquess of Lansdowne.[1] Henry was a commercial agent specializing in tea. Gerald's mother, whom Henry married in 1863, was Margaret McKenny, a member of a large and relatively prosperous family long established in Howth, with interests in the public house and hotel business, land, and construction. After his marriage, Henry moved to Dublin, where he entered into a partnership that operated from Fownes Street, which was lined with handsome buildings and located in the important commercial district of Dublin known as Temple Bar. Perhaps prompted by the business interests of his wife's family, in the early 1870s Henry Fitzmaurice also began to deal in French wine. Gerald was the second of at least five children, the first being his only brother.

Intended priest

Since Gerald Fitzmaurice came from a middle class Catholic family with business connections in France and a tradition of providing their

---

[1] *The Times*, 24 Mar. 1939, Obituary: Mr. G. H. Fitzmaurice. On the Petty-Fitzmaurices, Lord Newton, *Lord Lansdowne: A Biography* (Macmillan: London, 1929), pp. 1–4; Hugh Cecil, *Lord Lansdowne* (FCO: London, 2004).

sons with a good education,[2] his first destination was hardly surprising. He was sent to the French College, a fee-paying college at Blackrock, on the south side of Dublin Bay.

The French College, or Blackrock College as it was known after the end of the nineteenth century,[3] was established in 1860 by *Père* Jules Leman. Jesuit-trained, Leman was a member of the Congregation of the Holy Ghost and of the Immaculate Heart of Mary, a Paris-based Catholic order whose members were more usually referred to as the Holy Ghost Fathers—today, the Spiritans.[4] The chief purpose of the college was to find aspirants to the order—scholastics—and train them for missionary work in English-speaking Africa. Except for sharing classes with the lay students, the scholastics were completely segregated from them and subjected to a special religious regime. In the scholasticate they found themselves in the hands of a director whose duty was to train them in "habits of order, obedience and self-denial, to wean them from worldliness, to foster in them love for the priesthood, and ambition to serve the Church as Missioners".[5] In order to ensure that their instruction was undiluted and to prepare them for the long periods of isolation of the missionary's life, only in exceptional circumstances were they allowed home during the holidays. When a scholastic, after some years in the college, was thought to show a real vocation for the priesthood, he was allowed to wear the *soutane*. The parents of scholastics did not pay fees.

---

[2] At this period, less than one per cent of Catholics and only about seven per cent of Protestants in Dublin received any education beyond the primary level, Mary E. Daly, *Dublin: The Deposed Capital—A social and economic history, 1860–1914* (Cork University Press: Cork, 1985), p. 136. Nevertheless, in the previous twenty years the McKennys had sent two sons to the school run by the Benedictine monks at Ampleforth in Yorkshire. Information kindly supplied by the archivist of Ampleforth College.

[3] It continued to be known locally as 'the French College' until the end of the nineteenth century, even though its distinctive French system of education had been effectively extinguished by the end of the 1870s. Notable alumni of the twentieth century included Eamon de Valera and Bob Geldof. Except where indicated, the following account is based on Seán P. Farragher CSSp, *Père Leman (1826–1880): Educator and Missionary, Founder of Blackrock College* (Paraclete Press: Dublin and London, 1988); and Seán P. Farragher CSSp and Annraoi Wyer, *Blackrock College, 1860–1995* (Paraclete Press: Blackrock, Dublin, 1995).

[4] The Congregation Sancti Spiritus (CSSp) had its origins in the early eighteenth century and by Leman's time was, with the assistance of government patronage and Vatican endorsement, the chief supplier of missionaries to the French colonies.

[5] BCA, Fr. Laurence Healy, *History of Blackrock College 1860–1910*, unpublished mss., p. 138.

For financial and political reasons, the pragmatic Leman, however, was also anxious to attract the patronage of Catholic families who wanted their boys to have other careers. As a result, the college offered a general liberal education as well, and emphasis was placed on the humanities in general and languages in particular.[6] Leman was naturally anxious to suppress any outward show of extreme Irish nationalist ('Fenian') sentiment among his students but his own sympathies were clearly with the moderate Irish nationalists and it would be surprising if support for the Fenians themselves did not remain at least an undercurrent in the college.[7]

Assisted by its affiliation in 1862 to the struggling Catholic University, the French College was soon noted for the exceptional academic attainments of its students, and it expanded rapidly. In 1875 the college created a civil service department devoted to preparing students for the entrance examinations introduced for the Civil Service five years earlier; discipline remained strict and religious practice and instruction regular. Not long after this a university college was grafted on to the civil service department and in 1881 had great success with its candidates in the first examinations of the newly formed Royal University of Ireland. This represented attainment of a principle long sought by Leman: the ability of the French College "to prepare its students for university degrees without their having to attend any outside establishment".[8] What course did Fitzmaurice take through this remarkably self-contained institution, and how did he perform?

Coming from the other side of Dublin Bay, it was inevitable that when Fitzmaurice entered the French College in 1876, aged ten, he would be a boarder. This was just as well, for his mother had succumbed to tuberculosis over two years earlier, aged only 32, and his father—possibly an alcoholic—died in 1881.[9] When Fitzmaurice entered

---

[6] German, Italian and Spanish were offered, in addition to Latin, Greek and English. As for French, fluency in this was essential for a clerical student since it was the mother tongue of the Holy Ghost Fathers.

[7] Farragher, *Père Leman*, pp. 196, 214, 222, 298–300, and esp. pp. 306–7.

[8] Farragher and Wyer, *Blackrock College 1860–1995*, p. 67. The RUI was established in 1879 and significantly improved the opportunities for Catholics to obtain university degrees. It was an examining body rather than a campus university.

[9] Information kindly obtained by Caroline Mullan from Joyce House, Dublin. Henry died of cirrhosis of the liver.

the French College he was already living at his grandfather's modest hotel, the Royal, in Howth.[10]

Gerald Fitzmaurice was an outstanding pupil, showing a particular talent for languages, especially Latin, Italian, French, and Greek, and latterly winning exhibitions and a scholarship.[11] But despite all of this secular success, it seems likely that until at least shortly after he obtained his degree in 1887, Fitzmaurice remained set on becoming a priest.

Only a year after his entry to the college and still only 11 years old, he had transferred to the scholasticate, and remained in this special religious section until the end of his intermediate schooling. In 1882 he had been permitted to don the *soutane*, and he continued to wear this throughout his educational career.[12] Like most other graduates of the scholasticate, Fitzmaurice was also a junior master during his last two years in the university college, "a normal part of the training for the priesthood" and valuable for those who had to take charge of mission schools.[13] Why, then, some time shortly after graduating did he abandon his training for the priesthood and apply to become a student interpreter in the Levant Consular Service?

Since Fitzmaurice left no papers recording his thoughts at this time we are forced to rely on informed guesswork. Obviously, his great gift for languages must have been a strong factor. The Levant Service had been created ten years earlier[14] and, in contrast to the position with regard to clerks for the Foreign Office and attachés for the Diplomatic Service, selection for it was by open, competitive examination.[15] Moreover, these particular examinations had been among those for which the civil service department of the French College had been coaching students at least since 1881. Earlier students of the college had also embarked

---

[10] The Royal Hotel survives today as the two-star Baily Court Hotel.

[11] BCA, Fr. Laurence Healy, *History of Blackrock College 1860–1910* and the *Statistics Book*. As an exhibitioner and medallist between 1880 and 1883, Fitzmaurice's name litters the pages of these house publications.

[12] Information kindly supplied to the author by Fr. Farragher.

[13] Farragher and Wyer, *Blackrock College 1860–1995*, p. 278.

[14] Unless otherwise indicated, references to the origins and work of the Levant Consular Service are based on D. C. M. Platt, *The Cinderella Service: British Consuls since 1825* (Longman: London, 1971), ch. 4.

[15] 'Competitive' meant that there should be more than one candidate for each position; 'open' meant that candidates were not sifted by the need for prior nomination by the secretary of state. Arguing the singular sensitivity of its work, the FO resisted for longer than any other government department the trend at this time towards open examinations, Ray Jones, *The Nineteenth Century Foreign Office: An administrative history* (Weidenfeld and Nicolson: London, 1971), pp. 45–54.

on successful consular careers and no doubt served as models. There is, however, a further possibility: it would have been particularly easy for Fitzmaurice to square with his conscience giving up the priesthood for the *Levant* Consular Service. This is because during the Bulgarian crisis in 1876, the very year in which Fitzmaurice entered the French College, the great Liberal Party figure, W. E. Gladstone, had stirred up considerable moral outrage against the treatment of Christians in the much reduced though still sizeable Ottoman Empire. And the Levant Service was the chief instrument whereby the sultan was to be kept to his promises of future good behaviour made at the Congress of Berlin in 1878.

British consuls at remote outposts in the Ottoman Empire might not—unlike the missionary in Africa—have been seeking to convert the heathen to Christianity, but they were engaged in another important religious duty. This was protecting from Moslem violence those already converted, and—as we shall see—helping to restore to their faith forced Christian converts to Islam. It was also the duty of the consuls to protect the many missionaries in the Ottoman Empire and support their work.[16] Since consular work of this kind also involved long periods of isolation in difficult climates and a sometimes hostile environment, it was in this way, too, the kind of work for which missionaries themselves were trained at the French College at Blackrock. In short, Fitzmaurice's decision to abandon the priesthood and apply for the prestigious Levant Service, while it was certainly a change of direction, was not a change that was quite as radical as might at first sight appear.

Change of direction

The Levant consuls had formed an enclave within the General Consular Service ever since 1825, when the British government had taken over the network of consuls in the Ottoman Empire supported by the Levant Company. However, since their political tasks were thought to be more sensitive and important after mid-century, it had been finally decided in the late 1870s to reform their haphazard system of recruitment and training and generally put them on a firmer foundation. It

---

[16] Jeremy Salt, *Imperialism, Evangelism and the Ottoman Armenians, 1878–1896* (Cass: London, 1993).

had also been decided to rely in future on 'natural-born' British subjects. Promising candidates would be trained in oriental languages at the public expense, and thus would the existing need to rely uneasily on 'Levantines'—Ottoman subjects of European extraction—fall away.[17]

Candidates for the new service were to be aged between 18 and 24, unmarried, and to be of sufficiently robust health and physique to endure the rigours of life in the East. They were to be examined in handwriting, orthography, "reading aloud", arithmetic, English composition, French, and Latin, and could also offer themselves for examination in Ancient Greek, Italian, and German.[18] Since the modern languages had to be passed at "a very fair standard" it is clear that these examinations were designed to seek out men who had either been able to spend some years abroad or possessed special linguistic talents.

Successful candidates were to be sent directly to Constantinople, where they were to be placed under the authority of the British Ambassador and attend for two years at a modest school staffed by native teachers. The spot chosen for this establishment was Ortakeui, a village on the European side of the Bosphorus about three miles from the embassy in Pera; such a distance, it was thought, would prevent the students from being distracted by "the charms of the city".[19] Superintended by the senior second secretary at the embassy, who usually had a smattering of Turkish himself, they were to study Turkish, Arabic, Persian, modern Greek, and Bulgarian[20]—and also Moslem law. Having proved their competence in these subjects by further examinations, the student interpreters were then to be appointed to vice-consulates and ultimately to the more important consular posts in the Ottoman Empire, Persia, Morocco, and Greece. The dragomanates of diplomatic and consular

---

[17] David Morray, "The selection, instruction and examination of the student interpreters of the Levant Consular Service, 1877–1916", in J. F. Healey and V. Porter (eds.), *Studies on Arabia in Honour of Professor G. Rex Smith* (Oxford University Press: Oxford and New York, 2002). On British attitudes to Levantines, see G. R. Berridge, "Nation, Class, and Diplomacy: The Diminishing of the Dragomanate of the British Embassy in Constantinople, 1810–1914", in Markus Mösslang and Torsten Riotte (eds), *Outsiders in the Diplomats' World* (Oxford University Press for the German Historical Institute London: Oxford, forthcoming).

[18] TNA, Student Dragomans, FO, July 31, 1877, FO83/1486.

[19] TNA, Lowther to White 26 May 1890, FO78/4281.

[20] Only those students destined for service in Bulgaria were required to study Bulgarian, at least from 1879, Sir Robert Graves, *Storm Centres of the Near East* (Hutchinson: London, 1933), pp. 17, 29.

missions would also be desirable destinations for them, and eventually they would replace all of the native 'dragomans', the name given to the subjects of the sultan who served as interpreters and intermediaries between Europeans diplomatists and Ottoman officials.[21] The first examinations under this new scheme had been held in August and September 1877 and the first students arrived at the school at Ortakeui in November. They included Adam Block, himself destined to be chief dragoman at the British Embassy in Constantinople and subsequently a dangerous political rival to Fitzmaurice. Another was Justin Alvarez, with whom he was destined to have a delicate encounter in Tripoli in the winter of 1911–12.

By the time that Fitzmaurice sat the exams for student interpreterships, therefore, in late January 1888, the Levant Service was ten years old and 25 students had passed and gone on to the school at Ortakeui. The conditions for eligibility remained identical, and only a few minor changes in other areas had been made.[22] It was no surprise that Fitzmaurice, now aged 22 and unmarried—as he was to remain for the rest of his life—offered himself for examination in the optional as well as obligatory subjects. Out of 26 candidates he was ranked fourth overall,[23] but must have thought that he had just failed to gain a position when the results were first announced in late February. This is because at this stage only three situations were available, and on 10 March the three candidates above him were formally appointed. However, a decision was then taken to have a fourth student interpreter and two days later Fitzmaurice was deemed to have passed. His appointment, however, was delayed until 30 June.[24]

---

[21] TNA, Student Dragomans, FO, July 31, 1877, FO83/1486. The word 'dragoman' was a corruption of the Ottoman Turkish word for an interpreter: *tercüman*. The dragomanate (French: *drogmanat*) was the dragomans' section of a mission.

[22] TNA, Lowther to White, 12 May 1890, FO78/4281; see also papers in CS10/27 and T1/17127.

[23] His results were: Arithmetic 168/300, Orthography 175/200, Handwriting 120/200, English Composition 145/200, French 389/600, Latin 335/400, Ancient Greek 282/400, Italian 193/300, German 200/300, and Spanish 164/300. Only five candidates in all passed with a total of 2000 marks or more, TNA, CSC10/555.

[24] *FO List.*

Star student interpreter

When Fitzmaurice arrived in Ortakeui in summer 1888, he found a curriculum that had changed significantly from that of 1877. In addition to Turkish—the only language for which there was an oral examination and the emphasis on which was now generally greater—he was required to study Russian, Arabic, and Law.[25] To assist their legal studies, the students had to attend twice a week at the chambers in Galata of a local British barrister and part-time newspaper correspondent, Edwin Pears.[26] A man of strong liberal convictions and great moral courage, Pears had settled in Constantinople in 1873, and was now an important figure in the British community. In 1876 it was his letters to the *Daily News* that had first exposed the atrocities in Bulgaria on which Gladstone built his famous campaign, and since 1881 he had been president of the consular bar. Albert Wratislaw, who was at Ortakeui in the mid-1880s, subsequently wrote that "Mr Pears took an immense amount of trouble in preparing us for our future magisterial duties, and it would be difficult to overestimate the benefit we derived from his lectures".[27] Should Fitzmaurice pass the exams at the end of his two years, he could also look forward to an immediate improvement in his status and income. This was because in 1879 the foreign secretary, Lord Salisbury, had persuaded the Treasury to advance successful student interpreters to the rank of 'Assistant', with an increase in salary to £300.[28]

Fitzmaurice must have thought the omens favourable. Salisbury, who had early promoted the new scheme for student interpreters, was not only foreign secretary once more but also prime minister. Even more encouraging, the new student interpreter's more immediate master in the Turkish capital, Sir William White, who had been ambassador since 1885, was a diplomatist of the highest reputation—"the greatest British Ambassador since Stratford Canning", according to Harold

---

[25] MECA Oxf., Hallward Diary, Feb. 1, 1888, GB 165–0132.
[26] Platt, *The Cinderella Service*, p. 168.
[27] *A Consul in the East* (Blackwood: Edinburgh and London, 1924), p. 5.
[28] They also appear to have been given an allowance for lodgings while waiting for a posting, though they were usually pressed into service as soon as possible, TNA, FO to Treasury, 26 July 1879, T1/17127; FO to Treasury, 24 Sept. 1879, T1/17127; Layard to Salisbury, 2 Nov. 1879, T1/17127; and Salisbury to Layard, 26 Nov. 1879, T1/17127.

Nicolson.[29] No doubt of equal interest to Fitzmaurice, White was a devout Roman Catholic and the first member of this church to become a British ambassador since the Reformation.[30] He had also started his career as a consular officer. The chief dragoman in the embassy was Sir Alfred Sandison, a man who personified the transitional stage of the dragomanate at that time—he had been born and brought up in Turkey but his father was British. As for the superintendent of student interpreters, this was Gerard Lowther, who had been at the embassy since 1884 and was later to be ambassador himself. Like most of the other superintendents, he had a little Turkish.

What life did Fitzmaurice lead at Ortakeui? It was probably one that he found enjoyable as well as stimulating, even though the students were housed in an old wooden building that had no garden, a poor location, and was infested with bugs.[31] The regime was not a strict one and the locally-employed teachers were in general amiable and scholarly, if not in general gifted pedagogues. Though it was only occasionally that the students were permitted to join the social life of the embassy, the proximity of the alluring Bosphorus meant that the opportunities for other recreational activities were great. In consequence, a few students did not advance much at Ortakeui but those who were keen to learn could do so. They did this by interrogating their teachers; if necessary, by hiring additional ones at their own expense; and by practising at least their Turkish and modern Greek in the environs of the school and in Constantinople itself.[32] Donald Mackenzie Wallace, who was the correspondent of *The Times* in Constantinople from 1878 until 1884 and held a low opinion of the linguistic abilities of British

---

[29] Harold Nicolson, *Portrait of a Diplomatist: Being the life of Sir Arthur Nicolson First Lord Carnock, and a study of the origins of the Great War* (Houghton Mifflin: Boston and New York, 1930), p. 60.

[30] Sir Edwin Pears, *Forty Years in Constantinople: The recollections of Sir Edwin Pears 1873–1915* (Herbert Jenkins: London, 1916), p. 137; Colin L. Smith, *The Embassy of Sir William White at Constantinople, 1886–1891* (Oxford University Press: London, 1957), p. 5.

[31] Wratislaw, *A Consul in the East*, p. 9.

[32] Adern G. Hulme-Beaman, *Twenty Years in the Near East* (Methuen: London, 1898), pp. 2–3, 21–2; Graves, *Storm Centres of the Near East*, pp. 16–17; Wratislaw, *A Consul in the East*, pp. 3–11; and evidence of Halil Halid Efendi and Walter Baring, *Treasury Committee on the Organisation of Oriental Studies in London. Minutes of Evidence taken by the Committee*, Cd. 4561 (HMSO: London, 1909) [hereafter *Reay Committee, Minutes of Evidence*], QQ. 2548, 3795–6, 3812–17.

diplomatists in the Near East, thought highly of the educational value of the school at Ortakeui.[33]

Fitzmaurice, of course, was one of the hard-workers at Ortakeui, though he believed that he learned more outside the school than within it.[34] "He differed from most of his colleagues", recalled Pears years later, "by passing a considerable portion of his time in the really Turkish cafés, by which I mean cafés frequented almost exclusively by Turks or Turkish subjects. In that way he acquired a knowledge of colloquial speech which is generally recognised as unsurpassed".[35] Fitzmaurice was regarded as head and shoulders above his three contemporaries and passed out first in the final examinations by a large margin.[36] This was particularly gratifying, Lowther reminded White, "as he began his work at the school two months after the others".[37] Fitzmaurice also commended himself to the superintendent of student interpreters for another—and probably even more important—reason. He was the only one in his group who did *not* exhibit that "extreme nervousness" which, along with poor physique, Lowther regarded as too often the distinguishing feature of the middle and lower-middle class boys who were able to enter the Levant Service through the new system of open competition.[38] This attitude was by no means confined to Lowther. Indeed, it was summed up in a vintage Foreign Office minute on his reflections on the 1888–90 cohort and the student interpreter scheme in general:

> The merits and defects of the system resemble those of the Indian Civil Service under open competition. Many young men of the middle or lower middle class, indefatigable workers in grammar schools, examined at high pressure, obtain appointments: and come out without the moral and physical training of the best public schools, the social habits of the upper classes, or the active habits of country gentlemen.
>
> The natives do not look up to them: they marry early and go about on wheels instead of on horseback, so seeing little of the back country: they have often little bottom and in many cases go off their heads.

---

[33] *Reay Committee, Minutes of Evidence*, QQ. 5453–551.
[34] TNA, min. of Tilley, Nov. 27, 1909, FO369/261.
[35] Pears, *Forty Years in Constantinople*, p. 138.
[36] He scored 1790 out of a possible total of 2300, his nearest rival obtaining 1521. In conversational Turkish, he scored 180 out of 200, exactly twice as many marks as the second placed candidate, TNA, Lowther to White, 12 May 1890, FO78/4281; BCA, Blackrock College, *Prospectus and Annual 1907–8*, p. 54.
[37] TNA, Lowther to White, 12 May 1890, FO78/4281.
[38] TNA, Lowther to White, 26 May 1890, FO78/4281.

> Less exam and book learning: and more saddle and savoir faire would
> serve the state better.[39]

At the beginning of May 1890 Fitzmaurice was duly promoted to the
rank of consular assistant and grabbed by Sir William White to help
him out in the hard-pressed embassy dragomanate.[40] In June the Foreign
Office recommended that he be awarded a prize and the ambassador
happily concurred.[41] Fitzmaurice spent over a year in the dragomanate
in Constantinople, in effect as fifth dragoman or, as Wratislaw, an earlier
junior put it, "bottle-washer to the establishment".[42] He spent his time
translating Turkish documents, and—a most important activity—following up at the Porte to make sure that promised action on some question
had actually been taken. He also obtained the papers needed by British
archaeologists wishing to travel in the interior, smoothed out difficulties
experienced by other British subjects at the Custom House, and so
on—in each case reporting on his action to Sandison or Block, who
was in effect third dragoman. This much is evident from Fitzmaurice's
increasingly numerous reports in the dragomanate memorandum books
in late 1890 and early 1891.[43] No doubt, too, like Wratislaw before him,
he was required to mind the shop during holidays.[44] It was nevertheless
a most useful apprenticeship.

By the time that he was granted his first leave of absence, in the
second half of 1891,[45] Fitzmaurice was 26 years old. On the evidence
of later descriptions and the few photographs remaining in which he
appears, he was short in build but had a large head topped with red
hair. His face was strong and bony with a striking hooked nose, deep-
set blue eyes, and a fashionable, drooping moustache. Though it did
not jar on his listeners, his voice was hoarse, no doubt because he was
a great talker and smoked too many cigarettes.

---

[39] TNA, Sir James Fergusson, Parl. U-Sec., FO, 26 May 1890, FO78/4281.

[40] TNA, Lowther to White 4 May 1890, FO78/4281. By this time it appears to
have been customary for the star student to be placed in the embassy dragomanate,
while—as happened on this occasion—the other Ortakeui graduates were despatched
to the outlying consulates: Sir Telford Waugh, *Turkey: Yesterday, Today and Tomorrow*
(Chapman and Hall's: London, 1930), p. 23; and TNA, FO to White 2 June 1890,
FO78/4281.

[41] This was worth £40, TNA, FO to White 2 June 1890, FO78/4281.

[42] *A Consul in the East*, p. 32.

[43] TNA, FO195/1681, FO195/1716, and FO195/1717.

[44] *A Consul in the East*, pp. 31–3.

[45] TNA, Register of Correspondence, FO566/999. His last memo in the dragomanate is dated 6 July 1891, FO195/1717.

Fitzmaurice was already recognized by the British Embassy in Constantinople as a man of high intelligence and exceptional linguistic skills, hard-working, and resourceful. He also had the self-confidence born of winning prizes throughout his educational career and knowing that he enjoyed the good opinion of the diplomatic staff, though for many years—as a later ambassador noted—he remained socially ill at ease in elevated company. He was fortified by his strong attachment to the Catholic faith, and by circumstance and training was independent of family. Schooled in an atmosphere of moderate Irish nationalism and by teachers who encouraged debate on current affairs, he was also probably politically sophisticated above the average junior in the Levant Service. And yet as a middle class Irishman, as well as a Catholic, it is inevitable that his aspirations for advancement in the service of the British state would have been modest. It is in fact difficult to imagine anyone better suited to a career as interpreter, observer, and political fixer in the polyglot Ottoman Empire, with the formal rank of consular officer rather than diplomatist. However, as the progeny of the scorned system of 'open competition', he yet had to prove to the Foreign Office and the Diplomatic Service that he had some 'bottom', and that, when he was eventually sent into the interior, he would not go off his head. In other words, his real test was about to begin.

CHAPTER TWO

ARMENIA AND CONSTANTINOPLE, 1891–1902

At the end of 1891 Fitzmaurice was sent to eastern Anatolia, a remote region of the Ottoman Empire which abutted the Russian and Persian frontiers. This was peopled heavily by Armenian Christians, and though in none of the six *vilayets* where they were concentrated were they in a majority over their Turkish and Kurdish neighbours, it was often known in the outside world—to the great annoyance of the Turks—as 'Armenia'.[1] Over the next two years Fitzmaurice, covering for officers on leave of absence, served successively in Van, Erzeroum, and Trebizond, and thus gained intimate acquaintance with the problems that were to flare up so tragically at Sasun in 1894. After a brief interlude of more irksome duties in the embassy dragomanate, he was then indulged by promotion to vice-consul at the important consulate-general at Smyrna. However, while he was there, Armenian massacres and forced conversions to Islam reached a peak. This was the immediate background against which, at the beginning of 1896, he was chosen to represent the embassy on the Birejik Commission that was appointed by the sultan, Abdul Hamid II, to inquire into the forced conversions. This was his real baptism, and it made his reputation.

Political consul

Abdul Hamid had been sultan since 1876 and had soon secured control of the machinery of both central and provincial government. He did this by means of an elaborate set up of advisers, enforcers, and bureaucrats at his palace of Yildiz, not the least element of which was

---

[1] William L. Langer, *The Diplomacy of Imperialism, 1890–1902*, 2nd ed. (Knopf: New York, 1951), p. 147; Christopher J. Walker, *Armenia: The Survival of a Nation* (Croom Helm: London, 1980), p. 122; Sir Edwin Pears, *Life of Abdul Hamid* (Henry Holt: New York, 1917), pp. 215–18, 228, 232; Salahi Ramsdan Sonyel, *The Ottoman Armenians: Victims of Great Power Diplomacy* (Rustem: London, 1987), pp. 47–9, 66, 87; Salt, *Imperialism, Evangelism and the Ottoman Armenians, 1878–1896*, p. 54.

a secret police organization which he personally directed.[2] In 1878 he had promised the European powers that he would introduce reforms to ameliorate the condition of his Christian subjects, in particular the Armenians. The powers were to superintend their operation but only Britain showed willing. Finding itself forced to rely on its consuls to goad the *valis* into better ways, the British government even added to their ranks serving officers—'military consuls'. Unfortunately, this experiment had not proved successful, by 1880 it had already been decided to replace them, and it was not long after this before most of the military consuls had been withdrawn.[3] By 1891, then, much if not most of the British responsibility for encouraging reforms in Armenia was located squarely on the shoulders of the Levant Service. Where this task, plus intelligence gathering, was a consul's main duty, as in the eastern *vilayets*, such persons were known as 'political consuls'.[4] It was the ranks of such men that Fitzmaurice now joined.

Though it had been a mark of esteem to be employed in the dragomanate after passing his Ortakeui exams, Fitzmaurice was probably happy to be released. The work of the Constantinople dragomans was not popular with the members of the Levant Service. They were constantly at the beck and call of the senior diplomats and spent much of their time kicking their heels in Ottoman ministries, arguing at the Custom House, being bored out of their minds while observing in the courts, or serving as tour guides to visiting members of the English aristocracy. As a result, they dreamed of escape to one of the embassy's satellite consular posts, where they would have more independence, more leisure, and probably even a higher salary.[5] If escape

---

[2] Stanford J. Shaw and Ezel Kural Shaw, *History of the Ottoman Empire and Modern Turkey, Vol. II* (Cambridge University Press: Cambridge, 1977), pp. 212–20; F. A. K. Yasamee, *Ottoman Diplomacy: Abdülhamid II and the Great Powers 1878–1888* (The Isis Press: Istanbul, 1996), p. 53.

[3] W. N. Medlicott, *The Congress of Berlin and After* (Methuen: London, 1938), chs. 1 and 2; Sonyel, *The Ottoman Armenians*, pp. 30–40; and Andrew Roberts, *Salisbury: Victorian Titan* (Weidenfeld and Nicolson: London, 1999), chs. 10–12. It is important to stress that not all military consuls were removed and the issue of whether or not new ones should be appointed at posts of particular strategic significance (such as Erzeroum and Bitlis) for long remained a live one; see for example TNA, de Bunsen to Salisbury, 5 Sept. 1898, FO195/2007.

[4] Platt, *The Cinderella Service*, pp. 130–5.

[5] As it happened, it was in 1891 that Edward Law, a man of broad commercial and diplomatic experience sent to investigate the working of the consulate-general at Constantinople, drew official attention to the serious implications of this for the dragomanate, Berridge, "Nation, Class, and Diplomacy".

was Fitzmaurice's dream, it is also likely that Armenia was his preferred destination, since those with the best exam results were given greatest liberty of choice among the consular districts where additional men were thought to be needed.[6]

The Levant consuls displayed a strong consensus on the situation in Armenia. They certainly thought the Armenians had good cause for complaint about their treatment. However, they were always sceptical of claims of outrages against them since many were spread by 'paid agitators'. More importantly, they were firmly of the view that retaliatory violence and anti-government propaganda by young and ignorant 'hot-heads' of the Armenian lower classes was not merely wicked but seditious. As for the secret societies behind them,[7] their aim was not, believed the Levant consuls, an armed uprising against the Turkish authorities, which they knew to be hopeless, but to provoke both Turks and predatory Kurds into violent over-reaction. This in turn, the secret societies anticipated, would prompt military intervention on their behalf by the European powers. The result of this would be at worst an autonomous and at best an independent Armenia.

The judgement of the Levant consuls on this strategy, which in general they accurately captured, was harsh—and prescient. With no realistic prospect that it would work, these political 'malignants', whose leaders were based safely abroad, would, they believed, succeed merely in bringing terror and ruin on the heads of all Armenians in Turkey. It was therefore not part of the British consuls' job to discourage the *valis* from catching and punishing severely such persons—providing they got the right ones, gave them a fair hearing, and inflicted penalties proportionate to their crimes. As for their advice to the broad mass of loyal, hard-working Armenians, this was prudence and patience.[8]

---

[6] He had nurtured an early ambition to seek his first posting in Greece but changed his mind after a visit to Athens. The modern Greeks did not live up to the expectations fostered by his classical education, a common enough reaction among British visitors. He also seems to have concluded that Greece was now a political backwater and not a place where great careers were made, BCA, Blackrock College, *Prospectus and Annual 1907–8*, p. 54.

[7] On the *Hunchaks* and the *Dashnaktzutiun*, see Walker, *Armenia*, pp. 129–31; Langer, *The Diplomacy of Imperialism, 1890–1902*, pp. 155–7; and M. S. Anderson, *The Eastern Question, 1774–1923: A study in international relations* (Macmillan: London, 1966), p. 254.

[8] This view is most readily seen in Graves, *Storm Centres of the Near East*, p. 124ff (and in his despatches from Sivas in May 1893 in FO195/1804); and Hulme-Beaman, *Twenty Years in the Near East*, pp. 302–5. See also Walker, *Armenia*, pp. 135–6;

In Turkey's Asiatic provinces there was a British consulate at Trebizond, which supervised a vice-consulate at Samsoun, and another at Erzeroum, which supervised others at Van, Diarbekir, and Kharput. Fitzmaurice was first sent to Van, where he arrived in December 1891 and remained until the middle of the following year. Van was the principal town of the *vilayet* of the same name, which extended along the Persian border from the *vilayet* of Erzeroum in the north to that of Mosul in the south.[9] The town had an Armenian majority led by an educated and relatively worldly elite, and Graves described it later as "probably the most important centre of Armenian nationalist feeling in the Turkish Empire".[10]

In the more remote areas of the Van *vilayet*, where the writ of the Ottoman governor ran only with difficulty, if at all, Armenian peasant farmers were from time to time preyed upon by the nomadic or semi-nomadic Kurdish tribesmen, though in the previous two years there had been nothing on a major scale. The departing vice-consul was optimistic about future developments, and the acting vice-consul at Erzeroum believed that Bahri Pasha, whose appointment as the new *vali* had just been announced, was likely to be an improvement on Khalil Bey, the present holder of the post.[11] It looked as if Fitzmaurice would have a relatively undisturbed period in which to settle into his first post, as indeed proved to be the case.

Fitzmaurice's time in Van was confined largely to political reporting: the arrival of the new governor, Armenian political prisoners, developments across the nearby international frontiers, and cross border raids by Turkish Kurds into Persia and Persian Kurds returning the compliment. While for the most part his despatches were confined to factual reporting and detached political analysis, he did not hesitate to pass judgement—usually in the form of mildly sardonic understatement. For example, in a message to Erzeroum on 6 May 1892, the background to which was Abdul Hamid's recent decision to recruit great numbers of Kurdish tribesmen into regiments of irregular cavalry (the *Hamidiyeh*), he wrote:

Salt, *Imperialism, Evangelism and the Ottoman Armenians, 1878–1896*, ch. 5; and Sonyel, *The Ottoman Armenians*, ch. 4.

[9] H. F. B. Lynch, *Armenia: Travels and Studies*, in 2 volumes (Longmans, Green: London, 1901). Lynch visited Van in 1893 and stayed at the British vice-consulate, which he marks on his 'Plan of Van'; see vol. II, The Turkish Provinces, chap. 4.

[10] *Storm Centres of the Near East*, p. 124.

[11] TNA, Hampson to White, 22 Jan. 1892, FO424/172.

I have the honour to report that Bahri Pasha, the Vali of Van, has lately summoned to Van all the Aghas and Chiefs of the Kurdish tribes in this Vilayet.... While conversing with the Vali the other day on the subject, His Excellency told me that his object in summoning them to Van was to settle some intertribal differences and to warn them that, now that they have become regular troops, they must act on their good behaviour, and cease their raids. In fact, if the Vali can change them from people who do not sow but yet reap (the crops of their more peaceful Christian neighbours) into people who sow as well as reap, it will go far to remove the just causes of complaint of the Armenian villagers against the Kurds.[12]

Fitzmaurice had no faith that this would happen since the creation of the *Hamidiyeh* regiments had in effect licensed the violence of the Kurds, and had alarmed the Turks in the Asiatic provinces almost as much as the Armenians.[13] But their worst excesses were still in the future.

Robert Graves, who was appointed consul at Erzeroum in June 1892, must have heard good reports of acting vice-consul Fitzmaurice.[14] Anxious to take a long overdue leave, he requested his services as soon as he could be released by the return to Van of the vice-consul. Since the embassy had no other plans for him, this was granted and Fitzmaurice arrived in Erzeroum in late September 1892, just as a cholera outbreak was slackening. A month later he was 'Acting Consul for Koordistan'.

The *vilayet* of Erzeroum extended from the Persian frontier at Bayazid, all along the Russian frontier and westward into Anatolia at Baiburt and Erzinghian. The town itself, roughly a quarter of the population of which was Armenian, was gloomy and dirty, and had a winter described by a previous acting consul as "something appalling". On being finally relieved of his post, another had gone on his way "rejoicing".[15] It was on the route of the great Persian camel caravans that linked Trebizond on the Black Sea to Tabriz in Persia but its chief significance was strategic. "It was and is a great frontier stronghold," wrote Graves in his

---

[12] TNA, FO195/1766.

[13] Lynch, *Armenia*, vol. II, pp. 4–9; Sir Edwin Pears, *Life of Abdul Hamid* (Henry Holt: New York, 1917), pp. 226–7. Cf. Sonyel, *The Ottoman Armenians*, p. 126.

[14] Graves had graduated from Ortakeui almost ten years ahead of Fitzmaurice and had wide experience of the Balkans and Arabia. He remained at Erzeroum for six years and became an influential figure in the Levant Service and a friend and admirer of Fitzmaurice. He had spent some weeks in Constantinople in the spring of 1892, *Storm Centres of the Near East*, pp. 110–11, 123.

[15] Wratislaw, *A Consul in the East*, pp. 40, 49. On Erzeroum in this period, see also Lynch, *Armenia*, vol. II, The Turkish Provinces, pp. 207–9; Graves, *Storm Centres of the Near East*, p. 115; and *Encyclopedia Britannica*, 11th ed. (Cambridge University Press: Cambridge, 1910–11).

memoir, "protected from Russian attack by an outer chain of forts on all the commanding positions, and within the last century has stood repeated sieges with varying fortunes."[16] In the most recent war, Russian troops had been held by the Turks at the vital Devé Boyun pass and only succeeded in occupying the town following the general surrender. Not surprisingly, the Russians, who had a full-blown consulate-general in the town, tended to regard it as very much their own preserve,[17] an attitude the British Embassy in Constantinople was inclined to respect.[18] Nevertheless, Britain had had a military consul in Erzeroum until as late as 1889, and when Fitzmaurice arrived he had with him Captain F. R. Maunsell of the Royal Artillery.[19]

The consulate that Graves had left in Fitzmaurice's charge was in the crowded Christian quarter on the north-eastern side of the town, and was blessed with an experienced and able dragoman, the long-serving Yusuf Effendi, an Armenian Catholic.[20] Yusuf must have proved of great value to Fitzmaurice because, as an acting consul, his responsibilities were significantly heavier than those he had shouldered at Van. He was now supervising the subordinate vice-consulates and required to report directly to the ambassador in Constantinople. Moreover, he also found himself assuming the role of Italian Consular Agent in Erzeroum.[21]

Like Van, Erzeroum was a political consulate *par excellence*.[22] But as Graves had forecast in justifying his departure on leave, the district proved at first to be comparatively tranquil. As a result, Fitzmaurice was at first able to devote his attention to reporting on the death toll in the recent cholera outbreak and criticizing the weak and "senseless" measures adopted in an attempt to cope with it by the local authorities.[23]

---

[16] *Storm Centres of the Near East*, p. 115.
[17] Wratislaw, *A Consul in the East*, p. 65.
[18] TNA, White to Salisbury, 2 Aug. 1890, FO78/4281.
[19] Graves, *Storm Centres of the Near East*, p. 128. Maunsell subsequently became a consular officer in Armenia himself, and then military attaché in Constantinople from 1901 until 1905.
[20] Graves, *Storm Centres of the Near East*, pp. 115–18; and Wratislaw, *A Consul in the East*, p. 42. Yusuf was also esteemed by Lynch, *Armenia*, vol. II, The Turkish Provinces, pp. 198–9.
[21] TNA, Fitzmaurice to Ford (Constantinople), 17 Mar. 1893, FO195/1766. It appears to have been a custom for some time for the British Consul in Erzeroum to look after Italian interests there, TNA, Hampson (Erzeroum) to White, 2 Jan. 1892, FO195/1766.
[22] Graves, *Storm Centres of the Near East*, p. 116.
[23] TNA, Fitzmaurice to Ford, 31 Dec. 1892, FO195/1766. He was caustic on this theme in the depressing trade report that he submitted in May: "The cholera in itself has not done so much harm to trade as the futile system of land quarantine maintained

Later in the winter, however, the Armenian question began to hot up and it was not long before his reports became more political.

In early January 1893 seditious posters (*yaftas*) in Turkish appeared on the walls of towns in the *vilayets* of Sivas and Angora. This was blamed on the Armenians, and on 2 February part of the large American College at Marsovan in the Sivas *vilayet*—alleged by the *vali* to be implicated in the poster campaign—had been burned down in retaliation by none other than the chief of the Sivas gendarmerie.[24] Armenians were also swiftly imprisoned in large numbers and, as Graves records, "complaints of arbitrary arrest, torture to extort confession, and punishment without any form of trial came pouring into the Embassies".[25]

Erzeroum was soon feeling the backwash of the so-called 'affair of the *yaftas*', and in March Fitzmaurice sent the first of several long despatches to Constantinople on the Armenian question. In one he condemned a court martial that sentenced 23 Armenians to death and some 27 to penal servitude because there was no clear evidence that they had committed the crime with which they were charged: murdering three Turks. In another, he provided details on the general treatment of Armenians in his district. The situation, he told the ambassador, Sir Clare Ford, was not encouraging:

> There is scarcely an Armenian village...that does not suffer more than once a year from Kurdish lawlessness, and I may say that not one case in fifty meets with redress from the local Ottoman officials, partly from apathy, partly from unwillingness, if not actual connivance, and often from powerlessness....

There were 87 Armenian "political prisoners" in the Erzeroum *vilayet*. "I hear of large numbers in prison at Moush and Bitlis", he added, "but have so far no reliable information on the subject."[26] On 15 April he reported that Kurds had killed a considerable number of Armenians at Moush but that since the roads were still closed by snow, it was "very difficult to get accurate details on the subject". He also told the embassy

---

on the Russian and Persian frontiers.... Some attempt at local sanitation would, of course," he added, "be much more effectual than any quarantine, however rigorously enforced." Foreign Office. 1893. Annual Series. No. 1242. *Diplomatic and Consular Reports on Trade and Finance. Turkey. Report for the Year 1892 on the Trade of the Consular District of Erzeroum*. Presented to Parliament June 1893.

[24] TNA, Memorandum by Mr. Bertie on State of the Asiatic Provinces of Turkey, August 1892 to October 1893, FO881/6412. See also Walker, *Armenia*, pp. 135–6.

[25] *Storm Centres of the Near East*, p. 132.

[26] TNA, Fitzmaurice to Ford, 20 Feb., 11 and 25 Mar. 1893, FO195/1804.

of an upsurge of Armenians emigrating to Russia,[27] adding later that
Russian Armenians had been moderately successful in establishing a
revolutionary organization in the district of Khinis,[28] from which the
exodus had been particularly large.[29]

Fitzmaurice was expecting to be relieved at Erzeroum as soon as
the roads cleared in the spring but Graves's return was delayed until
the end of June. This made him responsible for compiling the Annual
Report for 1892 on the trade of the district. With this work finished
and Graves finally returned, by September Fitzmaurice was in charge of
the consulate at Trebizond,[30] formerly the exotic capital of the empire
of the Grand Comneni and at the end of the nineteenth century still
retaining a large Christian quarter.[31] Here, Fitzmaurice was fortunate
to find an experienced staff consisting of a dragoman, a clerk, and two
cavasses. All of them, including Alfred Spadaro, the trading agent in
Samsoun, were Turkish.[32] The consulate was also in close touch with
Dr Jewett, the American Consul in Sivas, who looked after British
interests there.[33] Fitzmaurice remained in charge at Trebizond until the
consul, Henry Longworth, returned, somewhat later than anticipated,
in late December.

Like Erzeroum, Trebizond had suffered badly from the cholera
epidemic in late 1892 and the consul had been actively involved in
bringing medicine to its citizens.[34] By the early spring of 1893, however,
he too had been distracted by the Armenian question. In March he
had reported that in Trebizond "Armenian affairs are comparatively
in a lull", thanks largely to the *vali*, Cadri Bey, who had "no taste for
tragedies".[35] However, Sivas was also in his district and one of the
provinces where the appearance of the *yaftas* had caused serious trouble.

---

[27] TNA, Fitzmaurice to Ford, 15 April 1893, FO195/1804.

[28] TNA, Graves to Nicolson (Constantinople), 27 June 1893, FO195/1804.

[29] Lynch, *Armenia*, vol. II, The Turkish Provinces, pp. 186–7, 219.

[30] TNA, Fitzmaurice (Trebizond) to FO, 26 Sept. 1893, FO526/12; Longworth to FO, July and 1 Sept. 1893, FO78/4498.

[31] This contained at least 10,000 Greeks and 7,000 Armenians, TNA, Longworth to Ford, 1 Dec. 1892, FO195/1769; see also *Encyclopedia Britannica*, 11th ed.

[32] Longworth to FO, 1 Jan. 1893, FO78/4498.

[33] TNA, Longworth to Ford, 14 July 1892, FO195/1769. It had been agreed at the beginning of the year, following an initiative by the United States, that Britain and America would act together on behalf of their subjects in Turkey, TNA, Rosebery to Ford, 15 Feb. 1893, FO195/1778.

[34] TNA, Longworth's reports to the embassy in the second half of 1892 in FO195/1769, especially that of 1 Dec. 1892.

[35] TNA, Longworth to Nicolson (Constantinople), 28 Mar. 1893, FO524/24.

As a result, Longworth had been under pressure from the embassy for information about it. He had not visited the *vilayet* recently, and at the end of March had told the embassy that his own sources of information on the region had been reduced "to nil".[36] The *vali* in Sivas was now Khalil Bey, of ill repute—at least to Fitzmaurice, who had known him in Van.

Ten days after his arrival in Trebizond, Fitzmaurice told the embassy that Khali Bey's penchant for intrigue and vindictiveness was making the Armenian question more acute and that the decision to appoint him *vali* of Sivas was "very ill-advised if not inexplicable".[37] Shortly afterwards, Fitzmaurice sought permission from the embassy to make a short journey of about 12 days in order to see for himself what was really going on in Sivas, particularly in Marsovan and nearby Amassia. There was, after all, still no certainty as to who was behind the trouble—Armenians or anti-Palace Turks, or both—or on the official reaction. His clerk, he said, was "thoroughly competent" and could safely be left in charge of the consulate.[38]

An expedition like this was the sort of thing expected of political consuls and is early evidence of Fitzmaurice's adventurous spirit but at this particular juncture the embassy thought it inexpedient and it was firmly vetoed.[39] He had to content himself with what was probably a more limited expedition in the middle of October.[40] Meanwhile, trouble had spread to nearby Erzinghian, and he found on his return that the embassy was anxious for any information he could obtain on this new hot spot.[41] In Trebizond, however, the political temperature remained low,[42] and thus did Fitzmaurice's first encounters with the Armenian question end on a quiet note when he was relieved by the return of the consul at the end of the year. After a very lengthy period of leave, extended by illness,[43] at the beginning of November 1894 he finally

---

[36] TNA, Longworth to Ford, 3 Apr. 1893; also Longworth to Nicolson, 21 Mar. 1893, and Longworth to Nicolson, 28 Mar. 1893, all in FO524/24.

[37] TNA, Fitzmaurice to Nicolson (Constantinople), 11 Sept. 1893, FO524/24.

[38] TNA, Fitzmaurice to Nicolson (Constantinople), 22 Sept. 1893, FO524/24.

[39] TNA, Nicolson to Fitzmaurice, 29 Sept. 1893 (tel. in cypher), FO195/1789.

[40] At the end of this month the clerk of the Trebizond consulate reported that he was probably at Ordou or Kerasond, small towns along the Black Sea coast to the west of Trebizond, TNA, Vivian to British Ambassador, Constantinople (tel.), 28 Oct. 1893, FO195/1812.

[41] TNA, Fitzmaurice to Ford, 31 Oct. 1893, FO524/24.

[42] TNA, Longworth to Nicolson, 31 Jan. 1894, FO524/24.

[43] TNA, Register of General Correspondence: Consular, 1891–1895, FO566/999.

returned to Constantinople, where—with a sinking heart—he resumed
his duties as a dragoman.

Anxious to escape the dragomanate

At the embassy there had been an important changing of the guard.
The brief tenure of Sir Clare Ford as ambassador had come to an
end and in January 1894 Sir Philip Currie took his place. Currie had
been much concerned with Near Eastern affairs during a long career
at the Foreign Office which since 1889 had seen him occupy the position of permanent under-secretary. He had served as secretary to Lord
Salisbury's special embassy to Constantinople in 1876–7, and as joint
secretary on the British delegation to the Congress of Berlin. Not surprisingly, his relationship with Salisbury was close.

Currie had obviously been sent to bully Abdul Hamid into better
treatment of the Armenians.[44] Alex Waugh, who was a few years senior
to Fitzmaurice in the Levant Service, says that he "came out to Turkey
with a great reputation", adding that "Sir Philip made no secret of his
determination to put things straight. He was a man of great energy,
self-confidence and decision, long accustomed to have his own way; and
he began by carrying things with a high hand".[45] Indeed the tone of
his embassy was set from the moment he arrived at Adrianople, where
it was a long established custom that new ambassadors were greeted
by Turkish officials. Arriving in the early hours of the morning, Currie
refused to emerge from the sleeping berth on his train.[46]

To begin with Fitzmaurice was not part of the new ambassador's
plans to whip the sultan into line over the Armenian question. Instead,
he found himself charged with the usual dreary tasks to which the denizens of the lower ranks of the dragomanate were generally condemned,
to which were now added arguments over the mooring of the embassy
stationnaire. He was at once promoted to acting third dragoman but
since the dragomans' section was unusually well staffed,[47] there was not
much prospect of further advancement either. Sandison, whom Currie

---

[44] Allan Cunningham, *Eastern Questions in the Nineteenth Century: Collected Essays*, vol. 2,
ed. E. Ingram (Cass: London, 1993), p. 229.
[45] Waugh, *Turkey*, pp. 36–7.
[46] CAC Cam., de Bunsen to O'Conor, 11 Aug. 1898, OCON 6/2/7.
[47] Berridge, "Nation, Class, and Diplomacy".

soon found lacking in zeal, was ushered into retirement[48] and in August Adam Block had been appointed chief dragoman in his place. Block, later described by Chaim Weizmann as "a renegade Jew of Galician origin" (see Ch. 9), was the son of an Indian civil servant and married to the daughter of a senior Levant consul of the previous generation. He was to become one of Fitzmaurice's most bitter enemies.

Within weeks of returning to the dragomanate Fitzmaurice was trying to get out. He was not only fed up with his irksome duties but also—he claimed later—had no wish to be connected with the Armenian reforms, which he predicted would lead to massacres.[49] Accordingly he asked Currie for appointment to the vacant post of vice-consul at the important but over-stretched consulate-general in Smyrna.[50] Fortunately, the consul-general, Frederick Holmwood, was anxious to add him to his staff, and Currie was willing to oblige. He arrived in March, and from the beginning of May until the middle of September 1895 was actually in charge while Holmwood took leave. However, his attention was soon diverted again.

The Birejik Commission

In the early autumn of 1894, shortly before Fitzmaurice returned to the embassy, violent clashes between Moslems and Armenians had flared up at Sasun. Subsequently spreading across eastern Anatolia, within a year there was virtually civil war. In Britain, where the Armenians had vocal and influential popular support but the Turks did not,[51] the massacres of Armenians provoked comparison in parliament and the press with the 'Bulgarian horrors' of 1876—though as on that occasion many Moslems also died, relatively unnoticed. As a result, in the course of 1895 there had been renewed diplomatic pressure on Abdul Hamid from the British government, seconded by Russia and France, for guaranteed reforms in the eastern *vilayets*. However, as the sultan well knew, the support of Russia, which for some years had seen dangers in

---

[48] Waugh, *Turkey*, p. 37.

[49] CAC Cam., Fitzmaurice to O'Conor, 15 Oct. 1903, OCON 6/2/27.

[50] TNA, Fitzmaurice to Currie, 29 Nov. 1894, FO195/1835.

[51] Contributing to this was the profound public ignorance of the aims and methods of the Armenian revolutionaries, Langer, *The Diplomacy of Imperialism, 1890–1902*, p. 161.

encouraging Armenian nationalism, was only nominal.[52] As for Britain itself, military intimidation was ruled out because the Admiralty was unwilling to risk forcing the Dardanelles without a promise of French neutrality.[53] This exasperated Lord Salisbury, the Tory leader, who had formed a new cabinet in the summer of 1895, won a clear majority in the election shortly afterwards, and was desperate to help the Armenians.[54] His only alternative was to continue the policy of relying on consular tutelage, and the sultan—whose "personal humanity" *The Times* still saw "no reason to doubt"[55]—was allowed to conduct a master class in procrastination.

In the following winter (1895–6) the slaughter resumed on an even greater scale. In fact, it was so much worse that in some towns, notably Birejik in the *vilayet* of Aleppo, Armenians converted to Islam in an attempt to save their lives.[56] This fresh twist to the rolling story of horror from Turkey stimulated further attention in Britain,[57] and Abdul Hamid—maintaining that the massacres were the result of spontaneous Moslem reactions to Armenian sedition that were beyond his control—clearly saw the need to deflect it. In January 1896 he indicated his doubts as to the sincerity of these conversions and invited the British Ambassador to nominate "some trustworthy person" to engage in a joint inquiry at Birejik with two local Ottoman officials.[58] Familiar

---

[52] Anderson, *The Eastern Question, 1774–1923*, pp. 254–5; Sonyel, *The Ottoman Armenians*, pp. 107–8, 136–7.

[53] France had been allied to Russia since 1891. See Roberts, *Salisbury*, pp. 605–7; Peter Marsh, "Lord Salisbury and the Ottoman massacres", *The Journal of British Studies*, 11 (2), May 1972, p. 79.

[54] Thwarted by the Admiralty over the Dardanelles, Salisbury was fertile in proposing other kinds of naval demonstration in order to intimidate the sultan. However, he lacked cabinet support. Armenia was not Bulgaria: it was much more remote, and the Armenians themselves were too scattered readily to form the basis of an autonomous province. Besides, first Russia and then Austria vetoed coercion of the sultan, Marsh, "Lord Salisbury and the Ottoman massacres", pp. 74–80; Roberts, *Salisbury*, pp. 607–9.

[55] 4 Dec. 1894.

[56] Walker discusses the significance of the forced conversions in his *Armenia* (p. 158) but mentions Bitlis and Gumush-khana rather than Birejik.

[57] Uncharacteristically outspoken, on 31 January Salisbury said publicly that Islam was "capable of the most atrocious perversion and corruption of any religion on the face of the globe". Quoted in Marsh, "Lord Salisbury and the Ottoman massacres", p. 75.

[58] Currie to Salisbury, 29 Jan. 1896, House of Commons Blue Books: *Turkey.* No. 5 (1896), vol. XCVI. Correspondence relating to the Asiatic Provinces of Turkey. Reports by Vice-Consul Fitzmaurice from Birejik, Urfa, Adiaman, and Behesni (June 1986) [hereafter '*Turkey* No. 5'].

with the Armenian question and only just returned to Smyrna from a mission to the district adjacent to Aleppo,[59] Fitzmaurice was the obvious choice. On the instructions of Currie, who was an enthusiast for consular representation on such commissions,[60] he left Smyrna for that town on 12 February. Significantly, he had already "arrived at the firm conviction, backed up by the testimony of several influential Mussulmans", that the sultan himself was behind the dramatic recent escalation in violence. No direct orders had been issued, he had told Currie, but clear hints had come down from Yildiz that "it would be desirable to give the Armenians a good lesson". In an oriental country, he said, this was all that was needed.[61] This was already suspected in the embassy,[62] and also by Salisbury.[63]

Membership of the Palace commission was not for the faint-hearted. Fitzmaurice had to face not only anti-Christian but also mounting anti-British sentiment. Indeed, the traditional friendship between Britain and Turkey was by now a thing of the past, eroded not only by the leading position Britain had taken on Armenian reform but also most notably by its failure to support Turkey in its war with Russia in 1877–8 and the occupation of Egypt in 1882.[64] His position was made even more delicate by a rumour that Armenian revolutionaries were being aided and abetted by London through the authorities in Cyprus,[65] and above all by the decision of Salisbury's government to resume publication of

---

[59] In January 1896 he had been sent by Currie to report on consular arrangements at Mersina in Cilicia, and had taken the opportunity to investigate the lot of its Armenians. This was not as bad, he reported, as in neighbouring Aleppo, consisting merely of wholesale plunder, frequent murders, and several "partial massacres", TNA, Fitzmaurice to Currie, 1 Feb. 1896, FO195/1946.

[60] He had earlier persuaded the sultan to attach European consuls to his commission of inquiry into the Sasun violence, with powers somewhere between observers and full members, Sonyel, *The Ottoman Armenians*, pp. 166–7. See also Graves, *Storm Centres of the Near East*, pp. 145–8.

[61] TNA, Fitzmaurice to Currie, 1 Feb. 1896, FO195/1946.

[62] Salt, *Imperialism, Evangelism and the Ottoman Armenians, 1878–1896*, p. 151. See also Sonyel, *The Ottoman Armenians*, pp. 190, 194; Langer, *The Diplomacy of Imperialism, 1890–1902*, pp. 159–61; and Walker, *Armenia*, p. 146.

[63] *The Times*, 11 Nov. 1895; Roberts, *Salisbury*, p. 606; Marsh, "Lord Salisbury and the Ottoman massacres", p. 78. The question of Abdul Hamid's personal responsibility for the Armenian massacres is as controversial today as it was at the time. Compare, for example, Walker, *Armenia*, pp. 141–73 with Salt, *Imperialism, Evangelism and the Ottoman Armenians, 1878–1896*, pp. 151–7, and Sonyel, *The Ottoman Armenians*, Conclusion.

[64] Cunningham, *Eastern Questions in the Nineteenth Century*, vol. 2, ch. 6; Sonyel, *The Ottoman Armenians*, p. 64.

[65] Salt, *Imperialism, Evangelism and the Ottoman Armenians, 1878–1896*, pp. 76–7.

consular reports from Turkey—a policy deliberately designed to cause serious embarrassment to the sultan.[66]

The first of a series of massive Blue Books containing diplomatic correspondence on the Armenian crisis, as well as reports from consular officers on the massacres, had actually appeared less than two weeks before Fitzmaurice left for Birejik, and the second one had been presented to parliament on the day after.[67] Only four days after this, on 17 February, a third appeared—ending with a despatch of the same day as his departure. All were fully reported in *The Times*[68]—as, in its "Latest Intelligence" column, were the vice-consul's subsequent movements. None of this would have escaped the attention of the sultan's numerous apologists in London, not to mention Costaki Pasha, the new Turkish Ambassador. Fitzmaurice's position was perilous, and Thomas Hohler, at the time a young attaché in Constantinople, reported embassy opinion that he was being sent "to his certain death".[69]

Fitzmaurice arrived in Birejik on 25 February. He reported that the local authorities, "urged by some of the well-disposed Moslems", had initially protected the Armenians from the Moslem mob when anti-Christian feeling spread to the town at the beginning of the previous November. Even during the general attack at the beginning of January, some Armenians who had escaped from the Christian quarter were sheltered in the houses of "one or two friendly Mussulmans". He added, too, that his Turkish co-investigators had not behaved in an entirely cynical or obstructive manner. Nevertheless, nothing that he found at Birejik altered his view of the responsibility for the treatment of the Armenians by the Turks, including the conversions to Islam; in fact

---

[66] Gordon Waterfield, *Layard of Nineveh* (John Murray: London, 1963), pp. 435–6. The publication of consular reports from Turkey had been discontinued in 1881, according to Walker because they were evidence of the failure of British policy to secure reform (*Armenia*, pp. 124–5), and had only re-appeared for a brief interval after that. The 'Sasun massacres' had soon made the resumption of their publication a prominent demand of Liberal backbenchers and the Anglo-Armenian Association but it had been resisted by the Liberal foreign secretary, Lord Kimberley, *The Times*, 28 Nov. and 12 Dec. 1894, 5 Feb. and 30 Mar. 1895.

[67] This was a measure of Lord Salisbury's despair over the sultan's attitude in the Armenian crisis, for his usual reflex was to give "as little information as possible to the House of Commons", Roberts, *Salisbury*, pp. 508–9. See also TNA, FO83/2415, which contains a revealing file of correspondence on the construction of the Armenian Blue Books ('Turkey: Armenia, 1882–1896').

[68] The Blue Books were *Turkey* No. 1 (1895), Parts I and II; *Turkey* No. 1 (1896); and *Turkey* No. 2 (1896). See *The Times*, 29 Jan., 14 and 18 Feb. 1896.

[69] Sir Thomas Hohler, *Diplomatic Petrel* (John Murray: London, 1942), p. 11.

rather the reverse. In the final massacre, he said, faced with a Moslem mob crying that "Our Padishah has ordered that the Armenians be massacred, and that no Christians are to be left in the country", the Ottoman official and reserve soldiers who had turned up in early December stood aside. As for the conversions, these were obviously forced.[70] In a private letter to Currie he described what had happened here as "a carefully planned war of extermination".[71]

But if what Fitzmaurice found at Birejik was bad enough, his discoveries were to be even worse at Urfa, where there had been a particularly high Armenian death toll in December, followed by the usual conversions to Islam. Ordered to proceed there by Currie, Fitzmaurice arrived on 10 March, and a week later sent the ambassador a vivid and detailed report. He found the Armenian quarter still wearing "the aspect of a town which had been ruined and laid waste by some scourge more terrible than any war or siege", and the Moslem population "openly threatening to 'wipe out' the remaining Armenian Christians during the Bairam holiday". Despite the fact that there had been little "actual disloyalty" on the part of the Armenians, he said, at least 8,000 of them had been massacred in two days in December, almost half of them deliberately burnt alive in the Cathedral. This, he observed, was:

> an act which for fiendish barbarity has been unsurpassed by any of the horrors of recent massacres of Armenians, and for which the annals of history can furnish few, if any, parallels.... During several hours the sickening odour of roasting flesh pervaded the town, and even today, two months and a-half after the massacre, the smell of putrescent and charred remains in the church is unbearable.

What was behind the Urfa massacres? Once more Fitzmaurice argued that the causes were remote as well as near. Certainly, he said, some Armenians, in despair at the sultan's failure to implement the promised reforms, had resorted to revolutionary methods. However, "[t]he Ottoman officials, instead of distinguishing between the guilty and innocent, chose, some from ignorance, many from motives of personal pecuniary gain, to regard all Armenians as traitors...", not least because they had encouraged the intervention of foreign powers. This was "criminally communicated" to the Moslem population, which, under Sheri law, regarded it as a "religious duty and a righteous thing to destroy the

---

[70] Fitzmaurice to Currie, 5 Mar. 1896, *Turkey* No. 5.
[71] TNA, FO195/1930.

lives and seize the property of the [traitorous] Armenians". In short, the Moslem population had been allowed "to usurp the prerogatives of Government by wreaking their blind and unreasoning fury on a, to a great extent, guiltless section of His Majesty's most intelligent, hard-working, and useful subjects". For good measure, continued Fitzmaurice:

> it appears orders were received here from the Central Government to the effect that should the Armenians attempt any disturbance, it was to be at once sternly quelled, and in the event of their offering resistance, they were to receive a terrible lesson...both Mussulmans and non-Mussulmans assert that the Government wished these massacres to take place, and that if it had not so wished they could not have taken place.[72]

In the last week of March Fitzmaurice arrived in Adiaman in order to investigate the killings and consequent conversions to Islam that had occurred in this place in the previous November. "The Government officials here, as elsewhere, might have easily prevented the massacre", he reported.[73] And by way of confirmation of his own claim, found that this was exactly what had happened in Behesni—"the only white spot on the map of this region"—where he arrived a few days later.[74]

Returning to Constantinople in April, Fitzmaurice was clearly determined that neither the Palace nor the Porte would be able to avoid the Birejik Commission's conclusions, and he was permitted to press his observations on them. The Armenians had converted to Islam "under the influence of terror", and would need to have their confidence restored if they were to be willing to return to Christianity, he maintained. The ill-disciplined reserve soldiers should be replaced by regulars, the leaders of the massacres punished or banished, and some high functionaries—ideally accompanied by one or more foreign delegates—sent to enforce order and oversee the re-conversions. With the ambassador actively pressing the same line, it was agreed that a commission of inquiry should proceed to Birejik.[75]

---

[72] Fitzmaurice to Currie, 16 Mar. 1896, *Turkey*. No. 5.
[73] Fitzmaurice to Currie, 25 Mar. 1896, *Turkey*. No. 5.
[74] Fitzmaurice to Currie, 27 Mar. 1896, *Turkey*. No. 5.
[75] Currie to Salisbury, 7 May 1896, *Turkey*. No. 5. The commission had four members: an assistant judge of the Constantinople Criminal Court of First Instance, an assistant judge of the Pera Correctional Court, and two senior military officers who were aides-de-camp of the sultan, TNA, Fitzmaurice to Herbert, 22 June, 1896, FO195/1930.

Fitzmaurice must have known that he would be in the frame again when he recommended that the commission include a foreign representative, and Sir Philip Currie quickly decided to send him. However, in the embassy there were by now even greater concerns over his personal safety. The content of Fitzmaurice's despatches from Armenia had since March been as well known in Constantinople as in London.[76] And at the end of April the correspondent of *The Times* had reported that "The plain unvarnished tale graphically unfolded by Vice-Consul Fitzmaurice … which Sir Philip Currie has communicated to his colleagues, has produced a strong impression upon the foreign Ambassadors".[77] Naturally, it was transmitted to the Porte as well. In London the government was under pressure in both houses of parliament to issue what was now being called the 'Fitzmaurice Report' as a parliamentary paper, and on 8 May Salisbury himself assured the House of Lords that it would be published.[78] A few days later George Curzon, number two at the Foreign Office and the coming man in his party, conveyed the gist of the report to the Commons, shortly afterwards making clear that its publication was imminent.[79]

Not surprisingly, the embassy reported that the Palace was hostile to Fitzmaurice joining the Birejik Commission,[80] and was the more anxious for his safety when it learned that the ringleaders of the massacres were not to be punished. It also had misgivings at his suggestion that he should be a full member of the commission since this would imply British endorsement of whatever actions it took. In agreeing to it nevertheless, it consoled itself with the thought that this would be likely to provide him with more protection as well as more influence over its proceedings.

Fitzmaurice left Smyrna for Birejik on 30 May and, with the assistance of the *vali* of Aleppo and embassy pressure on the Palace, appears to have bounced the Porte into accepting his presence.[81] By the middle of June he was back in Birejik and a full member of the commission; according to his own account, he was also soon on excellent personal

---

[76] *The Times*, 16 and 23 Mar. 1896.
[77] *The Times*, 2 May 1896.
[78] *Parl. Debs.*, 4th Ser. (Commons), 30 Apr. 1896, col. 201; *The Times*, 9 May 1896.
[79] *The Times*, 13 May; *Parl. Debs.*, 4th Ser. (Commons), 21 May 1896, col. 75.
[80] Memorandum by Mr. Block, 26 May 1896, *Turkey* No. 5.
[81] TNA, Fitzmaurice to Herbert, 12 June 1896, FO195/1930.

terms with its members.[82] This was just as well because his despatches of the spring had duly been presented to Parliament at the beginning of the month as a Blue Book in their own right,[83] and on 13 June they had been the subject of a full editorial in *The Times*.[84] Shortly after Fitzmaurice's arrival in the town, Michael Herbert, chargé d'affaires at the embassy, reported to Salisbury that "[a] very strong feeling against Mr Fitzmaurice unfortunately exists at this moment in Turkish official circles, owing to the recent publication of his reports". He added that a missionary visiting Birejik who had been mistaken for a consul was recently shot at, and that "in view of the spirit of fanaticism which prevails in the Birejik district, I confess that I shall be considerably relieved when his mission is concluded".[85] Hohler subsequently claimed that "two or three attempts were made to murder him".[86]

In Birejik Fitzmaurice at once sought to stiffen his fellow commissioners, and repeatedly telegraphed the embassy to demand clearer and more positive instructions from the Palace—not, he emphasised, from the Porte.[87] Conscious of the difficulties of his position, the embassy eventually succeeded in doing this. It also repeatedly pressed for an adequate guard for the vice-consul on his "most difficult and thankless mission",[88] though whether it was successful on this point is not clear.

By early July the new commission had made some progress in re-establishing the Christian community in Birejik. According to his own reports, Fitzmaurice had secretly persuaded the Armenian converts to Islam openly to declare themselves once more Christians and demand the protection promised by the sultan. This forced the hand of the Birejik authorities while the Palace commission was in the town. The church in Birejik, which had been converted to a mosque, was also returned to Christianity. This success led Fitzmaurice to hope that the Armenians in the neighbouring villages would be emboldened to reconvert, but he found them too fearful and so urged the commission to lend them its assistance.[89]

---

[82] TNA, Fitzmaurice to Embassy, 26 June 1896, FO195/1930.
[83] *Turkey* No. 5, advertised in *The Times*, 6 June 1896.
[84] 'Converts to Islam', 13 June.
[85] TNA, 24 June 1896, FO78/4709.
[86] *Diplomatic Petrel*, p. 11.
[87] Fitzmaurice to Herbert, 26 June 1896, encl. with Herbert to Salisbury, 7 July 1896, *Turkey* No. 5; see also Hohler, *Diplomatic Petrel*, p. 11.
[88] Memorandum of Mr. Block, 3 July 1896, encl. in Herbert to Salisbury, 8 July 1896, *Turkey* No. 5.
[89] TNA, Fitzmaurice to Herbert, 22 July 1896, FO195/1930.

The Turkish members of the commission were at first reluctant to proceed into the villages, and the embassy refused Fitzmaurice's request to go alone on the grounds that this was too dangerous. As a result, during the remainder of July and the first days of August he concentrated on preserving the precarious peace in Birejik and sorting out the complications (some matrimonial) produced by six months living as Moslems by the Armenians. However, in the second week of August the commission finally received instructions to proceed to the villages of RoumKaleh, thence to Urfa, and finally back to Birejik in mid-September. Fitzmaurice went with them. Armenian reconversions at three villages swiftly followed, as they did at Urfa.[90] On 24 September he reported to Currie that the situation remained tense but that the reconverts were "enjoying a tolerable freedom from molestation"—the more remarkable in view of the degree to which Moslem hostility had been fanned by reports of the Ottoman Bank incident in Constantinople.[91] Shortly after this he returned to his post at Smyrna.

The year 1896 was a very important one in Fitzmaurice's career. In the course of his three missions to the eastern *vilayets*, he had without doubt shown exceptional skill, tenacity, resilience, and physical courage. His achievements were also considerable. He had shone a powerful light on the massacres, and helped many Armenians to re-convert to Christianity. He had also probably strengthened the view in the embassy and in Britain generally that the wishes of the sultan were at the source of the indiscriminate attacks upon them. In its editorial devoted to his Blue Book, *The Times* itself came closer than it had done before to endorsing this view. "The reports of Vice-Consul Fitzmaurice on the massacres and forced conversions to Islam...show", it said, "the responsibility of the local *and the central authorities* for those crimes".[92]

Fitzmaurice was influential in some measure because he could write a graphic despatch, to which testimony was paid in the House of Lords in July 1896. Anxious that an insufficient number of his fellow peers had read the vice-consul's Blue Book, Lord Stanmore assured them that it was "more full of horror and interest than any sensational novel".[93] More important to his influence, though, was the fact that he visited the scene of the events on which he was required to report, and

---

[90] TNA, Fitzmaurice to Herbert, 13 and 29 Aug., and to Currie, 10 Sept. 1896, all in FO195/1930.

[91] TNA, FO195/1930.

[92] Emphasis added, 13 June, 1896.

[93] *Parl. Debs.*, 4th Ser. (Lords), 20 July 1896, col. 112.

used his excellent Turkish to interrogate Moslem as well as Christian sources. Indeed, he took care to emphasise that he had relied more on the former than on the latter. Where estimating the numbers of the dead was concerned, he was careful to show his scepticism of Armenian as well as Turkish estimates; and no doubt he benefited from his previous experience of documenting death during the cholera outbreak in Erzeroum. At Birejik in March, where he estimated that over 150 Christians were massacred, he added "I have in my possession a carefully checked list of their names".[94] Nor did Fitzmaurice have a Manichean view of the Christian-Moslem conflict,[95] and the idea that his reporting in 1896 showed him to be a Turcophobe is quite without foundation.[96] Like other British consuls in the Levant Service, he was quick to acknowledge Armenian sedition and provocation and equally quick to give credit to those Turkish officials and private individuals who behaved well in circumstances that were probably at least as difficult for them as they were for him. Nevertheless, over ten years later, he privately admitted that his reputation for being "a bit phil-Armenian" was deserved, adding that this was partly because the Armenians much preferred the British to the Germans and were so important to British trade with Turkey.[97] The other part was with little doubt a feeling of Christian solidarity.

Fitzmaurice's service on the Birejik Commission established his reputation not only as a political reporter but also as someone who could get results in dealings with Turkish officials. He had, in other words, shown the Foreign Office and the Diplomatic Service that he had 'bottom', and that he was not the sort to 'go off his head' in the remoter parts of Anatolia. The opinion that he was 'a bit phil-Armenian' did him no harm in Britain either. Indeed, he was warmly praised for his efforts and in January 1897—on Currie's recommendation—received a financial

---

[94] *Turkey* No. 5, p. 3. Though Salt tries to cast doubt on Fitzmaurice's account of the Urfa massacre by pointing out that he was not an eye witness, he does not challenge his estimate of the death toll, *Imperialism, Evangelism and the Ottoman Armenians, 1878–1896*, pp. 97, 101.

[95] On this typically Victorian view, see Part One of Salt's, *Imperialism, Evangelism and the Ottoman Armenians, 1878–1896.*

[96] With less than convincing logic, Sonyel levels this charge against him for laying the blame for the atrocities on the sultan himself, though, like Salt, he does not argue with Fitzmaurice's description of events at Urfa; see *The Ottoman Armenians*, pp. 191, 314.

[97] TNA, Fitzmaurice to Tyrrell (private), 27 June 1909, FO800/79.

gratuity from the Foreign Office.[98] Shortly afterwards he was granted leave of absence and returned to England. In June he was further honoured by being made a Companion of the Order of St Michael and St George (CMG), and then given the substantive—as opposed to acting—position of third dragoman in the embassy. However, he did not return to Constantinople until August, having been granted an additional month's leave.[99] It is probable that this is because while in Armenia he had contracted typhus, and almost died from it.[100]

Desperate to escape the dragomanate

Over the next three and a half years Fitzmaurice enjoyed great popularity in the embassy and beyond, and was marked out by a new ambassador for better things. He also had a most interesting visit to Persia while on leave in early 1902. Nevertheless this was a period of mounting frustration for him.

To begin with, he was once more condemned to the routine commercial work in Constantinople that was so despised by the diplomats in the embassy.[101] Much of this was concerned with sorting out delays in the inspecting and discharging of British goods by the Turkish customs authorities.[102] For the greater part of 1898 he also continued to suffer from poor health and had to have an operation that was only partly successful.[103] Moreover, all of the embassy's work was more uphill than usual because of the icy relationship now deeply entrenched between Sir Philip Currie and the sultan; until a stiff encounter in October 1897, they had not actually met for over a year. "The Porte is impotent", wrote Maurice de Bunsen, secretary of the embassy since January, to his friend Cecil Spring-Rice, "and the smallest matters are now referred to the Palace so that our 'cases' get stuck and our Dragomans tear their

---

[98] This amounted to £120, TNA, Fitzmaurice to Currie, 30 Jan. 1897, FO195/1971.

[99] TNA, Fitzmaurice to Salisbury, 29 June 1897, FO78/4839.

[100] Sir Reader Bullard, *The Camels Must Go: An autobiography* (Faber and Faber: London, 1961), p. 63.

[101] Pears, *Life of Abdul Hamid*, pp. 175–6.

[102] The nature of this work in the following years can readily be judged by his memoranda in TNA, 'Drogmanat via Chancery' in FO195/1971–3, 2015, 2051, 2052, 2080, and (to Aug. 1900) 2081.

[103] CAC Cam., Fitzmaurice to O'Conor, 30 May 1900, OCON 6/2/15.

hair and swear they were never so checkmated before".[104] On top of all this, the dragomanate remained firmly in the hands of Adam Block, the one man with whom Fitzmaurice was not popular at all.

Between Fitzmaurice and Block, who was almost ten years older than the Irishman and had been one of the first Ortakeui students, there was a clash of personalities. According to Aubrey Herbert, the eldest son of the second marriage of the Earl of Carnarvon, who joined the embassy as an honorary attaché in 1904, "Fitzmaurice was secretive, Block was outspoken. Fitzmaurice's brimming vitality was assertive; Block's self-reliance was harsh".[105] There were also differences over policy, Fitzmaurice having begun to look with a more jaundiced eye than the chief dragoman at the emerging movement of the Young Turks. It hardly helped their relationship either that Block had begun to take his home leave in the summer, thus forcing Fitzmaurice to take his in the English winter.[106] With Fitzmaurice's temper not assisted by his indifferent health and that of the ambitious Block not aided by mounting frustration over his own prospects, their enmity was soon to become legendary. When exactly the falling out occurred is difficult to say but it was certainly well established by the middle of 1899, when de Bunsen, telling Spring-Rice how perfect for once were things at the embassy, added: "Even Block and Fitzmaurice seem to have declared an armistice".[107]

Fitzmaurice was also increasingly irritated by the fact that while now formally third dragoman, in reality he was number two to Block because Hugo Marinitch, the second dragoman, was a Levantine. Marinitch was older and more experienced than Fitzmaurice and was respected in the embassy as "a most conscientious, painstaking official"[108] but—apart from lacking the Irishman's energy and his reputation for getting results in dangerous circumstances—he remained a Levantine and thus the object of prejudice by the British.[109] Lloyd Griscom of the American Legation had no doubt about Fitzmaurice's *de facto* position in the

---

[104] CAC Cam., de Bunsen to Spring-Rice, 8 Oct. 1897, CASR/1.
[105] Aubrey Herbert, *Ben Kendim: A Record of Eastern Travel*, ed. D. MacCarthy (Hutchinson: London, 1924), p. 271. Richard Graves, later briefly in the dragomanate, also found Block to have a "blunt and uncompromising manner", MECA Oxf.: Richard Massie Graves, Draft of Opening Chapters of an Autobiography, GB 165–0125.
[106] CAC Cam., Fitzmaurice to O'Conor, 30 May 1900, OCON 6/2/15.
[107] CAC Cam., de Bunsen to Spring-Rice, 13 June 1899, CASR/1.
[108] Waugh, *Turkey*, p. 28. He had been in the dragomanate since 1876.
[109] Berridge, "Nation, Class, and Diplomacy".

British Embassy.[110] Even the new ambassador, Sir Nicholas O'Conor, who replaced Currie in the summer of 1898, sometimes described Fitzmaurice as his second dragoman in his correspondence.[111]

One gleam of light for Fitzmaurice during this period—though it was not so long before this also turned into a shadow—was the arrival of O'Conor, who was more determined than his predecessor to get on to good personal terms with the sultan. As a result, his arrival led to an immediate improvement in relations and the burden on the drago-manate was accordingly lightened.[112] Furthermore, though the social gulf between Fitzmaurice and O'Conor was certainly broad and deep, for the O'Conor family carried an extremely ancient Gaelic title and numbered in its clan the last king of Ireland,[113] they were at least both Irish and devout Roman Catholics. O'Conor also had a great need for people of his third dragoman's skill and energy since he found the burden of work at Constantinople great and his health was no longer strong.[114] He soon encouraged him to believe that his patronage would be beneficent.

Fitzmaurice also acquired other useful acquaintances and good friends during these years. Maurice de Bunsen, who was four times chargé d'affaires during these years, was attracted to Fitzmaurice and became friendly with him. He also developed close relations with the American Legation, which was at this time almost entirely preoccupied with protecting American missionaries in Anatolia and seeking indemnities for the losses they had suffered in the turmoil of the mid-nineties. In the legation he struck up a friendship with the young Lloyd Griscom,[115] who was completely in awe of him. Fitzmaurice was a great raconteur and regaled Griscom with hair-raising stories of his experiences in the

---

[110] "Adam Block was chief dragoman, and his assistant was Gerald Fitzmaurice, a leading authority on Turkey", Lloyd C. Griscom, *Diplomatically Speaking* (The Literary Guild of America: New York, 1940), p. 138.

[111] For example, CAC Cam., O'Conor to Cromer, 25 Oct. 1902, OCON 6/1/38.

[112] "Our cases are certainly going through swimmingly now", de Bunsen wrote to Spring-Rice on 13 June 1899, CAC Cam., CASR/1.

[113] I am grateful to Caroline Mullan for this information.

[114] T. H. Sanderson, "O'Conor, Sir Nicholas Roderick (1843–1908)", rev. H. C. G. Matthew, *ODNB* [35288, accessed 20 Jan. 2007].

[115] Griscom was appointed US Secretary of Legation in July 1899 but became chargé d'affaires in December and remained in this position for the next fifteen months, John A. Garraty (ed.), *Dictionary of American Biography*, Supplement Six, 1956–1960 (Scribner's: New York, 1980).

eastern *vilayets*; he also no doubt enjoyed tutoring him in Turkish ways.[116] But these were meagre compensations for his life in the dragomanate and more than once he applied for a transfer to a provincial consulate not long after O'Conor's arrival.[117]

Unhappy though he may have been, Fitzmaurice's star remained clearly in the ascendant, and at the beginning of 1900 he almost became chief dragoman, the post believed by O'Conor to be the most important in the embassy[118] and "the plum of the [Levant] service".[119] Block had been disgusted with his salary for some time, believed that the status of first dragoman in the British Embassy compared unfavourably with that of those who held the same post in the other embassies in Constantinople, and was convinced that his career was at a dead end.[120] In 1898 he had unsuccessfully applied for the post of British representative on the Council of Administration of the Ottoman Public Debt, a body created some twenty years earlier in order to gather certain revenues of the government for distribution to the bondholders on whose loans it had defaulted. In early November 1899 he applied again when the position fell vacant once more. This time O'Conor felt he had a very good chance of getting it and, concluding that he would never get the best out of a miserable man and wanting a strong representative to work with on the Debt, lobbied hard in his support.[121] He was also confident that Fitzmaurice would slip readily into his place. "He [Block] is a first rate Dragoman and will be a great loss," the ambassador told Eric Barrington, who had responsibility for personnel matters in the Foreign Office, "but I rather expect Fitzmaurice whom I think of recommending in his place *on approval*, will show up well".[122] Elaborating rather more in a private letter to Valentine Chirol, the foreign editor of *The Times*, O'Conor said:

---

[116] Griscom, *Diplomatically Speaking*, pp. 145, 148, 173, 180. Referring to the same period, Graves said that "we never tired of hearing Fitzmaurice recount in thrilling terms his experiences at Orfa and Birejik", *Storm Centres of the Near East*, p. 166.

[117] CAC Cam., Fitzmaurice to O'Conor, 30 May 1900, OCON 6/2/15.

[118] CAC Cam., O'Conor to Villiers, 17 Jan. 1900, OCON 4/1/18.

[119] CAC Cam., O'Conor to Block 12 Aug. 1901, OCON 4/1/19.

[120] CAC Cam., Block to O'Conor, 15 Nov. 1899, OCON 6/1/21.

[121] CAC Cam., O'Conor to Cromer, 30 Nov. and 1 Dec. 1899, OCON 4/1/17; and O'Conor to Sanderson, 28 Dec. 1899, OCON 4/1/17.

[122] CAC Cam., O'Conor to Barrington, 2 Nov. 1899, OCON 4/1/17, emphasis in original. See also O'Conor to Sanderson, 2 Nov. 1899, OCON 4/1/17.

He understands the Turks quite wonderfully and constantly gets things through where others have failed.... His manner with Europeans is not good but it has improved immensely in the last 12 months as I have made it a point to invite him as much as possible with strangers and to introduce him.[123]

Sir Philip Currie, writing to O'Conor from Rome, agreed: "I think Fitzmaurice would be on the whole the best man to succeed Block. He is certainly a very able Dragoman and I daresay the 'Tenue' [polish] which was rather wanting will come with the increased dignity."[124] In the event, Block was once more rejected for the Debt, and Fitzmaurice, who was aware that he had been picked to succeed him,[125] had to wait for much longer for his elevation than at this point he anticipated.

Following this disappointment, Fitzmaurice wrote a long letter to O'Conor in which he begged him to help him "quietly to slip into a provincial post", even at the cost of a drop in salary, and replace him with someone with "greater tact and equability of temper". All he asked was that, in light of his more than four years of service in the interior of Asia Minor, it should be in European Turkey, Bulgaria, Syria or Egypt. Referring indirectly to the drudgery of his work and his insufferable position as *de facto* number two to Block, he admitted that he was ruining his prospects but that it had come to be a choice: "between ruining my career and ruining the best part of my life".[126]

This appeal obviously made some impression on O'Conor. In August 1900 he permitted Fitzmaurice a temporary reprieve from the dragomanate by appointing him acting consul-general to stand in for Sir Alfred Biliotti at the commercially important and (as we shall see) politically interesting post of Salonica in southern Macedonia. Here his tenure was disturbed by nothing more than an argument over the recognition of a British post office[127] but in the following January he was recalled slightly early in order to be available at the embassy when the ambassador returned from leave.[128]

At least when Fitzmaurice resumed his duties in the dragomanate his daily diet was more interesting—and much heavier after mid-June

---

[123] CAC Cam., O'Conor to Chirol, 5 Nov. 1899, OCON 5/3/4.
[124] CAC Cam., Currie to O'Conor, 14 Jan. 1900, OCON 6/1/23.
[125] CAC Cam., O'Conor to Villiers, 17 Jan. 1900, OCON 4/1/18; Fitzmaurice to O'Conor, 6 Dec. 1903, OCON 6/1/42, and 13 Sept. 1905, OCON 6/1/53.
[126] CAC Cam., Fitzmaurice to O'Conor, 30 May 1900, OCON 6/2/15.
[127] CAC Cam., Fitzmaurice to O'Conor, 23 Sept. 1900, OCON 6/2/16.
[128] TNA, de Bunsen to Lansdowne, 12 Jan. 1901, FO78/5127.

when for the first time he was appointed acting chief dragoman.[129] The occasion for this was the departure on long leave of the now seriously disgruntled Block.[130] O'Conor, who had not been impressed by what he found in the embassy on his return and thought that Block's "sulky" mood was impeding his work,[131] wrote to the permanent under-secretary at the Foreign Office, Sir Thomas Sanderson, that: "I am going to try Fitzmaurice as Acting first dragoman. He is a sort of Irish Turk and gets on well with the natives. I rather expect he will be a success."[132] Clearly, the ambassador hoped that he would help to improve the fortunes of his embassy, which had not fulfilled its early promise. This, then, was Fitzmaurice's chance.

As acting chief dragoman, Fitzmaurice was now dealing on a regular basis at Yildiz Palace with the sultan's first secretary, Tahsin Bey, and his second secretary, Izzet Bey, as well as with ministers at the Porte; and, until Block returned in late October, he was reporting directly to the ambassador. Political questions were now added to his plate, as well as important economic ones such as the Haifa-Damascus railway.

Some months after Block's return, in early 1902, Fitzmaurice was reluctantly released by the embassy to cover the vice-consulate at the Dardanelles, where Russian ship-spotting was the main preoccupation, but within eleven days it had got him back again.[133] Shortly afterwards, however, he was granted leave and this time, encouraged by Griscom, who had just been appointed American Minister in Tehran and invited him to stay at the legation, decided to use it to make an expedition to the Persian Gulf. He hired a tutor to teach him Persian and in March set out. Travelling problems prevented him reaching the Gulf but, in the company of Griscom and his new wife, he managed to get as far as Isfahan. He enjoyed the trip, broadened his knowledge of the region, and continued to make himself useful. In Tehran he was presented in

---

[129] Fitzmaurice's huge, varied, and complex work-load from January to December 1901 is readily observable in the memoranda in TNA, FO195/2103.

[130] CAC Cam., Block to O'Conor, 22 July 1901, OCON 6/1/27. By Christmas Day 1902 Block was in palpably angry mood, telling O'Conor that the issue of his treatment had reached a "critical stage", CAC Cam., Block to O'Conor, 25 Dec. 1902, OCON 6/1/31. See also O'Conor to Block 12 Aug. 1901, OCON 4/1/19; Block to O'Conor, 24 Aug. 1901, OCON 6/1/29; and Hardinge to O'Conor, 13 Mar. 1903, OCON 4/1/22.

[131] CAC Cam., O'Conor to Sanderson, 16 Jan. 1901, OCON 4/1/18. See also de Bunsen to O'Conor, 1 Jan. 1900, OCON 6/2/18.

[132] CAC Cam., O'Conor to Sanderson, 8 May 1901, OCON 4/1/18.

[133] TNA, Dardanelles Vice-Consulate. FO195/2119.

private audience to the shah by the British Minister, Sir Arthur Hardinge, and in Isfahan, where Hardinge happened to arrive on an official visit shortly after Griscom's party, Fitzmaurice rode out several miles to meet him. Having assisted the minister at certain of his engagements, he was able to inform O'Conor, with just a hint of false modesty, that he had "helped in a small way to swell his retinue".[134]

Following his return to Constantinople at the end of May 1902, Fitzmaurice found the rest of his year following a similar pattern to the previous one: routine, low level work in the dragomanate, punctuated by more challenging work in the summer when Block once more took leave and he became acting chief dragoman for the second time. Unfortunately, as Fitzmaurice later had occasion to complain, various factors impeded his efforts to live up to the ambassador's expectations. First, the considerable distance of the summer embassy at Therapia from the Porte and the Palace had made his work more arduous than it was for Block during the winter. Secondly, unlike Block, he had no 'Fitzmaurice' on whom to rely. Thirdly, Block, anxious to avoid invidious comparisons between what he was able to achieve prior to his departure and what his juniors might attain in his absence, briefed them inadequately before leaving. And fourthly, he "could not hustle poor old Marinitch in the cruel way Block used to do".[135] However, O'Conor was a notoriously exacting chief,[136] and both he and Fitzmaurice—as we shall see—had their own reasons for suggesting that he had not done particularly well as acting chief dragoman. In fact, the reputation he had made in Armenia had not been impaired and well before the end of 1902 O'Conor had decided to send him on another important special mission. That this was to the Aden hinterland, which was as near to a white man's grave as it was possible to get in the Near East, and that he was content to go, is a mark of how desperate by now Fitzmaurice was to escape from the dragomanate in Constantinople.

---

[134] CAC Cam., Fitzmaurice to O'Conor, 25 Apr. 1902, OCON 6/2/21; also 25 Mar. 1902, OCON 6/2/20, and Griscom, *Diplomatically Speaking*, pp. 206–10.

[135] CAC Cam., Fitzmaurice to O'Conor, 6 Dec. 1903, OCON 6/1/42.

[136] Lord Hardinge of Penshurst, *Old Diplomacy* (John Murray: London, 1947), p. 151; Edgar T. S. Dugdale, *Maurice de Bunsen: Diplomat and friend* (John Murray: London, 1934), p. 237; and Sir Andrew Ryan, *The Last of the Dragomans* (Bles: London, 1951), p. 47.

CHAPTER THREE

BETWEEN TWO FIRES: THE YEMEN FRONTIER, 1902–5

In 1902 there was considerable tension between Britain and Turkey in
south-western Arabia, and in sending Fitzmaurice there at the end of
the year Sir Nicholas O'Conor hoped that he would be able to preserve
the British position without risking war. It was to be a longer and even
more trying assignment than his work on the Birejik Commission, in
part because on the British side five different agencies of government
had a hand in it: the Foreign Office and the India Office in London,
the embassy in Constantinople, the 'Government of India' on the
subcontinent, and the Aden Residency. The affair also caused intense
exasperation to the ambassador, and—though it ended in success—in
the short run it damaged Fitzmaurice's career as well as his health. By
the time of his return to England in the late summer of 1905, when
he discovered that he had not won the honours to which he believed
he was entitled, he was a doubly embittered man.

The origins of the Anglo-Turkish tensions in this desolate territory
lay in the last half of the previous century, during which the Ottoman
Empire had been slowly driving south in an effort to make good a claim
to sovereignty over the whole of the Yemen.[1] This brought it into conflict
with the British because in 1839 Britain had seized Aden, the fortified
port at the tip of the peninsula, and extended its influence over the
hinterland in order to protect its rear and guarantee essential supplies.
After a narrowly avoided collision of arms in 1873, when Ottoman
forces were only 20 miles from Aden, the Turks had tacitly agreed to
recognize the independence of the nine tribes in the hinterland listed

---

[1] This was based on conquest and rule of the region from the sixteenth century until
well into the seventeenth, when the Ottomans were forced out by the Zaydi imams.
Anxiety to promote the claim was strengthened by Arabia's importance as the cradle
of Islam and the sultan's knowledge that his title of caliph was widely accepted. Unless
otherwise indicated, the historical background to this Chapter is based on R. J. Gavin,
Aden Under British Rule, 1839–1967 (Hurst: London, 1975); R. Bidwell, *The Two Yemens*
(Longman: Harlow, 1983); and John C. Wilkinson, *Arabia's Frontiers: The story of Britain's
Boundary Drawing in the Desert* (I. B. Tauris: London, 1991).

by the British and withdraw from their territory.[2] This represented the
establishment of a British protectorate in the Aden hinterland in all but
name. Unfortunately, the boundaries of the territory inhabited by the
nine tribes were vague and the border between the British sphere and
the re-established Ottoman *vilayet* of Yemen remained undefined.

For some time after the crisis of 1873 Turkey and Britain had been
content with a rather messy live-and-let-live arrangement along the
border. However, encroachments in the region by other European
powers in the 1880s led Britain to feel the need to stake out its sphere
more clearly, while Abdul Hamid, deeply suspicious of Britain's inten-
tions after the occupation of Egypt in 1882, had begun once more
to squeeze the territory of the nine tribes. A notable victim of this
advance was the Amir of Dhala, who was particularly aggrieved at
losing the frontier village of Al Jalela, which commanded the main
road through his territory north to Qataba. It was clear that matters
would come to a head when George Curzon became Viceroy of India
in 1899. This is because, as it happens, Aden was administered as part
of the Bombay province of the British Raj and Curzon's policy—while
not expansionist—was to employ vigorous diplomacy, and force when
necessary, in order to stiffen Britain's political position in all of the
areas that bordered his great fiefdom.[3] Moreover, Lord Lansdowne,
appointed foreign secretary in 1900 and himself a former viceroy, was
better disposed towards Curzon than some other cabinet ministers.

The conflict waiting to happen erupted at the end of 1900 when,
with the assistance of Turkish regulars, a tribal chief allied to the
Turks reoccupied a fort at Al Darayjah in hills 70 miles north-west
of Aden. It was only of late that this had been tacitly admitted to lie
in British-protected territory, and O'Conor was instructed to issue a
warning that Britain would respond with force if the position was not
surrendered. This threat went unheeded and in July British troops from
the Aden garrison drove the occupiers from the fort, which was then
blown up.[4] The situation was now dangerous. The number of British
troops at Aden had recently been increased, and in August—as rumours
circulated that the British were about to invade the Yemen—Turkish

---

[2] The nine tribes were the Abdali, Alawi, Amiri, Aqrabi, Awlaqi, Fadli, Hawshabi,
Subhayi, and Yafi.
[3] D. Gilmour, *Curzon* (Macmillan: London, 1995), pp. 194–5, 198–200; TNA,
O'Conor to Lansdowne, 19 Mar. 1902, FO78/5242.
[4] *The Times*, 27 Aug. 1901.

forces were concentrated to meet them. Both sides then thought better of it and in October it was agreed to establish a joint commission to delimitate the frontier, that is, survey the territory, negotiate a precise line, and—where necessary—mark it with pillars.

With Britain's war in South Africa going badly and plenty of other trouble spots to worry about, at this stage the Foreign Office and the ambassador in Constantinople took a broader view than Curzon (and his Resident in Aden Town) of the implications of a violent quarrel over what seemed to them relatively petty issues on the Yemen frontier. This also applied to the India Office in London, where—contrary to some popular belief—the Secretary of State for India occupied a constitution- ally superior position to the viceroy and the 'Government of India', with responsibility to parliament for Indian affairs generally.[5] Desiring a speedy settlement, all three of these different centres of decision—two in London and one in Constantinople—were anxious to avoid arguments over historical rights and agree simply on a frontier that corresponded with "the de facto limits at the present time of the respective spheres of influence of the two parties".[6] This rested on a line identified by an Aden Residency survey in 1891–2 and on "recognized practice or other proof of the existing boundaries of the nine cantons".[7] The rough *de facto* frontier extended from the Red Sea coast near Perim Island in the south-west to the natural barrier of the great sand desert in the north-east, and *in a straight line* was about 200 miles long.

The Aden Frontier Delimitation Commission, as it was formally known, had the first of its many meetings in February 1902 at the town of Dhala, a settlement about 100 miles north of Aden on a plateau roughly 4,500 feet above sea level, which at least gave this particular spot a good climate. Dhala was located on the central third of the frontier, in Amiri territory, and it was here through which the principal trade routes passed and the British-protected tribes came into most direct contact with the Turks. It was in the vicinity of Dhala that the boundary was most hotly disputed.

The British delegates on the boundary commission had made their camp at Dhala. They were appointed by and answered to Curzon via his political resident in Aden, Brigadier-General P. J. Maitland, and

[5] Gilmour, *Curzon*, pp. 149–51.
[6] TNA, O'Conor to Lansdowne, 19 Mar. 1902, FO78/5242.
[7] TNA, Lansdowne to Anthopoulos Pasha, 24 Mar. 1902, FO78/5242.

were led by Colonel R. A. Wahab of the Royal Engineers. Wahab
was an experienced, Arabic-speaking officer attached to the Survey
Department of the British Indian government and had been responsible
for the 1891–2 survey of the Aden frontier region. He was supported
initially by an officer from the Bombay Political Service. The Ottoman
delegates, who were based a little to the north, were led by Mustafa
Remzi Bey and included the notorious commandant and *kaimakam* of
Qataba, Khalil Bey.[8] Both sets of commissioners were supposed to have
only small military escorts for personal protection but the Turkish force
was significantly larger than that of the British and was commanded
by Abdullah Pasha, a Palace favourite.[9]

It had soon been apparent that no swift progress was going to be
made by the newly-established boundary commission. The Turks continued to insist on sovereignty over the whole of south-west Arabia,
while Maitland had concluded that the 1892 line was quite unreliable
in the Amiri country and directed his representatives to demand its
revision.[10] The result was that the Turkish forces continued to adopt
an aggressive posture, seizing new positions adjacent to the British
camp.[11] When Wahab's party attempted to survey the border in this
vicinity it was fired on by the Turks and their Arab levies, and soon
there were fears that the latter might even be instructed to attack the
Anglo-Indian camp—not a prospect to be taken lightly because the
Arab tribes were by now awash with modern rifles.[12] Wahab believed
that the British would lose all credibility with their own Arab allies if
they did not respond to this pressure with force, and he was strongly
supported by Curzon, who had been reduced—in his own words—to
"righteous fury" by what he saw as the weakness of British policy and
confusion in its application.[13] As a result, in August 1902 the Foreign
Office and the India Office had reluctantly deferred to the viceroy's

[8] In November 1902 murdered by one of his own men, IOL, Diary of the Aden
Boundary Commission [hereafter ABC Diary], R/20/A/1207, 28 Nov. 1902.
[9] TNA, O'Conor to Lansdowne, 18 Sept. 1902, FO78/5244; IO memorandum,
'Aden Boundary', 20 Jan. 1903, FO78/5315.
[10] TNA, Maitland to Bombay, 20 Nov. 1901, FO78/5169. Also IOL, Wahab to
Resident, 11 Feb. 1902; and Resident to S of S, 17 Feb. 1902, R/20/A/1196.
[11] TNA, Memorandum on the Boundary of the British Protectorate near Aden,
FO, 3 Jan. 1903, p. 2, FO881/9190.
[12] Gavin, *Aden Under British Rule, 1839–1967*, pp. 203–6.
[13] David Dilks, *Curzon in India*, vol. 1 (Rupert Hart-Davis: London, 1969), pp. 151–2;
Lord Ronaldshay, *The Life of Lord Curzon: being the authorized biography*, vol. 2 (Ernest
Benn: London, 1928), p. 239.

opinion that a frontier somewhat further north than the line of existing spheres of influence should be sought;[14] and in September de Bunsen told Spring-Rice that Britain might have to give Abdul Hamid a lesson over the Aden delimitation.[15] HMS *Harrier* was also thrown into the scales. Moved to a station off the Yemeni Red Sea port of Hodeida, it directly threatened the sultan's line of supply and reinforcement to his forces now embroiled in attempting to suppress an insurrection by the Zaydi imam, Yahya, in the northern highlands.

By October 1902 the menacing state of affairs in south-western Arabia was commanding top level attention in London as well as Calcutta. Indeed, O'Conor was instructed by Lansdowne to make it plain to Abdul Hamid that a serious conflict would ensue if he did not throw his weight behind a friendly settlement. This meant withdrawal of Turkish forces from positions occupied in the Amiri country since the boundary commission had been established, and cooperation in delimitation in a north-easterly direction to the desert[16]—a British priority designed to block Turkish penetration south to the Hadrumaut and the sea.[17] At a somewhat ill-tempered audience on 24 October, Abdul Hamid, who could not conceal from O'Conor that he was intimately acquainted with the affair, complained that the British were demanding territory that could mean little to them but meant a great deal to him.[18] "The fanatical element of the Palace are against compliance," the ambassador reported, "the Grand Vizier and the Porte are in favour of it—and His Majesty is hesitating between the two."[19] Plainly undecided on his best course of action, the sultan did what he generally did in these circumstances: he prevaricated, and then issued orders making token concessions. He promised a north-eastern delimitation and the withdrawal of regular troops (though not Arab levies) from points occupied since the appointment of the boundary commission.[20]

---

[14] TNA, mins. of meeting at FO, 6 Aug. 1902, FO78/5243. This was also attended by O'Conor and Maitland.

[15] CAC Cam., de Bunsen (Paris) to Spring-Rice, 15 Sept. 1902, CASR/1.

[16] TNA, Memorandum on the Boundary of the British Protectorate near Aden, FO, 3 Jan. 1903, p. 4, FO881/9190.

[17] TNA, S of S to Viceroy, 21 Apr. 1903, FO78/5317.

[18] TNA, O'Conor to Lansdowne, 25 Oct. 1902, FO78/5244.

[19] TNA, O'Conor to Lansdowne, 24 Oct. 1902, FO78/5244.

[20] TNA, Wahab to India, 8 Nov. 1902, FO78/5244; Memorandum on the Boundary of the British Protectorate near Aden, FO, 3 Jan. 1903, p. 4, FO881/9190.

Sent to perform miracles

In the spring of 1902 Sir Nicholas O'Conor had been optimistic about the Aden Boundary Commission but this mood had not lasted long.[21] In the early stages of the autumn crisis he had also begun to doubt Wahab's ability to handle the Turks. He concluded, as a result, that Fitzmaurice—who at this point was holding the Aden brief for him at the Porte in Block's absence[22]—should be sent out as his replacement. Confident that he could perform miracles, he told Sir Thomas Sanderson that Fitzmaurice "knows the situation here and how to deal with the Provincial Turk".[23] The proposal was accepted, though the Indian government—sensitive to the prerogatives of the Bombay presidency—insisted that Fitzmaurice must take rank after Colonel Wahab.[24] This was to be a mounting source of irritation to the ambassador, who had sent Maitland a glowing reference on his dragoman, adding to what he had told Sanderson that "many thousand Armenians are said to owe their lives to his address and savoir faire, while in riding through the more disturbed districts he carried his own in his hand".[25]

Defusing the Aden frontier crisis was by now a priority for O'Conor, who knew that an outbreak of fighting could result in the failure of his embassy. When, therefore, Fitzmaurice left Constantinople in late October he was instructed to proceed to the Yemen frontier as quickly as possible and obtain a *peaceful* settlement[26]—encouraged no doubt by a hint from the ambassador that the affair presented great opportunities for further honours.[27] En route at the Aden Residency he wrote to O'Conor something that must have returned to haunt him many times. A rapid solution to the boundary question would obviously suit British

---

[21] CAC Cam., O'Conor to Sanderson, 25 Mar. 1902.

[22] TNA, Fitzmaurice to O'Conor, 6 and 16 Sept. 1902, FO195/2124.

[23] CAC Cam., O'Conor to Sanderson, 23 Sept. 1902. See also TNA, O'Conor to Lansdowne, 28 Oct. 1902, FO78/5244.

[24] See the exchanges in TNA, FO78/5244, between O'Conor and the FO and the FO and the IO, Oct.–Dec. 1902.

[25] CAC Cam., O'Conor to Maitland, 7 Dec. 1902, OCON 4/1/19.

[26] TNA, O'Conor to Lansdowne, 28 Oct. 1902, FO78/5244; CAC Cam., Fitzmaurice to O'Conor, 30 Jan. 1903, OCON 6/1/36.

[27] It is instructive on this point that in the same period Robert Graves was invited by O'Conor to surrender his position as consul-general in Crete for the worse-paid and less independent post of consul-general in Salonica "in view of the opportunities of distinction offered by the disturbed state of Macedonia". This irritated Graves intensely, *Storm Centres of the Near East*, pp. 191–2, 193–4.

interests, he told the ambassador, but added that "[i]f I were actuated by personal motives, I suppose it would be more advantageous to me that matters should be spun out".[28]

Apostate to O'Conor[29]

Fitzmaurice arrived in Dhala in late November, to be greeted by four bullets fired by Turkish Arab levies falling near his tent.[30] However, the Turkish commissioners themselves—who were pleased to find that the British party had acquired someone who could speak their own language—received him more warmly. So, too, did Colonel Wahab, with whom Fitzmaurice quickly established a good relationship. This was no doubt in part because, having no knowledge of military matters or Hindustani and at this stage only rough Arabic, he did not share the ambassador's view that he should supplant him as leader of the British party.[31]

While at the Aden Residency Fitzmaurice had already begun to form a robust attitude towards the Yemen frontier question, and nothing that he saw or heard after his arrival caused him to alter it. On 22 December he submitted his views in a widely circulated formal report that probably surprised and certainly made unpleasant reading for O'Conor.[32] Britain, he maintained, had been deluded on the border question by emollient assurances from the Porte that were overridden by secret instructions from the Palace to the Turkish boundary commissioners to pursue a policy of intrigue and encroachment. In this the Palace had been encouraged by the embassy's desire not to wound the susceptibilities of the Ottoman Government. Britain had thereby given too much ground to the Turks since 1873 and was in danger of giving more. Its prestige with the nine tribes was in tatters, and Aden itself was in jeopardy. A firm stand had therefore to be made on the Amiri

---

[28] CAC Cam., Fitzmaurice to O'Conor, 15 Nov. 1902, OCON 6/1/35.

[29] I owe the idea for this sub-heading to Dilks, who says that Fitzmaurice proved "a real Balaam", *Curzon in India*, vol. 1, p. 153.

[30] CAC Cam., Fitzmaurice to O'Conor, 3 Dec. 1902, OCON 6/1/35; IOL, ABC Diary, 24 Nov. 1902, R/20/A/1207.

[31] CAC Cam., Fitzmaurice to O'Conor, 3 and 18 Dec. 1902, OCON 6/1/35. By the following summer he was "able to speak the local dialect of Arabic with tolerable fluency", CAC Cam., Fitzmaurice to O'Conor, 28 July 1903, OCON 6/2/26.

[32] TNA, FO78/5315.

border, which, he maintained, was "the crux of the whole boundary question". Contrary to the view of the ambassador, it was not enough to insist on reclaiming from the Turks only those positions which they had seized since the creation of the commission and postpone until later the delimitation of this sector. This would condone too much encroachment. The Amir of Dhala was in a permanent rage at the supine attitude of the British and proving immensely difficult for Wahab to restrain. Moreover, if his territorial rights were not re-instated before the joint commission left his country, argued Fitzmaurice, its departure would be seen by the tribes as a victory for the Turks and the British position would continue to unravel. The Yafi would block the north-eastern delimitation. Conversely, if the Amir's rights were restored the work of the commission would proceed "comparatively smoothly and rapidly". Following settlement of the Amiri section of the frontier, this should certainly proceed next, as the ambassador wished, in a north-easterly direction, and not—as the Turks were demanding—south-west to the sea. Trying to steer a course between the extremes represented by Maitland and O'Conor, Fitzmaurice was, however, careful to point out that he was not arguing for a *complete* restoration of the status quo of 1873 but only for reversing the comparatively recent encroachments of the Turks.

What tactics should be employed? Further negotiation for the time being was not only useless, thought Fitzmaurice, but damaging to British interests. Nor could anything be anticipated from the cash bribery of the Turkish commissioners suggested by O'Conor.[33] Fear of the Palace made them immune to this, as he had established after two formal conferences with them and "a couple of long private yarns". A show of force during the present cool season was thus imperative. The ambassador should not worry that it would lead to war because the sultan, whose position in the Yemen was already precarious and who was in any case distracted by events in Macedonia, was bluffing and would back down if called out. "Remember," he concluded a private letter to the Foreign Office, "if this Turkish nettle is grasped, it won't sting, and their obstructive attitude will collapse all along the line."[34]

---

[33] CAC Cam., O'Conor to Sanderson, 11 Jan. 1902, OCON 6/1/32.
[34] TNA, Fitzmaurice to Tyrrell, 12 Dec. 1902, FO78/5244. In addition to Fitzmaurice's formal report to O'Conor of 22 December in TNA, FO78/5315, see also CAC Cam., Fitzmaurice to O'Conor, 15 Nov., 3 and 12 Dec. 1902, OCON 6/1/35.

Despite his confidence in a peaceful outcome, Fitzmaurice was aware that he was recommending tactics likely to be thought too provocative by the ambassador. He was also probably a little nervous at having implied that—like his predecessors—O'Conor had been duped by the sultan on the boundary question. His letter of 12 December thus contained a plea that it was no more than his duty to express his view plainly, together with some judicious flattery of the ambassador's achievements in extracting encouraging promises from the sultan. However, shortly afterwards he could not entirely conceal his exasperation when he realized that O'Conor still expected him to make the Turks turn somersaults by pure diplomacy. He had seen a good deal of the Turkish commissioners and established excellent relations, he said, but emphasised that "they cannot stir without an Iradé, unless indeed they are prepared to throw off their Turkish uniforms and desert to us".[35]

Aware that O'Conor's wishful thinking about Aden had its adherents in the Foreign Office, Fitzmaurice had also been canvassing support for a more robust policy by means of private letters to London. It must at once be made clear that these did not include letters to the foreign secretary himself, despite the fact that they were remotely connected by family and that Lord Lansdowne, though a Protestant, appears to have held no animus against Catholics.[36] The fact is that the social distance between Fitzmaurice and the great Victorian aristocrat who was his ultimate chief was immense, and it is unlikely that he would have even dreamed of writing to him. Among his correspondents instead were Ronald Hamilton, Lansdowne's assistant private secretary[37] and, most notably, William Tyrrell, Sanderson's private secretary for the last seven years.[38] Tyrrell, also a Roman Catholic and almost exactly the same age as Fitzmaurice, was to prove a figure of great significance in the projection of the latter's opinions. In 1903 he was appointed acting secretary to the Committee of Imperial Defence and by 1907 was private

---

[35] CAC Cam., Fitzmaurice to O'Conor, 25 Dec. 1902, OCON 6/1/35.
[36] The family name of Lord Lansdowne, the 5th Marquess, was Petty-Fitzmaurice, and the Petty-Fitzmaurice's, like Fitzmaurice's father, came from Kerry. (The wealth of the Lansdowne Fitzmaurices came from a marriage alliance with the family of the great 17th Century Irish land-grabber, Sir William Petty.) According to Cecil, Lansdowne was "not fervently religious...and never troubled himself much about creeds or dogmas", *Lord Lansdowne*, p. 11.
[37] TNA, Fitzmaurice to Hamilton, 16 Dec. 1902, FO78/5244. Hamilton had been acting third secretary in Constantinople in 1897–8.
[38] TNA, Fitzmaurice to Tyrrell, 12 Dec. 1902, FO78/5244.

secretary to Sir Edward Grey, becoming his closest confidant—"the Grey Eminence in the Foreign Office".[39] Tyrrell acquired immense influence and has been described as "a dangerous and unforgiving adversary".[40] The letter he received from Fitzmaurice about the Aden Boundary Commission was included in the Foreign Office's Confidential Print and circulated on 31 December, two days following its receipt.

Fitzmaurice's campaign for a show of force on the Amiri border, which had culminated in his report of 22 December, was decisive in swinging opinion behind this tactic. O'Conor, it is true, in a despatch prompted by Fitzmaurice's report, claimed that his own approach was making progress at the Palace.[41] But his tone was markedly defensive and his position had been weakened by his failure to have the assurances he had been given translated into cooperation on the frontier. In London there was exasperation at the year-long deadlock and Fitzmaurice's report had been grudgingly admired. As for Curzon, who in 1896 had launched Fitzmaurice's report on the forced conversions to Islam in the eastern *vilayets*, he regarded the conversion of O'Conor's dragoman to the need for a show of force with "huge amusement".[42] "Every representation we have hitherto made has been endorsed by Mr. Fitzmaurice's report", he telegraphed gleefully from India. "We emphatically urge", he concluded, "that the political pivot of the whole question is the Dthali plateau, and that any settlement which leaves its future in protracted doubt will be valueless."[43]

Already on 12 December district orders had been issued in Aden for the organization of a 400–strong movable column stiffened by artillery. Formed chiefly by a detachment of the Second Battalion Royal Dublin Fusiliers, who had distinguished themselves in South Africa and were on their way home to Ireland, its appearance in Dhala in early January naturally cheered Fitzmaurice immensely.[44] British policy was now looking more muscular but the Turks had reinforced their own

---

[39] Sir Francis Oppenheimer, *Stranger Within: Autobiographical pages* (Faber and Faber: London, 1960), p. 206.

[40] Erik Goldstein, "Tyrrell, William George, Baron Tyrrell (1866–1947)", *ODNB* [36608, accessed 20 Jan. 2007]. See also Zara S. Steiner, *The Foreign Office and Foreign Policy, 1898–1914* (The Ashfield Press: London, 1986), pp. 118–20.

[41] TNA, O'Conor to Lansdowne, 13 Jan. 1903, FO78/5315.

[42] Dilks, *Curzon in India*, vol. 1, p. 153.

[43] TNA, Viceroy of India to S of S, 20 Jan. 1903, FO78/5315.

[44] CAC Cam., Fitzmaurice to O'Conor, 30 Jan. 1903, OCON 6/1/36. See also Majors C. F. Romer and A. E. Mainwaring, *The Second Battalion Royal Dublin Fusiliers in the South African War with a Description of the Operations in the Aden Hinterland* (A. L. Hum-

positions.[45] For a while, therefore, counsels continued to be divided between those who wanted a showdown on the Amiri border near Dhala and those who argued that the British commissioners should head off for the north-east, showing the mailed fist only if unavoidable. The north-east-first party was now clearly led by O'Conor, who in this as in other matters was painstaking in his attention to detail and stubborn in refusing to abandon any policy on which he had resolved.[46] However, Curzon kept up the pressure and at the end of January was told that he could use force in Amiri territory should the sultan continue to be obstructive. Shortly after this the British column at Dhala was further reinforced,[47] and the cruisers *Hermione* and *Intrepid* were ordered to proceed to Aden in order to be in a position to choke the Turkish ports in the Red Sea.

With these steps in progress, on 9 February the embassy—with O'Conor, fortunately for him, on leave—was required to issue an ultimatum to the Turkish government. This demanded that the irregular Arab levies in Turkish pay should be totally disbanded, the whole of the Yafi tribes (including the Shaibi sub-division) recognized as forming part of the nine tribes, arrangements made for the safe delimitation of the border to the north-east, and that "immediate and effective recognition [should] be given to the rights of the Amir of Dthali as exercised by him previous to October 1901". These demands should be met by 14 February, failing which the British government would be "compelled to use force".[48]

On the following day the Turks capitulated on all points. However, the instructions to their boundary commissioners to make a withdrawal on the Amiri frontier did not include the village of Al Jalela,[49] which was

---

phreys: London, 1908), part 3, ch. 1; TNA, IO memorandum, "Aden Boundary", 20 Jan. 1903, FO78/5315.

[45] TNA, IO memorandum, "Aden Boundary", 20 Jan. 1903, FO78/5315.

[46] Pears, *Forty Years in Constantinople*, p. 217.

[47] TNA, Report on the demarcation of the frontier between the tribes in the Protectorate of Aden and the Turkish Province of Yemen, by Major-General P. J. Maitland, C. B., Resident at Aden, 11 May 1904, FO78/5376 [hereafter 'Maitland Report, 11 May 1904'].

[48] TNA, Aide-memoire to be presented to Turkish Minister for Foreign Affairs on Aden frontier question, 9 February 1903, FO78/5315; confirmation that this *was* presented (by the chargé d'affaires, James Whitehead) on 9 February is found in O'Conor to Lansdowne, 10 Mar. 1903, FO78/5316.

[49] IOL, ABC Diary, 14 Feb. 1903; CAC Cam., Fitzmaurice to O'Conor, 24 Feb. 1903, OCON 6/1/36.

not surprising since, as the embassy pointed out, they had occupied it with British acquiescence since 1885. This did not impress Wahab and Fitzmaurice, who refused to contemplate demarcation north-eastward until the settlement was evacuated. An embarrassed Lansdowne was thus forced hurriedly to fall into line with their position by instructing the embassy on 16 February to clarify for the benefit of the Turks that the British did indeed include Al Jalela in the Amiri territory to be restored.[50] This did not move the Turks and another naval demonstration was inevitable. "Whether the Turks give in quietly or compel us to use force," Fitzmaurice reassured O'Conor, "I shall use my endeavours to make the settlement as quiet and peaceful as possible."[51]

The British camp now received warning that the Turkish troops at Dhala were encouraging "mad mullahs" to stir up the Arabs to a *jihad* against it. "I suppose we shall get no sleep tonight either as another attack is expected", Fitzmaurice told O'Conor after the troops had already been stood to arms for a night. This situation made it even easier for the Amiri border-first party to persuade the Foreign Office and O'Conor to fall in with swift action. "The iron is hot now", Fitzmaurice added, "and we need scarcely strike to settle the Amiri question once for all."[52] The British force assembled at Dhala now boasted 2,500 men and eight mountain guns[53] and could probably have seized Al Jalela without any great difficulty, even pushing on further to Qataba to secure the Amir's more extensive territorial claims. However, this was unnecessary because the naval demonstration at Hodeida threatened the collapse of the sultan's whole position in the Yemen.[54] Faced with this prospect, and denied support by the German emperor,[55] on 17 March Abdul Hamid reluctantly signified his compliance with British demands—though reserving his sovereign rights at Al Jalela.[56] The

---

[50] TNA, Whitehead to Lansdowne, 14 and 17 Feb. 1903, FO78/5316.

[51] CAC Cam., Fitzmaurice to O'Conor, 14 Feb. 1903, OCON 6/1/36.

[52] CAC Cam., Fitzmaurice to O'Conor, 24 Feb. 1903, OCON 6/1/36; and IOL, ABC Diary, 23 Feb. 1903.

[53] Maitland Report, 11 May 1904.

[54] The warships were not withdrawn until May, TNA, Memorandum respecting the Aden Frontier Delimitation. March 1906, FO881/8644, p. 5.

[55] TNA, Waters (Military Attaché, Berlin) to Lascelles (Berlin), 16 Mar. 1903; Lascelles to Lansdowne, 18 Mar. 1903, FO78/5317.

[56] TNA, O'Conor to Lansdowne. 19 Mar. 1903, FO78/5317; CAC Cam., O'Conor to Sanderson, 17/18 Mar. 1903, OCON 4/1/20.

Dhala plateau was to be evacuated, and no further obstacles placed in the way of the work of delimitation.[57]

Fitzmaurice learned by field telegraph of the sultan's announcement on the day following its issue but the news did not reach the Turkish commissioners until 21 March, as he anticipated. "I rode over to Jalela on a camel and found they had read the Iradé an hour before and had already given orders for everything to be ready to leave during the night", he told O'Conor. "The wrench was a hard one for them but they took it like men and said they only wished it had come a year ago."[58] In the early hours of 22 March, the Turks evacuated Al Jalela and set up a new camp at Qataba. In order to re-establish British authority quickly and put a stop to looting, Fitzmaurice immediately returned to the village, this time with two companies of the Bombay Rifles. Having negotiated the terms of Britain's re-entry with the Arabs who initially blocked his approach, he then oversaw the hoisting of the Union Jack on the village flag tower.[59] He was exultant but careful in his report to give due credit for the success to the ambassador's diplomacy in Constantinople.[60] A week later he accompanied a British survey party which established a new camp at Sanah.[61] This was close to Qataba and so made it easy for him to keep in contact with the Turkish commissioners.

The Turkish withdrawal enabled the delimitating of the central sector of the frontier finally to commence at the beginning of April. However, the understandings reached remained fragile, and so as not to risk disturbing them, on 30 March Lord Lansdowne—who together with Sanderson had regarded the rush to hoist the British flag over Al Jalela as needlessly provocative[62]—wisely refused to lay before parliament any papers on the subject.[63]

---

[57] Gavin, *Aden Under British Rule*, pp. 223–4; CAC Cam., Fitzmaurice to O'Conor, 23 Mar. 1903, OCON 6/1/38.

[58] CAC Cam., Fitzmaurice to O'Conor, 23 Mar. 1903, OCON 6/1/38.

[59] IOL, ABC Diary 22 Mar. 1903; Romer and Mainwaring, *The Second Battalion Royal Dublin Fusiliers in the South African War*, p. 211.

[60] CAC Cam., Fitzmaurice to O'Conor, 23 Mar. 1903, OCON 6/1/38.

[61] IOL, ABC Diary, 29 Mar. 1903.

[62] TNA, mins. of Sanderson and Lansdowne, 23 Mar. 1903, FO78/5317. This view was not shared by Curzon, TNA, Viceroy to S of S, 29 Apr. 1903, FO78/5317.

[63] *Parl. Debs.*, 4th Ser. (Lords), vol. 120, col. 548.

Between two fires

Well before Jalela Fitzmaurice had begun to feel himself caught between the assertiveness of the Indian government and the preference for pure diplomacy of O'Conor and the Foreign Office. The nervous tension that this created, together with the climate and fever, began to take its toll on him, especially as the delimitation soon ran into trouble again.

While O'Conor and the Foreign Office tended to see Fitzmaurice's sensitivity to the connection between military power and local prestige as evidence of his conversion to the bellicosity and tunnel-vision of the Anglo-Indians, Maitland mistook his increasing insistence on the political necessity of a *joint* delimitation[64] with the Turks for proof that he was a supporter of the "half measures" advocated by London. "I find I am between two fires", he complained to O'Conor,[65] though it was the heat from the Aden Resident that was to prove the greatest.

While the ambassador had been on leave in London Maitland had actually kept back one of Fitzmaurice's telegrams to him in the hope that he could be induced to stiffen its recommendations.[66] They had also had a serious altercation on the eve of the peaceful Turkish withdrawal from Al Jalela, when a sleepless Fitzmaurice had been forced to ride south a day's journey to intercept Maitland riding north and discourage him from taking precipitate military action.[67]

With the Anglo-Indian commissioners seeking to sustain the momentum of their advance at Al Jalela, it was only a matter of weeks before the fragility of the March settlement was exposed. This was occasioned by their demand—prompted said Fitzmaurice later by their simple desire to establish a "margin for barter"[68]—that an Amiri frontier to the *north* of Qataba, and significantly beyond what the British had previously claimed, should be discussed. The Turkish commissioners rebelled at this, and a few days later insisted on suspending delimitation.[69] O'Conor also thought that the claim to Qataba was "rather

---

[64] CAC Cam., Fitzmaurice to O'Conor, 30 Jan. 1903, OCON 6/1/36.
[65] CAC Cam., Fitzmaurice to O'Conor, 23 Mar. 1903, OCON 6/1/38.
[66] CAC Cam., Fitzmaurice to O'Conor, 23 Mar. 1903, OCON 6/1/38.
[67] CAC Cam., Fitzmaurice to O'Conor, 17 Mar. 1903, OCON 6/1/38; IOL, ABC Diary, 14 and 15 Mar. 1903. In his Report of 11 May 1904, Maitland had the decency to concede that Fitzmaurice had been right.
[68] CAC Cam., Fitzmaurice to O'Conor, 1 and 8 June 1903, OCON 6/2/24.
[69] IOL, ABC Diary, 20 Apr., and 26 June 1903, R/20/A/1207; CAC Cam., O'Conor to Sanderson, 7 Apr. 1903, OCON 4/1/20.

doubtful and certainly impolitic".[70] The Foreign Office and even Curzon agreed,[71] and the suggestion was dropped. However, just as cooperation on demarcation with the Turks was resuming, the British commissioners found themselves immobilized by the upshot of an acrimonious dispute with Maitland over priorities and who was actually in charge of the boundary work.

Maitland, like Curzon himself, had long believed that the delimitation would only rest on secure foundations if *treaty relations* with the frontier tribes, providing British guarantees against Turkish encroachment and regular payments, were first established. Choosing at this point to resurrect this argument, Maitland now urged that the demarcation north-east to the desert should be delayed until treaties with the troublesome tribes here were signed, which he estimated would take about six months; meanwhile, the commission should remain where it was until the dispute over Qataba was resolved and then proceed south-west to the sea through territory where close British relations with the tribes already existed.[72] Wahab and Fitzmaurice, however, wanted to complete their hot and dangerous work as quickly as possible, pushing on at once to the north-east while the Yafi tribes remained in awe of the demonstration of British power at Al Jalela, then returning to complete the job in the south-west in the cool season. Maitland's plan, upon which—they pointed out—they had not been consulted, was based on ignorance of the situation on the frontier and prompted by personal ambition. It would merely incite the "cupidity" of the tribes, lead up blind alleys, waste money on a heroic scale, and, by introducing confusion and delay, completely sabotage their work.[73] Their exasperation therefore was complete when in June, just as the Turks were ready to resume boundary cooperation, Maitland, supported by Curzon, got his way. The India Office agreed that in the north-east treaties were to take precedence over delimitation, and the boundary commissioners were

[70] TNA, O'Conor to Lansdowne, 15 and 18 May, 1903, FO78/5317; O'Conor to Lansdowne, 16 June 1903, with a long, important minute by Lansdowne on "this valuable despatch", FO78/5318.
[71] TNA, Viceroy to S of S, 19 May 1903, FO78/5317.
[72] TNA, Viceroy to S of S, 19 May 1903, FO78/5317, and Wahab to India, 26 June 1903, FO78/5318; CAC Cam., Maitland to O'Conor, 28 Jan. 1903, OCON 6/1/36; IOL, Maitland to Wahab, 13 Apr. and to Fitzmaurice, 26 Apr. 1903, R/20/A/1199; and IOL, Resident to India, 3 May 1903, R/20/A/1200.
[73] CAC Cam., Fitzmaurice to O'Conor, 11 May 1903, OCON 6/2/24.

to take their cue from the resident.[74] Meanwhile, the commissioners should concentrate on the delimitation of the central section of the frontier. At least once the Bana River was reached they might be in a position to provide the information about the line to the desert which, together with Maitland's new treaties, would make possible presentation of a credible notification to the Porte on the north-east boundary. This was the second-best solution that the commissioners had actually come up with themselves.[75]

There was now "open war" between the commissioners and the resident, Fitzmaurice told O'Conor. It meant, he told him, either "shaking ourselves free of his thraldom or smashing the Commission".[76] For good measure, Fitzmaurice reported that Maitland was so indifferent to the suffering of his men that "all the officers detest him—find him impossible and pray for his removal or death".[77] Shortly afterwards, on 24 June, both he and Wahab became incandescent on discovering that Maitland had for months been blocking or selectively quoting their outbound messages in order to make them suit his own purposes. As a result they took the extraordinary step of sending Curzon a short telegram of protest *en clair*. Two days later they elaborated on this in a secret telegram—clearly drafted by Fitzmaurice—and concluded with the observation that Maitland was a more serious obstacle to the success of the boundary commission than the Turks. In the absence of a remedy to "the evil", they effectively offered their resignations.[78] For his part, Maitland, who greatly resented this "monstrous" attempt by the commissioners to go over his head to the viceroy, told Curzon's secretary exactly what he thought of them. "Wahab's chief characteristic", he said, "is want of backbone", while Fitzmaurice could well have "gone a little bit off his head".[79]

---

[74] TNA, Viceroy to S of S, 18 May 1903, FO78/5317; IOL, ABC Diary 26 June; CAC Cam., O'Conor to Sanderson, 8 July 1903, OCON 4/1/20, and Fitzmaurice to O'Conor, 11 Aug. 1903 [covering a 20-page account of this 'dust storm'], OCON 6/2/26.

[75] TNA, Viceroy to S of S, 24 July 1903, FO78/5318; IO to FO, 29 July 1903, FO78/5318.

[76] CAC Cam., Fitzmaurice to O'Conor, 10 June 1903, OCON 6/1/39.

[77] CAC Cam., Fitzmaurice to O'Conor, 8 June 1903, OCON 6/2/24.

[78] TNA, Wahab to Govt. of India, 26 June 1903, FO78/5318; also, CAC Cam., Fitzmaurice to O'Conor, 8 July 1903, OCON 6/2/26—a letter full of talk of the need for them to resign.

[79] IOL, Maitland to Secretary to Govt. of India, 12 July 1903, R/20/A/1199.

Maitland's opinion of Fitzmaurice's mental state at this juncture probably had some foundation. By his own account, he had never worked so hard since the Birejik Commission. Already by March he had been "very much run down" and was advised by the camp doctor that he needed to take leave. It was only the tonic of the Jalela triumph, he told O'Conor, which had picked him up again.[80] This had been short-lived, and the summer temperature was mounting in step with the frustrations of the work. Dhala, at its higher altitude, may have been slightly cooler than Aden town but this did not alter the fact that the temperatures there were often unbearable for Europeans, especially if they were living under canvass. In mid-June he reported that it was rarely less than 100 degrees in the shade and that any kind of movement had to be undertaken at night, which added dangers of a different kind.[81] In early July it was 110. "The ink dries on one's pen as one writes—while what with dust storms, mosquitoes, scorpions, myriads of locusts which overcloud the sky often at a height of 3000 ft., our lot is not an enviable one."[82] Insect-borne diseases, notably dengue fever, were rampant. The summer of 1903 also experienced a more than usually severe drought, with rainfall down well over fifty per cent on the previous year. In the middle of July the British were forced by scarcity of water to move their camp back south from near Qataba to the site of the supporting column at Dhala in order to be near a better well. From this point until the end of August the drought became a regular theme of Wahab's diary, and the lightest shower worthy of comment.[83]

Neither was it as if during this period of stalemate Fitzmaurice could take it easy during the heat. Wahab's diary for the spring and summer of 1903 is full of records of his activities: keeping up contacts with the Turks at Qataba, visiting the British party surveying the particularly feverish Tiban Valley, and cementing relations with tribal chiefs. In early August he had the first of a number of bad attacks of fever plus "one or two other disorders", and did not leave his tent for twelve days—except for one night when, delirious, he was found wandering about the camp "saying quaint things". For 48 hours he was

[80] CAC Cam., Fitzmaurice to O'Conor, 5 Apr. 1903, OCON 6/1/38.
[81] CAC Cam., Fitzmaurice to O'Conor, 15 June 1903, OCON 6/1/39.
[82] CAC Cam., Fitzmaurice to O'Conor, 9 July 1903, OCON 6/2/26.
[83] IOL, ABC Diary, e.g. 14 July, 24 Aug. 1903; and CAC Cam., Fitzmaurice to O'Conor, 15 July 1903, OCON 6/2/26.

in a state of complete collapse.[84] The start of the rainy season at the end of August was a mixed blessing, for intense heat in the mornings was followed by downpours in the afternoons, leaving the nights damp and chilly. Due to leave to assist the survey work in the Tiban Valley, he told O'Conor that they would all have to "live on quinine".[85] He never fully recovered from the damage which this interlude inflicted on his health.[86]

Meanwhile, the India Office had rapped Maitland over the knuckles in response to the commissioners' protest in June,[87] though Curzon—who of course agreed with the resident on the treaties—had shown him much more indulgence. Indeed, though he did not exonerate Maitland completely, in late July he told the commissioners that he had found their charges unwarranted and their conduct in putting them forward "unjustifiable and improper".[88] Shortly after this the viceroy, whose patience with the whole boundary affair was about at an end,[89] broadened his offensive, now singling out for attack the very man whose support he had welcomed so warmly in January—Fitzmaurice. On 31 July, in a long telegram to O'Conor, Fitzmaurice had replied rather tartly to Curzon's criticism, suggesting that the viceroy had been misled by Maitland and had thus overlooked, among other things, the international character of the boundary commission.[90] Stung by this, on 8 August Curzon telegraphed to the India Office that Fitzmaurice's remarks showed a "complete misapprehension of position. Unless there is material change in his attitude", he added menacingly, "I may be driven to recommend a change".[91]

For his part, O'Conor had throughout the summer also been getting more and more agitated by the virtual paralysis inflicted on the boundary commission, though his view was that this was the fault of Curzon's man, the Aden Resident.[92] Maitland should be withdrawn and the commissioners allowed at once to get on with the delimita-

---

[84] CAC Cam., Fitzmaurice to O'Conor, 24 Aug. 1903, OCON 6/1/40.
[85] CAC Cam., Fitzmaurice to O'Conor, 31 Aug. 1903, OCON 6/1/40.
[86] Ryan, *The Last of the Dragomans*, p. 86; Bullard, *The Camels Must Go*, p. 63.
[87] TNA, Foreign Secretary (Simla) to Political Resident Aden, 24 July 1903, FO78/5319; IO to FO, 29 July 1903, FO78/5318.
[88] TNA, Foreign Secretary (Simla) to Political Resident Aden, 24 July 1903, FO78/5319 [for forwarding to Commissioners].
[89] TNA, Viceroy to IO, 11 Aug. 1903, FO78/5318.
[90] TNA, Fitzmaurice to O'Conor, 31 July 1903, FO78/5318.
[91] TNA, Viceroy to IO, 8 Aug. 1903, FO78/5318.
[92] CAC Cam., O'Conor to Sanderson, May–Aug. OCON 4/1/20.

tion in the north-east. He refused to believe that either the tribes or the Turks would attempt any serious obstruction, as both were "aware that behind them there is an army of two thousand British troops".[93] When Lansdowne, who admitted to finding it difficult to carry the complicated history of the affair in his mind, finally declared against the north-east frontier,[94] O'Conor suggested that at least Fitzmaurice might be allowed to make a personal inspection of it.[95]

With O'Conor insisting on the ejection of Maitland, and Curzon now threatening to demand the withdrawal of Fitzmaurice, something clearly had to be done urgently. Accordingly, in the middle of August the India Secretary, Lord George Hamilton, announced that either the British commissioners or Maitland—or both—would be removed if they did not cooperate.[96]

Though 'loyal cooperation' was now the official order of the day, Fitzmaurice's private attitude towards Maitland soon became if anything even more venomous. In September he told O'Conor that the resident was to blame for the death of a surveyor and provoking an attack by 1000 Yafi tribesmen ("mainly his treaty friends")[97] on the British camp in which five men were killed, for wasting money on a stupendous scale, and for a disingenuous stream of comments on his policy that made him sick. "The Turks are jubilant. It makes one's blood boil", he told O'Conor in a letter full of sarcasm and bitterness, "to think that the Gov[ernmen]t of India still believes in a man who so unscrupulously mismanages everything he touches."[98]

Passed over for chief dragoman

In mid-September 1903 Adam Block finally achieved his ambition of being appointed British representative on the Ottoman Debt and

---

[93] TNA, O'Conor to Lansdowne, 8 Aug. 1903, FO78/5318.

[94] TNA, min. of Lord Lansdowne, n.d. (circa early Aug. 1903), FO78/5318.

[95] TNA, O'Conor to Lansdowne, 24 Aug. 1903, FO78/5318. This came to nothing. Fitzmaurice was opposed, as was Curzon, TNA, Viceroy to IO, 11 Sept. 1903, FO78/5319.

[96] IOL, S of S to Resident Adviser, 14 Aug. 1903, R/20/A/1199; Lansdowne to O'Conor, 14 Aug. 1903, CAC Cam., OCON 6/1/439.

[97] CAC Cam., Fitzmaurice to O'Conor, 20 Sept. 1903, OCON 6/1/40.

[98] CAC Cam., Fitzmaurice to O'Conor, 14 Sept. 1903, OCON 6/1/40.

resigned as chief dragoman at the embassy.[99] Thereupon Sir Nicholas O'Conor took a decision that hurt Fitzmaurice deeply. He passed him over for appointment to the vacancy. He did this despite Fitzmaurice's long and broad experience, despite the public recognition of his achievements in Armenia—and despite the fact that as *de facto* second dragoman he was heir apparent. Instead, O'Conor appointed Harry Lamb, at the time 'Consul for Koordistan' in Erzeroum.[100]

It is true that Lamb was older than Fitzmaurice and was nine years his senior in the Levant Service. Those who knew him well thought that he had sound judgement and was easy to work with. He also had experience at consular missions throughout the Ottoman Empire.[101] On the other hand, he had as yet received no honours, at least one person who knew him thought his Turkish no more than adequate,[102] and he had no experience at all of the dragomanate in Constantinople. Why did O'Conor prefer him over Fitzmaurice?

O'Conor clearly did not find it easy to make his decision, and was devious with Fitzmaurice, who—unlike his rivals[103]—seems to have been kept in the dark about the whole business. What O'Conor did was write to Fitzmaurice on 6 September and ask him whether, in light of the fact that "there might be a sudden pressure of work" in the embassy, it was "necessary" for him to stay on the Yemen frontier. He appears not to have elaborated[104] but it is too much of a coincidence to believe that he did not have in mind Block's imminent departure. It may be of course that at this point O'Conor had not closed his mind to appointing Fitzmaurice. But by not telling him *why* the pressure of work in the embassy was likely to increase, he was also more likely to elicit from Fitzmaurice a properly modest hesitation about returning—especially since the delimitation work at last had prospects of some progress and cooler weather was in view.

---

[99] By this move he virtually tripled his salary, and four years later received a knighthood.

[100] CAC Cam., O'Conor to Lamb, and O'Conor to Sanderson, 11 Sept. 1903, OCON 4/1/20.

[101] Ryan, *The Last of the Dragomans*, p. 118; Pears, *Forty Years in Constantinople*, pp. 346–7.

[102] MECA Oxf., Draft autobiographical chapters of Richard M. Graves, p. 32, GB165–0125, Graves 1/1.

[103] The other was Edward Blech, dragoman-archivist in the embassy.

[104] His own letter has not survived and it is necessary to rely on Fitzmaurice's reply: CAC Cam., Fitzmaurice to O'Conor, 28 Sept. 1903, OCON 6/1/40.

"I am naturally the worst judge of the value of my services and consequently whether it was <u>necessary</u> I should stay on," was Fitzmaurice's reply to O'Conor's clever letter. Wahab, however, he informed the ambassador, believed strongly that he should and had told him that, if he left, he would himself resign. "General Maitland to my astonishment", Fitzmaurice added, "endorsed Wahab's statement."[105]

Of course, before O'Conor received this letter from Fitzmaurice the die had already been cast, and he had privately explained his preference for Lamb both to his wife and to Sanderson. "Fitzmaurice who in many ways is a very clever fellow is away and will not be back for some time", he told Lady O'Conor, "besides which he has not managed affairs near as well as I expected at Aden where that blessed commission is still footling about."[106] A month later he elaborated to Sanderson: "Fitzmaurice is...a sort of Irish Turk on whose temper you cannot always count. I was sure of getting on with him but another Ambassador might not hit it off as well."[107]

O'Conor had certainly been disappointed by his dragoman's inability to perform miracles in Aden and initially at any rate angered by his desertion to the Amiri border-first party.[108] However, after Al Jalela, and even after the deadlock had resumed, the ambassador conceded that Fitzmaurice was in a very difficult position, and in his letters to Sanderson not only refused to tar him with the same brush as "Wahab and Co." but continued to defend his *indispensability* to the success of the delimitation work.[109] He even persuaded the Foreign Office to pay him an extra £100 a year while he remained in the Yemen, plus an outfit allowance.[110] All things considered, it is difficult to avoid the conclusion that O'Conor had really made Lamb chief dragoman principally because he could not afford to withdraw Fitzmaurice from the Yemen. De Bunsen tactfully congratulated the ambassador on his choice of Lamb as chief dragoman but seemed to sense this when he added:

---

[105] CAC Cam., Fitzmaurice to O'Conor, 28 Sept. 1903, OCON 6/1/40.

[106] CAC Cam., O'Conor to Lady O'Conor, 11 Sept. 1903, OCON 3/5/5; see also O'Conor to Sanderson, 23 Sept. 1903, OCON 4/1/20.

[107] CAC Cam., O'Conor to Sanderson, 23 Oct. 1903, OCON 4/1/20.

[108] "I'm afraid from the tone of your Excellency's last two letters, you are a bit displeased with me and may wish me to cease my connection with this boundary work", CAC Cam., Fitzmaurice to O'Conor, 23 Mar. 1903, OCON 6/1/38.

[109] CAC Cam., O'Conor to Sanderson, 7 Apr. and 24 June 1903, OCON 4/1/20.

[110] CAC Cam., Fitzmaurice to O'Conor, 5 Apr. 1903, OCON 6/1/38.

"I still think Fitzmaurice, *if he were available*, has the capacity for making a first rate one, if his temper could be kept under control."[111]

Fitzmaurice received the bleak news of Lamb's appointment when he picked up two letters from O'Conor in the middle of October. He had just returned to the British camp at Sanah from a successful expedition to the mountainous Shaibi-Mares section of the border, where he had been climbing for 10 to 13 hours a day in the boiling sun and even swinging a pickaxe himself to cut stones for boundary pillars. It was, he told O'Conor, "the worst blow I have received for a long time". He had only stayed in the dragomanate, he said, because Currie had reformed it and made it "a career in itself".[112] He had tolerated the work—and Block—for years on the assumption that he would succeed his rival. Block himself had told him this, as had de Bunsen and Sir Charles Eliot, and he had thought it was agreed. Since an "outsider" had now been appointed, he continued, it appeared that he must have some defect of character that made him unsuitable for the post. Not wishing to become "a second Marinitsch, to be shelved when worn out", and loathe to face the humiliation of a return to Constantinople, where everyone thought that he would succeed Block, he begged O'Conor to give him a provincial post. Erzeroum, where his knowledge of Russian would prove useful, was his preference but, failing that, the vice-consulate at Philippopolis. Here he could have "a few years rest after nearly fifteen years roughing it", which had perhaps made him old before his time. It was the letter of a man deeply hurt but also acutely conscious that his correspondent was still his chief patron. Fitzmaurice was not about to burn his bridges with O'Conor.[113]

Unfortunately for Fitzmaurice, in a telegram of 4 October O'Conor had already told him that he was to remain with the boundary commission "for the present". The result was that three subsequent requests for release—lent urgency by his mounting exasperation with Wahab's military cast of mind and lack of drive, not to mention his own exhaustion—fell on deaf ears.[114]

---

[111] Emphasis added. CAC Cam., de Bunsen to O'Conor, 2 Oct. 1903, OCON 6/2/27.

[112] On this, see Berridge, "Nation, Class, and Diplomacy".

[113] CAC Cam., Fitzmaurice to O'Conor, 15 Oct. 1903, OCON 6/2/27.

[114] CAC Cam., Fitzmaurice to O'Conor, 12 and 22 Nov. 1903, OCON 6/1/42.

South-west to the sea

In September 1903 the joint commission had at least regained some momentum in delimitating the central section of the frontier. However, the work was often extremely dangerous because incidents with hostile tribesmen had become more serious, and there was even fear of an uprising in the rear of the commission. Maitland, to the irritation of both London and Calcutta, asked for reinforcements. Fitzmaurice, whose health remained poor and who was once more finding Maitland obstructive, believed that the tribal animosity had been encouraged not only by the ineptness of the resident's treaty-seeking policy but by his increasingly rough methods.[115] The British force, ostensibly sent to support the commission, was, he believed, doing more harm than good.[116]

As for O'Conor, his gloom about Aden only deepened, especially when—under parliamentary pressure—it was decided to postpone the delimitation to the north-east and instead drive south-west to the sea.[117] The ambassador also had to suffer being disabused by Fitzmaurice of a seriously inflated notion of Britain's relative military strength in the protectorate.[118] And always there was Maitland. "We are spending about £80 a day on the Commission, we are courting an enquiry, and a business which, if properly managed on the spot, would have been a brilliant success, is likely to end in a ghastly failure", he told Sanderson, once more urging that the only answer was to give Fitzmaurice overall responsibility.[119]

The push to the south-west was able to begin in January 1904 but difficulties with the Subhayi tribe and the Turkish commissioners led the commission once more, in the middle of March, to grind to a halt.[120] According to Fitzmaurice, this was entirely the fault of Wahab, whose baseless fears of the Subhayi allowed Maitland's excessive militarism to sabotage peaceful demarcation. High-handed behaviour by his troops was also antagonizing friendly tribesmen, and he complained that he

---

[115] CAC Cam., Fitzmaurice to O'Conor, 14 Sept. 1903, OCON 6/1/40; and 12 Nov. 1903, OCON 6/1/42.
[116] CAC Cam., Fitzmaurice to O'Conor, 26 Oct. 1903, OCON 6/2/27.
[117] CAC Cam., Sanderson to O'Conor, 29 Oct. 1903, OCON 6/1/41; TNA, O'Conor to Lansdowne, 24 Nov. and 1 Dec. 1903, FO78/5319.
[118] CAC Cam., Fitzmaurice to O'Conor, 22 Nov. 1903, OCON 6/1/42.
[119] CAC Cam., O'Conor to Sanderson, 9 Dec. 1903, OCON 4/1/20.
[120] TNA, Wahab to India, 29 Mar. 1904, FO78/5375.

was spending more time pacifying the Arabs—who had named him 'FarisMaris'—than demarcating with the Turks.[121]

Fortunately, the Turkish commissioners were as anxious as Fitzmaurice to end their Yemeni exile, and after the British had succeeded in intimidating them by blowing up towers belonging to one of their clients, the commission regained momentum.[122] Thereafter, by dint of night marches to avoid the appalling heat of the day, keeping rifles pointed at their camel men day and night,[123] abandoning some guns and stores, searching relentlessly for water, and providing flour, small luxuries and camels to the poorly supplied Turkish party,[124] the exhausted and scurvy-threatened joint commission finally reached the sea in the middle of May.[125] Fitzmaurice, whose health seemed to have improved, was overjoyed. The bargaining along the route with the Turks had been interminable but their condition, together with the general military situation in the Yemen and the despatch of a British warship to the entrance to the Red Sea,[126] had given him a strong hand to play. It had even, he boasted, allowed him to employ the Sibylline books principle with them.[127] He was extremely pleased with the boundary that had been agreed and was confident of a favourable settlement of the remaining details and exchange of maps before long.[128]

O'Conor rejoiced that the commission, against all expectations, had reached the sea. He was quick to congratulate Fitzmaurice, told the Foreign Office that his dragoman had earned a further honour, and

---

[121] CAC Cam., Fitzmaurice to O'Conor, 22 Mar. 1904, OCON 6/2/28.

[122] TNA, Memo. by Mr Fitzmaurice respecting Turkish encroachments in Wadi Sha'b, enclosed in Barclay to Grey, 14 Dec. 1906.

[123] On 7 April 139 of them, together with their animals, had fled at the prospect of the hardships they anticipated on the rest of the march, and only 5 were recaptured, TNA, Wahab's Diary, 1st to 13th April inclusive, FO78/5376. On 11 April, Wahab noted that 20 more camel men had deserted.

[124] On 20 April, Wahab noted in his Diary (14th–23rd April 1904 inclusive, TNA, FO78/5376) that the Turks were on half rations.

[125] IOL, Wahab's Diary, 11th May to 11th June, R/20/A/1207; TNA, Wahab to Aden, 25 May 1904, FO78/5376.

[126] IOL, FO to Admiralty, 21 Apr. 1904, and Resident to S of S, 31 May 1904, R/20/A/1203.

[127] Sibyls were prophetesses of the ancient world. In a famous myth, one of them sold the books of prophecies in her possession to Tarquin the Proud. She first offered him nine. He refused this, so she burned three and offered him the remaining six at the same price. When he persisted in refusing to strike a deal, she burned three more and offered him the remaining three still at the same price. At this point a resigned and now seriously disadvantaged Tarquin agreed to the purchase.

[128] CAC Cam., Fitzmaurice to O'Conor, 6 June 1904, OCON 6/1/42.

pressed Sanderson in the meantime to arrange an accolade from Lord Lansdowne.[129] This was the least that the ambassador could do, for he had whipped him on quite ruthlessly. In late April he admitted to Sanderson that he had been "urging him almost beyond his physical force, and that he may be bowled over by fever, to which he is somewhat subject".[130] However, in virtually the same breath O'Conor said that after a short rest on completion of the south-western boundary, Fitzmaurice was the man to lead the delimitation to the north-east.[131]

But where should the commission go to conclude the details of the south-westerly project? Wahab, whose own health had been poor for some time and was desperate to escape the climate, wanted it wrapped up at Constantinople or Simla, the summer capital of British India.[132] Fitzmaurice, however, thought the commission should stay where it was on the Red Sea. It made the sultan uneasy, he argued, and thus kept him under pressure. If it went to Constantinople he "would procrastinate till doomsday". For his own part, he said rashly that he could stay on as long as necessary.[133] O'Conor agreed about Constantinople and, after flirting with the idea that in order to spare the sultan's blushes Fitzmaurice should settle everything with the *vali* of the Yemen in Sanah,[134] accepted his dragoman's recommendation.

Castaway on Perim Island

On reaching the sea in May, the Anglo-Indian party had encamped on Perim, a British-occupied island in the Bab el Mandeb strait, while the Turks had installed themselves in their fort at Turba on the adjacent mainland. Though Perim was the most civilized place Fitzmaurice had seen since departing for the interior, it was only about five square miles in area, rocky, barren, and devoid of fresh water. It was also surrounded

---

[129] TNA, O'Conor to Fitzmaurice, 13 May 1904, tel. encl. in O'Conor to Lansdowne, 13 May 1904, FO78/5376; CAC Cam., Fitzmaurice to O'Conor, 28 May 1904, OCON 6/1/48; O'Conor to Sanderson, 25 May and 1 June, 1904, OCON 4/1/21.

[130] CAC Cam., O'Conor to Sanderson, 26 Apr. 1904, OCON 4/1/21.

[131] TNA, O'Conor to Lansdowne, 19 Apr. 1904, FO78/5375.

[132] TNA, Wahab to Maitland, 7 May 1903, encl. in Resident, Aden to Viceroy, 12 May 1903, FO78/5376.

[133] CAC Cam., Fitzmaurice to O'Conor, 6 June 1904, OCON 6/1/42.

[134] CAC Cam., O'Conor to Sanderson, 1 and 14 June 1904, and O'Conor to Fitzmaurice, 18 June 1904, OCON 4/1/21.

by some of the most treacherous waters in the Red Sea.[135] When he
arrived in May it was slightly cooler than the mainland but the rocks
were too hot to touch during the day and the humidity was appalling.
This was no place for Fitzmaurice to linger but once more he had been
hoist by his own petard, for linger he did.

On 9 June Curzon released Wahab and, believing there was little
left for the boundary commission to do, finally agreed that Fitzmaurice
should lead the British side.[136] Even O'Conor had concluded by now
that demarcation of the north-east frontier was dead.[137] However, there
remained the possibility that concessions to the British on understandings about the allegiance of the north-east tribes might be traded for
concessions to the Turks on the Red Sea coast. The negotiations thus
dragged on and O'Conor, always fearful that any turn of the sultan's
mood might cause all of the commission's work to be lost, once more
became anxious. "The Aden business is at a critical stage", he told
Sanderson,[138] and informed Fitzmaurice that he wanted him "at any
cost or inconvenience to come to an agreement on the whole frontier
right down to the sea".[139]

Fitzmaurice was again feeling unwell and angling, not for the first
time, to be allowed to recuperate during a period of leave on an
Indian hill station.[140] It was perhaps wishful thinking, therefore, that
led him to predict a swift conclusion.[141] However, the sultan began to
procrastinate, and by October Lord Lansdowne was so exasperated
that he arranged for another naval demonstration.[142] The Turks still
proving obdurate, in February 1905 they were warned by Lansdowne

---

[135] Gavin, *Aden Under British Rule, 1839–1967*, pp. 95–6, 181.
[136] TNA, Viceroy to IO, 9 June 1904, FO78/5376; Govt. of India (Foreign Dept.)
to Brodrick, 10 Nov. 1904, FO78/5377.
[137] CAC Cam., O'Conor to Sanderson, 29 June 1904, and O'Conor to Percy,
29 June 1904, OCON 4/1/21. Sanderson confirmed this: "The Govt. have always
been very half-hearted about it", he told O'Conor, "and anxious to bring the expedi-
tionary part of the business to a close. I cannot help feeling", he added, "that with all
Fitzmaurice's judgment and power of management it would have been a somewhat
hazardous undertaking", CAC Cam., Sanderson to O'Conor, 4 July 1904, OCON
6/1/47.
[138] CAC Cam., O'Conor to Sanderson, 14 June 1904, OCON 4/1/21.
[139] CAC Cam., O'Conor to Fitzmaurice, 18 June, 1904, OCON 4/1/21.
[140] CAC Cam., Fitzmaurice to O'Conor, 22 Mar. 1904, OCON 6/2/28; 3 Sept.
and 28 Oct. 1904, OCON 6/2/29.
[141] CAC Cam., Fitzmaurice to O'Conor, 3 Aug. 1904, OCON 6/1/48.
[142] TNA, min. of Lansdowne, c. 25 Oct. 1904, FO78/5377; H. M. S. *Proserpine* at
Perim to Admiralty, 9 Nov. 1904, FO78/5377.

that failure to conclude would force the British government to resort to a unilateral solution of the frontier question—and a warship was sent back to the Red Sea.[143] For theatrical effect, and at Fitzmaurice's own suggestion,[144] this vessel was also employed to convey him to one of his routine meetings at Turba.[145] According to the report sent to the Porte by the Turkish commissioner, Remzi Bey, Fitzmaurice then used "violent language" towards him—though it seems that the sultan had at last probably already capitulated.[146]

On 14 March, less than two weeks after returning from a five months' absence in Britain during which he had undergone a serious operation, O'Conor extracted from the sultan a *note verbale* suggesting a favourable response to the boundary commission's proposals. As a result, on 20 April at Turba, Fitzmaurice and Remzi Bey duly signed copies of maps and the minutes of their final meeting.[147] Together with side letters dealing with a slice of Subhayi-claimed territory that Britain had conceded on condition that it would never be transferred by the Turks to a third power,[148] these documents constituted the greater part of the written agreement on the Aden-Yemen frontier delimitation. With them the British had to be content.[149] "I do not think we could have achieved better terms," Lansdowne told O'Conor, "but I am appalled when I think of the length of time during which the negotiations have dragged on."[150] So was Fitzmaurice, whose ordeal on Perim reminded him, he told the ambassador, of the trial of Warren Hastings.[151]

---

[143] TNA, Lansdowne to Townley, 7 Feb. 1905, FO78/5440; Memorandum respecting the Aden Frontier Delimitation. March 1906, FO881/8644, p. 7.

[144] TNA, Fitzmaurice to O'Conor, 3 Mar. 1905, FO78/5440.

[145] TNA, Fitzmaurice to O'Conor, 12 Mar. 1905, FO78/5440.

[146] CAC Cam., Fitzmaurice to O'Conor, 17 Mar. and 4 Apr. 1905, OCON 6/1/50.

[147] TNA, Fitzmaurice to Govt. of India, 30 Apr. 1905, FO78/5441; Memorandum respecting the Aden Frontier Delimitation. March 1906, FO881/8644, pp. 8–9. As to the north-east sector of the frontier, these documents said nothing more than that this was "generally in a line north-east from Lakmet-es-Shah to the desert".

[148] TNA, O'Conor to Lansdowne, 10 June 1905, FO78/5441.

[149] It was reluctantly judged inexpedient at this stage to press the sultan to give any more formality to the agreement than this in view of his sensitivity to the charge that he was surrendering swathes of Moslem territory to infidels. However, this was finally achieved in the 'Anglo-Turkish Convention respecting the boundaries...' signed in London on 9 March 1914 and ratified by exchange of instruments on 5 June, FO881/10517.

[150] CAC Cam., Lansdowne to O'Conor, 21 Mar. 1905, OCON 6/1/51; TNA, Lansdowne to O'Conor, 23 Apr. 1905, FO78/5440.

[151] CAC Cam., Fitzmaurice to O'Conor, 4 Apr. 1905, OCON 6/1/50. This lasted six years.

The joint commission had been kept at Perim to delimitate the last 60 miles of the border but in practice this did not give Fitzmaurice much to do. To make matters worse, he had practically nobody to speak to and nothing to read, and was unable even to venture to Aden until the spring of 1905 because of the plague. His kidneys had been permanently damaged, and he had another bad attack of fever.[152] At the end of February 1905 he told O'Conor that he had even given up writing letters since he had had no news of the fate of his negotiations for two months.[153] His only consolations were being able to live under a roof rather than canvass, shark fishing in the relative cool of the evening, and a pat on the back from the Foreign Office.

O'Conor had sought in January to cheer Fitzmaurice up by telling him of the efforts he had been making to obtain recognition from the Indian government for his achievements.[154] However, he was served notice that his dragoman would expect something substantial when Fitzmaurice replied that he now attached more importance to this sort of thing than he used to do, pointedly observing that he had heard that "Wahab is expected to get a K".[155]

At the end of April 1905 Fitzmaurice was able to leave Perim Island for the last time. Back in Constantinople he lost no time in asking O'Conor to be appointed to the consulate at Monastir, and in the meantime for six months' leave of absence.[156] With the former request pending, he was back in England at the beginning of July, two years and eight months after leaving Constantinople for Aden.

Dark mood in London

Fitzmaurice must have been reasonably confident that he would receive some significant accolades when he returned to London. Despite the early arguments, he had ample evidence that his achievements on the Yemen frontier had finally come to be appreciated in London and Cal-

---

[152] CAC Cam., Fitzmaurice to O'Conor, 4 Feb. and 22 Apr. 1905, OCON 6/1/50.
[153] CAC Cam., Fitzmaurice to O'Conor, 28 Feb. 1905, OCON 6/1/50.
[154] CAC Cam., Fitzmaurice to O'Conor, 4 Feb. 1905, OCON 6/1/50; and O'Conor to Barrington, 18 Jan. 1905, FO800/143.
[155] CAC Cam., Fitzmaurice to O'Conor, 4 Feb. 1905, OCON 6/1/50.
[156] TNA, Fitzmaurice to O'Conor, 13 June 1905, FO78/5395.

cutta, as well as in the embassy in Constantinople.[157] However, things were not to turn out quite as he had hoped.

He arrived in London on 1 July and appears to have installed himself, at least for a few weeks, in the St. James's Club at 106 Piccadilly. This was much favoured by diplomats and Foreign Office staff, who—unlike ordinary members—could be elected without ballot and enjoyed financial discounts if employed abroad. It provided him, of course, with first class opportunities to make the kind of contacts he needed to mark his social progress and advance his career. He was not the only member of the Levant Service to be a member of the St. James's Club.[158]

As it happened, the Birthday Honours List had appeared in *The Times* on the day before Fitzmaurice arrived in London. One of the first things that he must have discovered, therefore, was that he had not been knighted. Instead, at the instigation of the Foreign Office, he had been made a Companion of the Order of the Bath (CB). This only pushed him two steps up the general table of precedence but would perhaps have made him content since Wahab had not been knighted either. However, his former colleague had received a *double* award: a CMG from the Foreign Office as well as a CB from the India Office. Convinced that it was he rather than Wahab who had been largely responsible for the eventual success of the boundary commission and that his service to Calcutta had been rendered at high personal cost, Fitzmaurice felt himself the victim of a serious injustice. Why had not the India Office given him an award to match the award given to Wahab by the Foreign Office? Hearing from Lansdowne's private secretary that it had been a mistake to give a double award to Wahab did not mollify him.[159]

A second blow followed hard on the first. This was the news that the Monastir post for which he had asked O'Conor, and which paid significantly more than his miserable third dragoman's salary,[160] was

---

[157] TNA, Wahab to Secretary to Govt. of India, Foreign Dept., 10 June 1904, and Foreign Dept. of Govt. of India to Brodrick, 10 Nov. 1904, FO78/5377; Mason to Govt. of India, 7 May 1905, FO78/5441.

[158] Robert Graves notes in his memoirs how valuable it was for him in making contacts with members of the FO, and British and foreign diplomatists, *Storm Centres of the Near East*, p. 186.

[159] CAC Cam., Fitzmaurice to O'Conor, circa late July 1905 and 22 Aug. 1905, OCON 6/1/53.

[160] At this point, Fitzmaurice received the maximum for the third dragoman (£550); Marinitch as second dragoman received £750; while Lamb as chief dragoman received £1100, CAC., Cam., min. of Cockerell, 13 May 1905, OCON 6/1/52.

not only to be filled by another but by a person he believed to be his junior. Three days after arriving in London and approaching his fortieth birthday, Fitzmaurice wrote to O'Conor to complain of his treatment and repeated his doubts about his qualifications for advancement in the dragomanate.[161]

On his appearance at the St. James's Fitzmaurice had been told that he looked "thin and a bit fine drawn" but he was soon beginning to feel better as a result of "good British food and native air".[162] Moreover, during the first few weeks of his leave he appears not to have had too much time to brood on his grievances for there were many embassy matters to engage his attention. He met someone recently in Military Intelligence to discuss the Baghdad Railway, and had a long talk on the same subject with Henry Babington Smith, Secretary to the Post Office, whose departure from the Ottoman Debt had created the vacancy into which Block had stepped. He also attended the House of Lords to hear Lansdowne on the Macedonian question, visited the Khedivial offices, and met senior figures at the India Office.

Fitzmaurice also discovered that he had acquired minor celebrity status in certain crevices of the political world, and was clearly flattered by the number of important people who were interested to hear first-hand of his exploits—and pick his brains. At the Foreign Office Lord Lansdowne was too busy to see him but he was warmly received by Sir Thomas Sanderson, who invited him to dinner to meet the famous Austrian adventurer Slatin Pasha.[163] It was at this juncture, too, that he first met the young Aubrey Herbert. He dined with the influential Sir Edward Law, until recently Finance Member of the Indian government, and even lunched with the Chancellor of the Exchequer, Austen Chamberlain. He took obvious pride in relating these encounters to O'Conor[164] but there was calculation in it, too, for this aspect of his treatment did not sit well with the way the India Office had refused him recognition or with the dead end at which his career had arrived. He was still *third* dragoman. His mood soon darkened again, and he wished O'Conor to know it.

---

[161] CAC Cam., Fitzmaurice to O'Conor, 4 July 1905, OCON 6/1/53.

[162] CAC Cam., Fitzmaurice to O'Conor, 4 July 1905, OCON 6/1/53.

[163] CAC Cam., Fitzmaurice to O'Conor, 4 July 1905, OCON 6/1/53. Slatin Pasha had served under both Gordon and Kitchener in the Sudan.

[164] Detailed in Fitzmaurice's three letters to O'Conor in July 1905, CAC Cam., OCON 6/1/53.

His resentment at the India Office in London was fed further by seeing Wahab receive his two awards at the investiture at Buckingham Palace on 24 July. He had also learned that he enjoyed the support of the government in the sub-continent, especially Curzon. As a result, in a pungently expressed letter of exceptional bitterness written to O'Conor shortly after the investiture, Fitzmaurice begged the ambassador once more to press his case for an Indian distinction, however small, "for work done on Indian soil".[165] O'Conor seems to have done his best for him but it was to no avail. St. John Brodrick, the Secretary of State for India, had set his face firmly against it. He probably knew that Lansdowne was lukewarm;[166] and he is unlikely to have been impressed by the view of Curzon, with whom he had fallen out and who in any case had just resigned as viceroy.[167]

Though Fitzmaurice accepted finally that no Indian distinction was to come his way, he refused to give up on Monastir. "I do hope you will send me there", he wrote to O'Conor in late August, "as returning to the Dragomanate would be not only distasteful but repugnant to me". He would rather be consul at Monastir than second dragoman in Constantinople when Marinitch retired. "Surely", he concluded, "my past failures have been adequately punished by being passed over and above all by that eleven months' nightmare and mental torture at Perim."[168] In mid-September he made a further impassioned plea for Monastir[169] but O'Conor would not relent.

Despite his deep unhappiness, Fitzmaurice appears to have given no serious consideration to another career, so there was no alternative for him but to return to his position as third dragoman in Constantinople. O'Conor probably held out the prospect of advancement in the

---

[165] CAC Cam., Fitzmaurice to O'Conor, circa late July 1905, OCON 6/1/53. As late as mid-September the Indian government was still trying to persuade the IO to give Fitzmaurice "further credit", TNA, Govt. of India (Foreign Dept.) to Brodrick, 14 Sept. 1905, FO78/5441.

[166] Lansdowne had formed the view that the performance of the boundary commissioners was "not one of which we can boast" and that therefore "our approval of the conduct of these officers should be expressed in very measured terms", TNA, min. of Lord Lansdowne, 21 Dec. 1904, FO78/5377; and draft letter from FO to IO [amended in Lansdowne's hand], 6 Jan. 1905, FO78/5440.

[167] CAC Cam., Fitzmaurice to O'Conor, 22 Aug. 1905, OCON 6/1/53; TNA, Walpole (IO) to Sanderson (FO), 12 Oct. 1905, and min. of Sanderson 24 Oct. 1905, FO78/5441.

[168] CAC Cam., Fitzmaurice to O'Conor, 22 Aug. 1905, OCON 6/1/53.

[169] CAC Cam., Fitzmaurice to O'Conor, 13 Sept. 1905, OCON 6/1/53.

dragomanate and threw him a few crumbs: a further special allowance for his time on the frontier,[170] and, effective from the end of August, promotion to consul at Constantinople—though *without* any increase in salary.[171] These were paltry consolations for having to return to the tedious and unrelenting work in the dragomanate and with which he believed that his long spell on the Yemen frontier had left him physically and mentally unable to cope.[172] The ambassador had made a bad enemy.

---

[170] CAC Cam., Cartwright to O'Conor, 2 Feb. 1906, OCON 6/2/32, and 26 Mar. 1907, OCON 6/1/60.

[171] *FO List*; TNA, Fitzmaurice to O'Conor, 17 Mar. 1907, FO195/2249.

[172] CAC Cam., Fitzmaurice to O'Conor, 13 Sept. 1905, OCON 6/1/53.

CHAPTER FOUR

CHIEF DRAGOMAN AT LAST, 1906–7

Following a final month of leave spent in Ireland, Fitzmaurice returned to Constantinople at the beginning of 1906, three years since his departure for the Yemen frontier. The political situation was much as he had left it. Abdul Hamid chafed under the financial tyranny of the European-staffed Ottoman Debt but had no visible *domestic* opponents of whom to speak. His spies, for whom he was now infamous, were everywhere; troublemakers were being exiled to the nether regions of the Empire; and the press suffered from the strictest censorship. Few would have thought that Aubrey Herbert was greatly exaggerating when he later remarked that "there was a pall of fear over the city of Constantinople".[1]

Rumblings of growing opposition to the sultan stimulated by émigrés abroad and cells in the provinces were certainly heard but for the most part the city remained tranquil. Privileged by the regime of the capitulations, the life of the large foreign community went on much as usual, with its senior members rubbing shoulders with the diplomatists at the exclusive *Cercle d'Orient*.[2] The British colony, which numbered probably about 2,000,[3] was not alone in still wishing its government to be gentle with the sultan. There were large contracts to be won from his ministers and long overdue debts to be paid. Moreover, the competition from other countries was increasing, especially from Germany, which usually treated the feelings of Yildiz Palace with exceptional tenderness.

In the dragomanate Fitzmaurice found the personalities unchanged since the time of his departure—except, of course, that Harry Lamb had replaced Block as chief dragoman. In the embassy hierarchy, to which all claimed indifference but many brooded over in the small hours of the morning,[4] Fitzmaurice was 22nd: below the consular dragoman,

---

[1] Herbert, *Ben Kendim*, p. 37.
[2] Consuls tended to frequent the *Club de Constantinople*.
[3] Many of these were Maltese, Ryan, *The Last of the Dragomans*, p. 32.
[4] TNA, Precedence at British Embassy at Constantinople, 18 June 1907, FO372/84.

Alex Waugh; below the dragoman-archivist, Edward Blech; and of course below the second dragoman, Hugo Marinitch. Lamb at 5th was quite out of his sight. The only dragomans he outranked were Andrew Ryan and Onik Effendi Parseghian. Ryan—melancholy but humorous and also a devout Catholic from southern Ireland—was eleven years his junior and, though capable and diligent, had worked only in the consulate-general.[5] As for Onik Effendi, he was an Armenian whose position was not officially recognised.

Lamb, a decent man, was uncomfortable with his position relative to Fitzmaurice[6] and Sir Nicholas O'Conor had grown to be even more so. Indeed, the ambassador had been deeply disappointed with Lamb's performance as chief dragoman, and had been trying for a year to insert Fitzmaurice in his place.[7] Lamb, he later wrote, "was a conscientious hard working but lugubrious chap who at times was rather trying. He had no driving power and did not in the least know how to get on with the Turks".[8] These deficiencies must have been underlined for O'Conor even more after Fitzmaurice's return, for it is difficult to imagine a more complete contrast. Nevertheless, it was to be another two years before the ambassador was able to get his way and, in the meantime, Fitzmaurice just had to make the best of things.

Among the diplomatic staff of the embassy Fitzmaurice found a few old faces. In addition to O'Conor, apparently quite recovered from his serious illness of the previous winter, there was Charles Marling, an old Constantinople hand, who headed the chancery.[9] Ernest Weakley, who had been appointed commercial attaché as long ago as 1897, and whose ability, industry and selfless devotion to duty was much admired by Fitzmaurice, was also still there. However, the new faces greatly outnumbered the old, which is significant because it was one

---

[5] MECA Oxf.: Richard Massie Graves, Draft of opening chapters of an autobiography, GB 165–0125.

[6] CAC Cam., "I occasionally have a severe twinge of remorse when I think of Fitzmaurice…", Lamb to O'Conor, 14 May 1906, OCON 6/2/33.

[7] CAC Cam., O'Conor to Douglas, 6 Oct. 1907, OCON 5/5/9.

[8] CAC Cam., O'Conor to Douglas, 6 Oct. 1907, OCON 5/5/9. Richard M. Graves, acting third dragoman at Constantinople 1907–8, described Lamb as "a quiet, reserved man…He had never acquired the art of talking for effect…", MECA Oxf., GB165–0125, Graves 1/1.

[9] In September 1906 Marling was replaced by John Tilley, who had been sent out from the FO in order that he might have experience of the embassy before assuming a higher position in London, Sir John Tilley, *London to Tokyo* (Hutchinson: London, nd.), pp. 43–7.

of the sources of Fitzmaurice's influence that Constantinople—perhaps the greatest of all centres of international intrigue—was regarded as a valuable diplomatic training ground.[10] Few young diplomatic secretaries needed a second bidding to go there either. It was tinged with the exotic, spectacularly situated, and abundant in its opportunities for pleasures of every sort. With recent improvements in the Orient Express, first introduced in 1883, it was also now only three days from London. The high throughput of diplomatists—some of whom were not much better than tourists—both increased the chancery's dependence on the dragomanate and swelled the numbers of those who became Fitzmaurice's admirers and then went on to important posts.[11] Many of them were also grateful to Fitzmaurice for testing and passing them as competent in conversational Turkish, for which they received an annual allowance of £100.

Francis Stronge was now counsellor, James Macleay second secretary, and Colonel Herbert Conyers Surtees the military attaché. Lancelot Oliphant was acting third secretary, and Percy Loraine and Patrick Ramsay paid attachés—and all three became Fitzmaurice's disciples.[12] Perhaps most significantly of all for his future career, however, was the remarkable triumvirate of wealthy young honorary attachés, all subsequently Conservative politicians, whom he also found on his return: the half-blind, engagingly eccentric Aubrey Herbert;[13] the forceful and multi-talented Mark Sykes;[14] and George Lloyd. These men were also attracted by the personality, reputation, and eagerness to tutor them of Fitzmaurice,[15] who was soon to spend much time in their company

---

[10] Bullard, *The Camels Must Go*, p. 61.

[11] Sir Lancelot Oliphant, *An Ambassador in Bonds* (Putnam: London, 1946), p. 17.

[12] Gordon Waterfield, *Professional Diplomat: Sir Percy Loraine of Kirkharle Bt.* (Murray: London, 1973), pp. 12–13.

[13] Aubrey Herbert was a compulsive traveller in the Ottoman Empire, subsequently colourful campaigner for Albanian independence, and the model for Sandy Arbuthnot in John Buchan's novel *Greenmantle*, John Buchan, *Memory Hold-the-Door* (Hodder and Stoughton: London, 1940), p. 205. By the autumn of 1905 he had already decided against a diplomatic career but, coming from a family of great influence and recommended by Sanderson, he was permitted to retain a desk in the chancery provided he wrote the occasional memorandum and report, M. FitzHerbert, *The Man Who Was Greenmantle: A biography of Aubrey Herbert* (John Murray: London, 1983), pp. 47–73.

[14] Captain Mark Sykes, a Catholic, was heir to a baronetcy and large estates in Yorkshire, and the man behind the name subsequently made famous in the secret Anglo-French Sykes-Picot Agreement of the First World War (see Ch. 9).

[15] John Charmley, *Lord Lloyd and the Decline of the British Empire* (Weidenfeld and Nicolson: London, 1987), p. 12; Roger Adelson, *Mark Sykes: Portrait of an Amateur* (Cape: London, 1975), p. 115; FitzHerbert, *The Man Who Was Greenmantle*, p. 83.

and write them many letters when they were separated. It was, however, George Lloyd, who had come to Constantinople determined to launch a political career on the basis of expertise in Turkish finance and German schemes in the Near East,[16] to whom as we shall see he became closest.

Mention should also be made of the short-stay diplomats and consular officials, that is, those who stayed for only a week or so at the Embassy while journeying to or from postings elsewhere in the region, particularly Cairo and Tehran. Fitzmaurice was quite capable of making a lasting impression on them as well. For example, en route to Persia in early 1907, Robert Vansittart, the controversial future permanent under-secretary at the Foreign Office, stayed for a week at the embassy. O'Conor's staff was "strong", he remarked in his memoirs half a century later but added that perhaps "the finest figure was one of whom the world never heard, Fitzmaurice the Chief Dragoman, who knew The Sick Man as a specialist, could tell the endless twists of corruption... He carried the Near East in his head, though information was extracted not volunteered". He had, he said, "seen plenty of horror at which imagination baulked, though his voice was level".[17]

Numerous important and well connected private travellers also dropped in at the embassy and expected it to provide them with assistance: guides, introductions, and—especially if they had archaeology in mind—permits from the Porte for excavations. These, too, were a source of Fitzmaurice's influence. Companionable, steeped in local knowledge, without any demands of family on his spare time, and obviously aware of the political value of such contacts, he was often the man who would, to use his own words, "trot them around". The former Liberal prime minister, Lord Rosebery, and later his son, were among those looked after by Fitzmaurice. However, one of the most significant was Gertrude Bell, who had a large circle of influential friends, not least in the Foreign Office and the Diplomatic Service,[18] and was first encountered by Fitzmaurice when she visited Constantinople in July 1907. Only a few years his junior, she was brilliant and

---

[16] Charmley, *Lord Lloyd and the Decline of the British Empire*, pp. 10–12.

[17] Lord Vansittart, *The Mist Procession* (Hutchinson: London, 1958), pp. 68–9.

[18] H. V. F. Winstone, *Gertrude Bell* (Cape: London, 1978), pp. 22–5, 29–30, 90, and 106. She was also already a close friend of the influential Valentine Chirol.

rich, had a talent for languages, and a reputation already established as a mountaineer, writer, traveller and archaeologist in the Middle East. She also had a reputation for being intellectually aggressive, and, unused as he was to mixing with women, she was a person of whom Fitzmaurice was initially afraid.[19] This was also apparent to Gertrude Bell, who described him in a letter to her father as "a nervous little red haired Irishman". However, his apprehensions were misplaced because they got on famously. After taking her to meet Ferid Pasha, the grand vizier, she told her father that:

> I then spent the day with Mr Fitzmaurice who knows more about Turkey than most people, and we talked without stopping till 7 o'clock in the evening when he went away.... I like him particularly.[20]

At the end of her visit, during which she had been introduced to "many interesting people", she told her step-mother that:

> The only person I have not seen enough of is Mr Fitzmaurice the second dragoman, whom I think the most interesting man in C'ple. But as soon as I go back there I shall make him come and spend many hours with me.[21]

Redeemed by George Lloyd

George Lloyd, who after the First World War was Governor of Bombay and then High Commissioner in Egypt,[22] was the younger son of a wealthy Birmingham steel-making family with Welsh origins. In 1903 it had merged its interests with a Scottish rival to form Stewarts and Lloyds Ltd., a company that remained one of the most important in the British steel industry for almost another century. Lloyd had attended Eton and Trinity College Cambridge and was only 26 when he arrived in Constantinople in November 1905; Fitzmaurice had just turned 40. In other respects, however, they had much in common. Both were middle class, albeit from opposite ends of this social stratum. Both had lost

---

[19] CAC Cam., Fitzmaurice to Lloyd, 15 July 1907, GLLD 7/1.
[20] GBP, Letters, 30 July 1907.
[21] GBP, Letters, 27 July 1907.
[22] On the first of these appointments he became Sir George Lloyd and on the second Lord Lloyd of Dolobran.

their parents early and sought solace in life abroad. Both were highly intelligent, determined, and energetic—and impatient with slackers and flabby institutions. Both were devoutly Catholic in religion, even though Lloyd remained in the Church of England. Both were from the Celtic fringe but both believed strongly in the civilizing mission of the British Empire. Both were fervent supporters of Joseph Chamberlain's campaign for tariff reform and strongly anti-German. Both based their careers on the Near East and paid a price in terms of their health. Both were acutely aware of the tension in British policy caused by the ambition to reform the administration of the Ottoman Empire while preserving British influence at the Palace—and were also inclined to think that Britain was too far out of step with the other powers in the emphasis it put on the former. Both disliked O'Conor: Fitzmaurice for reasons that we already know, George Lloyd because "he fancied that the Ambassador did not properly appreciate his talents".[23] Lloyd preferred the company of men to women,[24] and it is probable that so did Fitzmaurice—though there is no proof that they had a homosexual relationship. That they were soon on extremely affectionate terms, however, there is little doubt.

There is sparse evidence of the relationship between Fitzmaurice and Lloyd in the winter of 1905–6 but plenty of it after they moved in the spring to the summer embassy at Therapia, where they shared a house with the other unmarried members of the chancery, Percy Loraine and Pat Ramsay. The atmosphere of this house, christened by its denizens the *Bodega*, was adored by Fitzmaurice and repeatedly invoked as a golden age in his later private correspondence with them. The setting was idyllic, his companions were high-spirited and included stimulating conversationalists, and they had many shared enthusiasms, particularly riding and polo, bathing in the Bosphorus, and collecting velvets and Persian carpets with which to adorn their rooms. They were also united by a common contempt for the ambassador's vanities and annoyance at what they believed to be the unreasonable demands he made on them. In private they called themselves the embassy's *tilkis*

---

[23] Tilley, *London to Tokyo*, pp. 48–9. Lloyd, adds Tilley, already had "a reputation for brilliance", and "was somewhat consciously at the beginning of a great career".

[24] Charmley, *Lord Lloyd and the Decline of the British Empire*, p. 11; Jason Tomes, "Lloyd, George Ambrose, first Baron Lloyd (1879–1941)", *ODNB* [34567, accessed 1 Feb. 2007].

(foxes), and their way of life was christened 'tilkidom' by Fitzmaurice. It is in this setting that his friendship with George Lloyd blossomed and it was subsequently sustained by an intense correspondence that began when Lloyd went on home leave in the autumn of 1906 and resumed during his five months' expedition to the Persian Gulf in the first half of 1907.

The third of the four letters Fitzmaurice wrote to George Lloyd in late 1906 is particularly interesting for the refinements it contains of political views to which he knew his young friend would be receptive. It is also from this letter onwards that "My dear Lloyd" was dropped in favour of a pet name, sometimes *Yavri* (cub) but more routinely *Tilki* or *Tilki Pasha*. Tariff reform, the "true creed", was bound to come, Fitzmaurice argued, and it might be better that it should be introduced by an enlightened Liberal government that could sway some people who would never be convinced by the Conservatives. It would remove "the rottenness and flabbiness which has grown around the nation's heart" and breathe a new spirit into the Empire.[25] Less than a week later he added that the "big motive power" for tariff reform might come from the colonies rather than the mother country.[26]

In November 1906 Lloyd returned to Constantinople, where he appears to have shared winter quarters in Pera with Fitzmaurice and Pat Ramsay, but at the end of January he left on the first stage of his expedition to the Persian Gulf, Ramsay initially accompanying him.[27] Within three days Fitzmaurice was mailing him a pair of his old puttees; they "are no use to me", he wrote, "as they can't be applied to my ungainly legs whereas they ought to be just the thing to clothe your graceful calves...Chok-Chok lonely old man since the two teelkees left. Last night I moved into your bedroom...".[28] Henceforward, Fitzmaurice addressed his letters as from the *Bodega*, the next of which followed hard on the first. This was a very remarkable one:

[25] CAC Cam., Fitzmaurice to Lloyd, 23 Sept. 1906, GLLD 7/1.
[26] CAC Cam., Fitzmaurice to Lloyd, 29 Sept. 1906, GLLD 7/1.
[27] Adam, *Life of Lord Lloyd*, p. 36.
[28] CAC Cam., Fitzmaurice to Lloyd, 1 Feb. 1907, GLLD 7/1.

BRITISH EMBASSY,
CONSTANTINOPLE.
"Bodega",
Feb. 4th 1907

My dear Yavri,

You see the change of address and behold the abomination of desolation is standing in the holy place! I had just settled down in the 'Bodega' when your note from Athens reached me and it produced in me an earthquake of mingled feelings of distress and pleasure. The latter soon conquered as it usually does in sluggish tempered creatures like myself and I reckoned what you said in it as one more kindness added to the thousand and one nice deeds you have done to this unworthy one during the alas! too brief period you were here—deeds that were all the nicer and more pleasant that they were done in an almost imperceptible way. Yavri, it has been a very great privilege and a very deep pleasure to me to have been here with you during the last year and in my dull way I shall never forget it. The pleasant nice memories remain and 1906–7 has been a red-letter year to me. But surely the obligation is all the other way. I am deeply sensible that it is so. The thought that one thousandth part of what you say may be true almost releases this poor "devejo" from the death rattle which has been in my throat for some time back because of the impossibility of your ever forgiving the amount of boredom I have inflicted on you....

When I say the obligation is all the other way I mean what I told you once or twice before. For some fifteen-seventeen years I was animated in my work with what, according to my lights, I imagined to be the correct spirit and proper conception of what a Britisher should feel and do in matters broadly imperial, but 3 years under canvass up country from Aden coupled with the tricks O'Conor played me warped my reason and shrivelled my heart so that I fell away from my ideals. Shortly after I met you, Tilki, I recognized in you a higher and truer form of what I had failed to attain. I felt ashamed of myself and my backsliding and repented. I had fallen and you saved me. This I can never repay. You did me 'good' and through me you have done good to others. For it is given to humble instruments at times to help others to do what they themselves cannot attain....

Tho' we may never meet again there is one little way, Tilki, in which I shall endeavour to requite what you have done to and for me here. I shall use my energy and the spirit you have restored to me to work here on the lines you would like. If from time to time I may write and tell you that something has been done in the right way or that things are improving, I feel that it will give you pleasure while it will be a selfish way for me to perpetuate the very pleasant memories of the past year. It *has* been a pleasant year and I have enjoyed it inordinately. There is now a very big void in the embassy and a big void in the 'Bodega' tho' I have filled it with pretty things. Ce n'est plus la même chose....

There was much more in this ten-page letter: more *Bodega* house-keeping matters, embassy news, and especially a fervent statement of Fitzmaurice's belief that George Lloyd was "destined to do great things". He ended with a characteristically long postscript and signed off: "Tamam [perfection]. Yours ever, G. H. Fitzmaurice."[29] It was as if he had been writing to a young god.

Back to the "Byzantine dungheap"

Morally restored though Fitzmaurice may have been by George Lloyd, his enthusiasm for the dragomanate was not increased in the same degree—or so quickly. Nine months after his return and shortly after Lloyd had left for home leave, he ended a letter to him by saying: "I suppose we shan't see you for a while as you must hate returning to our Byzantine dungheap".[30]

Railway concessions—especially the vexed question of the Baghdad Railway that was so central to the geopolitical designs of Germany—had been pitch-forked onto the dungheap well before Fitzmaurice's return and were still assaulting the senses of the embassy staff.[31] It was, however,

---

[29] CAC Cam., Fitzmaurice to Lloyd, 4 Feb. 1907, GLLD 7/1.
[30] CAC Cam., Fitzmaurice to Lloyd, 23 Sept., 1906, GLLD 7/1.
[31] O'Conor wished to secure for Britain the final section, from Baghdad to Basra, of this German-controlled project. He was also keen to obtain the concession for an extension to the British-owned Smyrna-Aidin railway, the negotiations for which had been going on for almost two years.

having to record and somehow wrestle with the anarchy and violence in the ethnically and religiously mixed territory of Macedonia—the three *vilayets* of Salonica, Uskub, and Monastir—that made them pinch their noses most of all.[32] These questions were entangled in protracted and complex negotiations between the European embassies and the Porte over a long-standing Turkish demand for an increase in customs duties from 8 to 11 per cent—the '3 per cent' question.[33] What had Fitzmaurice gasping for clean air more than anything else, however, at least to begin with, was the discovery that the sultan had decided to probe another section of only vaguely defined frontier between his own dominions and British-occupied territory; this was in the Sinai Desert. With the Aden success behind him, would not O'Conor think he was just the man to handle this as well?

The British occupation of Ottoman Egypt in 1882 had continued to rankle with the sultan and, since his suzerainty was still admitted by Britain, there had always been the risk that the *de facto* frontier on the north-eastern edge of the Sinai peninsula would surface as a bone of contention in Anglo-Turkish relations. This had in fact already happened and in January 1906 happened again when it emerged that the Turkish authorities, claiming that they were responding to an Egyptian move, had sent troops to occupy the village of Taba. This was about seven miles from Akaba on the western side of the eponymous gulf, and was firmly believed by the British to lie in Egyptian territory, that is, south of the line running from Akaba to Rafeh on the Mediterranean coast. Taba was uninhabited but of some strategic importance because of its position and the fact that it possessed one of the few wells in the area.[34] Turkish troops had also occupied other posts believed by the British to be Egyptian and had destroyed boundary pillars at Rafeh, it duly emerging that Abdul Hamid wished to press claims to the northern half of the Sinai peninsula that would bring Turkish troops to the banks of the Suez Canal. Lord Cromer, the British proconsul in Cairo, believed that a threat was posed not only to the security of the canal

---

[32] On the Macedonian question at this time, see H. N. Brailsford, *Macedonia: Its races and their future* (Methuen: London, 1906); Graves, *Storm Centres of the Near East*, chs. 12 and 13; Pears, *Forty Years in Constantinople*, pp. 194–201; Ryan, *The Last of the Dragomans*, pp. 42–5; Waugh, *Turkey*, pp. 77–8, 106–8.

[33] Britain's ability to block, or at least delay, this increase was believed to give it a major lever to gain Turkish agreement both to Macedonian reform and more international control of the Baghdad Railway.

[34] *The Times*, 8 May 1906.

but to Egypt generally, where an increase in unrest was also believed to be connected to the Turkish action.

How Britain should react to the Taba incident was now the responsibility of Sir Henry Campbell-Bannerman's recently installed Liberal government. In this Sir Edward Grey, a representative of the imperialist wing of the Liberal Party who favoured continuity in foreign policy and was suspicious of Germany, had been appointed foreign secretary, a post he was to hold continuously for the next eleven years.[35] Grey demanded withdrawal of the Turkish troops and proposed the appointment of a joint commission to delimit the frontier along the *de facto* line, initially dropping only a hint at the use of force by way of encouragement. Naturally, Abdul Hamid proved obdurate. In consequence, the Egyptian garrison was strengthened, British warships began to appear at each end of the disputed boundary, and a minor crisis was in train. Hard on the heels of the German-inspired first Moroccan crisis, this was intensified by rumours that Abdul Hamid's Egyptian adventure had been encouraged by Berlin. These rumours were given credit in the Foreign Office and were probably nourished by Fitzmaurice.[36]

Following discussion by the British cabinet, on 30 April O'Conor was instructed by the Foreign Office to tell the Ottoman government that it had ten days to comply with Britain's demands, failing which it could anticipate "grave" consequences.[37] This was music to the ears of the ambassador because—grown wise in the ways of Abdul Hamid and probably encouraged by Fitzmaurice—this was the course he had already been urging. Indeed, he favoured stronger action than either the Foreign Office or Cromer were willing to contemplate, arguing first for military pressure on the Yemen and then for the threat of a

---

[35] Keith Robbins, *Sir Edward Grey: A biography of Lord Grey of Fallodon* (Cassell: London, 1971), ch. 7. Grey emphasised his attachment to continuity in policy towards Turkey in a private letter to O'Conor: "...we want to pursue what I think was Lord Lansdowne's policy—keeping with the other Powers and getting them to go as far with us as we can", CAC Cam., 22 December 1905, OCON 6/1/54.

[36] CAC Cam., Fitzmaurice to Lloyd, 13 Sept. 1906, GLLD 7/1; Robbins, *Sir Edward Grey*, pp. 164–5. However, O'Conor reported that he could find no evidence of this in the actions of the German Ambassador in Constantinople and Grey thought that at most the sultan had been encouraged by a presumption that he could rely on Germany. He also thought that Abdul Hamid's forward policy may have been a pre-emptive one inspired by a genuine fear of British expansion, TNA, Grey to O'Conor, 9 Apr. 1906, FO800/79; O'Conor to Grey, 24 Apr. 1906, FO371/61 and 15 May 1906, FO371/63; Grey to Lascelles, 30 Apr. 1906, FO371/61; and Viscount Grey of Fallodon, *Twenty-Five Years, 1892–1916*, vol. I (Hodder & Stoughton: London, 1925), pp. 123–30.

[37] TNA, Grey to O'Conor, 30 Apr. 1906, FO371/61.

land action to drive the Turks from Taba and even from Akaba itself.
Something like this was needed, O'Conor thought, because naval
demonstrations seemed to have lost some of their potency to alarm the
sultan.[38] This was rejected as too risky[39] but he was given a big enough
stick to brandish to make him confident of success: the Mediterranean
fleet was moved eastwards and, in the event of a Turkish refusal, plans
were laid to occupy numerous important Turkish islands and stop all
Turkish transports in the Mediterranean outside the limits of the Suez
Canal.[40] On 3 May he delivered the ultimatum: Turkey had until 13
May to comply with Britain's demands. As the ambassador anticipated,
at the eleventh hour Abdul Hamid capitulated. An added bonus was
that he accepted formally for the first time that Britain had a right to
intervene in Egyptian affairs.[41]

In the early weeks of the Akaba crisis Lamb had acted for the
embassy while Fitzmaurice had resumed his usual round of assisting
British companies wrangling with the Porte or the Custom House and
securing permits for British archaeologists to excavate Hittite sites.[42] It
is evidence of the erosion of O'Conor's faith in his chief dragoman,
however, that on 2 April—precisely the date on which the ambassador
had concluded that a real crisis was now unavoidable[43]—Lamb was
permitted to depart on three months' leave of absence.[44] Fitzmaurice
was promptly made acting chief dragoman, and thus played the key
role for the embassy as the crisis came to a head, though this did not
mean that he was allowed to abandon his routine work.[45]

On 13 May, a Sunday, with only hours left before the expiry of the
ultimatum, Grey was confined resentfully to his London house with

---

[38] TNA, O'Conor to Grey, 23 and 26 Apr. and 2 May 1906, FO371/61.
[39] TNA, Cromer to Grey, 27 Apr. 1906 and Grey to O'Conor, 2 May 1906, FO371/61.
[40] TNA, AR 1906, p. 6, in Barclay to Grey, 18 Jan. 1907, FO195/2363.
[41] On the Taba incident generally, see TNA, Turco-Egyptian Frontier: Rafeh-Akaba. Summary of Negotiations, 1892–1906, FO, 31 May 1906, FO881/8713; O'Conor to Grey, 3 May 1906, FO371/62 [O'Conor's own view of the development of the crisis up to the delivery of the ultimatum on 3 May]; Pears, *Forty Years in Constantinople*, pp. 111–14; and Grey, *Twenty-Five Years, 1892–1916*, vol. I, pp. 123–34.
[42] TNA, From Dragomans 1906, FO195/2221.
[43] TNA, O'Conor to Grey, 3 May 1906, FO371/62.
[44] TNA, O'Conor to Grey, 9 Apr. 1906, FO371/148.
[45] In the middle of April he could still be found bribing a Turkish officer to supply a map wanted by the Royal Scottish Museums and drafting a promemoria in Turkish in order to convince the grand vizier that 295 cases of British safety matches detained by the Basra customs were not "explosives".

two senior officials awaiting the Turkish response.[46] At the same time in Constantinople, while O'Conor was occupied in the embassy with a flurry of telegrams, it was Fitzmaurice who negotiated directly with the grand vizier and other ministers at the decisive meeting which recommended acceptance of the British demands.[47] Of course, O'Conor claimed the credit and made no mention of the role of his dragoman in his despatches. George Lloyd took a different view. Writing to Gertrude Bell a week after the Turkish capitulation, he said that "The undoubted success we have gained is due to 3 men[:] Cromer, Hardinge and Fitzmaurice (and the Ambassador)...".[48] The parenthetical afterthought was eloquent. In a brief and less than effusive telegram on 14 May, Grey congratulated O'Conor for the "steady way" in which he had applied pressure to the Porte and for securing a settlement which was "in principle satisfactory".[49]

The joint boundary commission to which the Turks had now finally agreed was duly set up. It gathered at Akaba at the end of May and worked north-west up to Rafeh. Fortunately for Fitzmaurice, who on the retirement of Marinitch at the beginning of July was finally promoted to second dragoman, London and Cairo considered the joint commission to be an Egyptian government responsibility, and the British side was composed exclusively of Egyptian officials.[50] Compared to the Aden affair, the Sinai Commission was also relatively plain sailing. Nevertheless, the predictable hitches occurred, and in mid-July the commissioners reached a deadlock.[51]

Anxious to get away to Ireland, O'Conor was greatly annoyed by this impasse on Sinai because he was told both by Grey and the unsympathetic Sir Charles Hardinge—the new broom who had recently replaced the ambassador's old friend Sanderson as permanent undersecretary—that he could not leave until the affair was concluded.[52] Bemoaning the inevitable complications of a triangular negotiation

---

[46] Grey, *Twenty-Five Years, 1892–1916*, vol. I, pp. 127–9.
[47] TNA, AR 1906, p. 7, in Barclay to Grey, 18 Jan. 1907, FO195/2363; Fitzmaurice to O'Conor, 15 May 1906 (no. 129), FO195/2221.
[48] CAC Cam., Lloyd to Bell, 21 May 1906, GLLD 29/1.
[49] TNA, Grey to O'Conor, 14 May 1906, FO371/62.
[50] They were led by Emir Lewa Ibrahim Fathi Pasha and Captain R. C. R. Owen.
[51] TNA, Report on Sinai Boundary Commission, 1906, by Captain R. C. R. Owen, encl. in Cromer to Grey, 2 Nov. 1906, FO371/64 [hereafter 'Owen Report'].
[52] TNA, Grey to O'Conor, 4 Aug. 1906, FO800/79; CAC Cam., O'Conor to Sanderson, 21 Aug. 1906, OCON 4/1/23.

between the Porte, the embassy, and Cairo, made worse by what he believed to be the naivety of the Khedive's representative, O'Conor twice suggested to Grey that Fitzmaurice should be sent to sort things out on the spot.[53] Grey initially favoured this idea but in the end the Foreign Office decided against it on the somewhat obscure grounds that it might encourage discussion of what was the status quo when the issue of the boundary last came up, in 1892.[54] O'Conor then asked instead to be given a free hand to get the best terms he could for the Egyptian government via negotiations in Constantinople.[55] Aware that Fitzmaurice would be at the sharp end of any such talks, and subject only to some largely routine conditions, the Foreign Office promptly agreed.[56]

Though Lamb had returned at the end of June, it was thus Fitzmaurice who for the next two weeks was kept working night and day on Sinai at the Palace and the council of ministers. On 11 September the sultan finally signed an *iradé* signifying agreement in principle on the course of the boundary that met British wishes.[57] "It is somewhat of a bitter pill to the Turks and indirectly a knock to Germany as it will make the Turks chary of listening to any German whisperings about Egypt", Fitzmaurice told George Lloyd.[58] The joint commission was then able to wrap up its business and on 1 October the detailed agreement (including maps) was signed by the commissioners at Rafeh.[59]

Following signature of the *iradé*, Fitzmaurice had also reported it to Aubrey Herbert, adding that since settlement of the Aidin Railway extension was also imminent, O'Conor would go on leave "amid a shower of Iradés and a blaze of glory which will dazzle the F.O. and

---

[53] CAC Cam., Letter Books. Summaries by Lisle: O'Conor to Grey, 7 and 22 Aug. 1906, OCON 4/2/7; O'Conor to Sanderson, 21 Aug. 1906, OCON 4/1/23. Fitzmaurice also thought that Mansfeldt de Cardonnel Findlay, who was acting agent and consul-general in Cairo from early July until the end of September, was causing confusion by second-guessing his commissioners on the basis of poor information, CAC Cam., Fitzmaurice to O'Conor, 17 Sept. 1906, OCON 6/2/35.

[54] TNA, FO mins. 7, 14–16 Aug. 1906, FO800/79.

[55] TNA, O'Conor to Grey, 27 Aug. 1906, FO371/64.

[56] TNA, Grey to O'Conor, 29 Aug. 1906, FO371/64.

[57] TNA, O'Conor to Grey, 22 Aug. 1906, FO371/64; AR 1906, pp. 9–10, in Barclay to Grey, 18 Jan. 1907, FO195/2363; CAC Cam., Fitzmaurice to Lloyd, 9 and 13 Sept. 1906, GLLD 7/1.

[58] CAC Cam., Fitzmaurice to Lloyd, 13 Sept. 1906, GLLD 7/1.

[59] TNA, Owen Report. The agreement can also be found in *British and Foreign State Papers 1905–1906*, vol. XCIV (HMSO: London, 1910), pp. 482–4.

dissipate any clouds of mistrust on his going which may have gathered in that quarter".[60]

Indeed, the ambassador also hoped to win another Foreign Office laurel before leaving Constantinople by gaining Turkish acceptance of a *note verbale* that he had persuaded the powers to present to the Porte on the 3 per cent question.[61] The Turks obliged but instead of a laurel a "bombshell" arrived for O'Conor in the shape of a message from the Foreign Office informing him that the concessions he had obtained from the Porte on this were wholly insufficient. "Elchi's dovecote has been fairly fluttered", George Lloyd was informed by Fitzmaurice, who shared the fear that the sultan planned to use the extra customs revenues to subsidise the Baghdad Railway.[62]

Chief dragoman at last

With the excitement and pressures of the Sinai dispute over, in the next 12 months Fitzmaurice returned to his more usual diet: bribing officials in order to obtain confidential documents, including despatches from the Ottoman ambassadors in Paris and Berlin; pursuing arrears of pay on behalf of British officers in Ottoman service; grappling with problems thrown up by the Protestant Cemetery in Basra; and so on.[63] He also wrote a lengthy memorandum on "The Turkish Press and Its Influence" for inclusion in the embassy's Annual Report, which was sent to London in the middle of January 1907.

The Turkish press, wrote Fitzmaurice in this memorandum, was a servile and yet effective instrument of the sultan, which consolidated and strengthened his position by exalting his role as caliph and encouraging the "deep-rooted and secret antagonism" of the true believers, especially among the lower classes, towards everything Western and

---

[60] SCA, Fitzmaurice to Herbert, 12 Sept. 1906, DD HER 41.

[61] A few days earlier, Fitzmaurice had reported to George Lloyd that O'Conor had managed to get his colleagues to agree to a "joint 3% note" and was "quite pleased with himself", though he had expressed pessimism that the Turks would accept it and said there were rumours that shortly they would "enforce" the increase, CAC Cam., Fitzmaurice to Lloyd, 9 Sept. 1906, GLLD 7/1.

[62] CAC Cam., Fitzmaurice to Lloyd, 13 and 23 Sept. 1906, GLLD 7/1.

[63] Between the end of September 1906 and the end of September 1907, Fitzmaurice drafted 36 of the 'Drogmanat to Chancery' memoranda, most of them on different subjects, TNA, From Dragomans 1906, FO195/2221 and From Dragomans 1907, FO195/2249.

Christian. It also reached well beyond the Ottoman Empire, to Russia, Afghanistan, India, Egypt and North Africa. Extended by word-of-mouth in the cafés, and translated into vernaculars abroad, it was, he said—describing it with a typically exaggerated invocation of the mysterious aspect of the Orient—"a powerful though invisible medium for transmitting the Pan-Islamic current to distant Mahommedan communities".[64] This was sure to catch the official eye in London because the ideology of Islamism and its promotion abroad ('Pan-Islamism'), which included contacts with foreign Moslem groups and leaders, had been deliberately cultivated by Abdul Hamid as a weapon to intimidate his European tormentors.[65]

At least by now Fitzmaurice was required to do less customs work but this did not prevent him from once more brooding on his personal situation in the dragomanate. He remained bitter that he had been given a consul's rank but, until his promotion to second dragoman in July 1906,[66] denied anything like a consul's pay. He was even more incensed about this because he believed that in 1906, mainly in connection with the Sinai boundary dispute, he had—contrary to regulations—been employed on first dragoman's work without commensurate reward.[67] In any case, his promotion to second dragoman still left him well down the embassy order of precedence—below the 'gilded youths' dignified as honorary attachés, as well as below the chaplain and the embassy doctor. It must have been at this juncture that he supplied the publishers of *Who's Who* with the false information that he had been second dragoman since 1897.[68] This was astonishingly risky for his career since it was unlikely to have been missed in the Foreign Office, where the Library continued to publish the truth about his record in the *Foreign Office List*. This was eloquent of Fitzmaurice's mood, which was made less sunny still because not only were valuable members of the dragomanate lost but the replacements chosen for them by O'Conor were,

---

[64] TNA, AR 1906, pp. 38–42, in Barclay to Grey, 18 Jan. 1907, FO195/2363.

[65] Shaw and Shaw, *History of the Ottoman Empire and Modern Turkey, Vol. II*, pp. 259–60.

[66] This saw him jump from £550 per annum to £700–£800 but he believed that he would have been earning this since the autumn of 1905 had he been given a consular post in the provinces.

[67] CAC Cam., Fitzmaurice to Lloyd, 11 May 1907, GLLD 7/1.

[68] Fitzmaurice commenced the falsification of his entry in *Who's Who 1907*, the copy deadline of which appears to have been 30 September 1906.

he believed, deplorable.[69] At the end of 1906, Lamb told the chargé d'affaires that Fitzmaurice and Onik Effendi had been doing work that really needed "at least four men".[70] But worse was to follow because in early May 1907 Onik Effendi died suddenly, after giving "24 years faithful and good service" to the embassy.[71]

Nominally only a messenger, whose pitiful salary was paid from the embassy's secret service funds and carried no pension rights, Onik had been extremely valuable, particularly in resolving the complicated problems that arose at the Custom House, which were increasing both in number and importance. Liked and respected by Turkish officials, he also dealt with most questions of real property, drew up documents in Turkish for presentation to the Palace and the Porte, and followed them up.[72] Of recent years his responsibilities had grown considerably, not least because he had in effect been required to do the work of third dragoman while Fitzmaurice was on the Yemen frontier, and then take over the embassy's Slave Department after the retirement of Marinitch. "He is of course an irreparable loss to us all", Fitzmaurice told Lloyd, "…he was the mainstay of the dragomanate out of which I feel the bottom, so to speak, has fallen."[73] He was not replaced until July and then by a "raw" individual whom Fitzmaurice thought would need two years to break in.[74]

Incredibly enough, Lamb was then allowed by O'Conor to go on leave. Feeling bloody-minded, Fitzmaurice, who had not had any leave since 1905, applied for two months' leave himself and wheeled out the embassy doctor in support of his case. Of course, he was turned

---

[69] Marinitch had already gone and in November 1906 was followed by Blech, who was replaced by a man described by Fitzmaurice as "so impossible that the Chancery…almost revolted and O'C[onor] had to admit his mistake" and get rid of him. He also thought that O'Conor's second stab at replacing Blech was not much better and this man only lasted for eighteen months. Fitzmaurice himself was not replaced as third dragoman until the spring, when—without consulting him—O'Conor gave the post to Richard Graves, the young and inexperienced nephew of Robert Graves. Fitzmaurice thought Richard not suited to the work and in less than a year he had gone as well, CAC Cam., Fitzmaurice to Lloyd, 21 June and 15 July 1907, GLLD 7/1.

[70] TNA, Lamb to Barclay, 29 Dec. 1906, FO195/2221.

[71] CAC Cam., Fitzmaurice to Lloyd, 20 May 1907, GLLD 7/1.

[72] TNA, Memoranda by Marinitch and Lamb, June 1906–June 1907, FO195/2221.

[73] CAC Cam., Fitzmaurice to Lloyd, 20 May 1907, GLLD 7/1. This view was shared unreservedly by both Lamb and Marinitch.

[74] This was another Armenian, called Tchamitch, a contraction of 'Tchamitchian'. He had been Turkish Clerk in the consulate-general.

down.[75] Now under intense pressure of work, in the summer of 1907 he was forced to remain in the heat of the town rather than go with the chancery to enjoy the delights of Therapia.[76] He felt utterly left in the lurch.[77]

Fitzmaurice was also miserable because his close friends George Lloyd and then Percy Loraine had left Constantinople earlier in the year. Loraine had been posted to Tehran and set off in a blizzard on 14 March. "In the Custom house, where the usual pandemonium was reigning", he later wrote, "I found Fitzmaurice, perfectly blue with cold, who had sacrificed himself to come and see me off."[78] He also began to complain of a serious weakness in his left knee, and with less need of his horse because tennis players had replaced polo players in the chancery, eventually sold it. No wonder that when the high-spirited Aubrey Herbert dropped in with his brother Mervin in June Fitzmaurice reported sadly to George Lloyd that "I'm afraid he found me in a rather lugubrious state of mind...".[79]

Fitzmaurice now re-doubled his efforts to get off the dungheap. In the previous September Cecil Spring-Rice, newly appointed minister in Tehran, had virtually offered him the improved post of oriental secretary in his legation but he seems not to have been seriously tempted.[80] It was still an 'independent' post in the provinces that he really wanted. Once more he asked O'Conor for the consulship at Monastir. Once more he emphasised his weakened physical condition: "Every day I am more and more convinced of my inability to replace Marinitsch...."[81] Once more he was denied—but his moment was now imminent.

In no doubt as to Fitzmaurice's restlessness,[82] at the beginning of 1907 O'Conor had again tried to persuade the Foreign Office to find some more money for him. This produced a tetchy reply from Chauncy

---

[75] CAC Cam., Fitzmaurice to Lloyd, 21 June 1907, GLLD 7/1; TNA, Fitzmaurice to O'Conor, 22 June 1907, FO195/2249. O'Conor minuted on the latter document that he could not possibly go on leave while Lamb was away, adding: "He might have gone away two months ago without inconvenience". Following this in Fitzmaurice's hand is: "What rot!"

[76] This saved him three hours a day in travelling up and down the Bosphorus, CAC Cam., Fitzmaurice to Lloyd, 21 June 1907, GLLD 7/1.

[77] CAC Cam., Fitzmaurice to Lloyd, 15 July 1907, GLLD 7/1.

[78] TNA, Transfer Constantinople to Tehran 1907, FO1011/120.

[79] CAC Cam., Fitzmaurice to Lloyd, 21 June 1907, GLLD 7/1.

[80] CAC Cam., Fitzmaurice to Lloyd, 23 Sept. 1906, GLLD 7/1.

[81] CAC Cam., Fitzmaurice to O'Conor, 4 Oct. 1906, OCON 6/2/35.

[82] TNA, Fitzmaurice to O'Conor, 17 Mar. 1907, FO195/2249.

Cartwright, the chief clerk of the Financial Department. "There really is no end to Fitzmaurice's complaints", he told the ambassador. "Fitzmaurice is no doubt very capable", he continued, "but, besides that, he is well known and personally popular here as well as at Constantinople." Nevertheless, he said, he had already been treated generously and the Treasury would not entertain another approach. "I hope you will tell him in the most courteous and friendly way", concluded Cartwright, "to 'shut up.'"[83]

Anxious to appease his indispensable dragoman, and showing patrician irritation at failing to get his way, O'Conor ignored this advice. Assisted by Tilley, he proposed several different ideas to improve Fitzmaurice's position: fiddling with outfit allowances and giving him the local rank of second secretary. However, Foreign Office fear of establishing worrying precedents stood in the way, and an appeal to Grey himself proved fruitless.[84] What in the end came to the rescue of both ambassador and dragoman was the appearance of a vacancy for the position of consul-general at Beirout. Fitzmaurice at once applied for it but was then told by O'Conor that he intended to propose Lamb for this post and nominate him as his successor. In conveying this "*dead secret*" to George Lloyd, Fitzmaurice said that he did not thank the ambassador for the offer because he regarded himself as entitled to it. What he did say to him was that he was flattered and hoped for the sake of British interests that he was not appointing the wrong man:

> My words said one thing—my tone of voice a second and my eyes and looks a third—but the result was that he has written home—I don't know what or to whom. The upshot is a toss up for Elchi's proposals are not always acted on nowadays.[85]

On this point, however, O'Conor was pushing at an open door and it was only a few months later, in October 1907, that Fitzmaurice finally became chief dragoman at the embassy.[86] He was now formally fourth

---

[83] CAC Cam., Cartwright to O'Conor, 26 Mar. 1907, OCON 6/1/60.

[84] CAC Cam., Barrington to O'Conor, 1 June 1907, OCON 6/1/64; TNA, Precedence at British Embassy at Constantinople, 18 June 1907, FO372/84.

[85] CAC Cam., Fitzmaurice to Lloyd, 15 July 1907, GLLD 7/1; emphasis in original.

[86] Lamb agreed to go to Beirout even though it would entail the expense and inconvenience of a very short initial posting to Salonica. In the event, after finding that Salonica was to his liking and protesting strongly against being forced to move on again so quickly, it was decided by Grey—over the objections of O'Conor, who clearly thought the post too important for him—that he could stay there, CAC Cam.:

in its hierarchy and earning double what he received on returning from Aden. The ambassador was so delighted that he told the story *twice* to his friend Greville Douglas.[87] On the second occasion he wrote: "I have got at last Fitzmaurice as 1st Dragoman in place of Lamb...He is", he continued, using an oft-repeated phrase, "a sort of Irish Turk and is rapidly making quite a position for himself in Office circles and will one day rank with the great Dragomans of the past—Urquhart, Alison, Lionel Moore, etc." It added to O'Conor's pleasure that he had been at the same time able to move Andrew Ryan from the consulate-general to the embassy dragomanate, and make Richard Graves the acting third dragoman. "All Irish! Curious isn't it?", remarked O'Conor. In the following spring Fitzmaurice was given the local rank of first secretary in the Diplomatic Service. He was at the pinnacle of his career and the beginning of his period of real influence, and it was perhaps as a gesture of contempt for those who had failed to give him recognition for so long that he did not bother to have his new status confirmed in *Who's Who* until the edition of 1911—or perhaps he was just too busy.

"The beast must *go"*

In the course of 1906 O'Conor's credit both in the Foreign Office and the Diplomatic Service had diminished significantly. This reflected the ambassador's own declining influence with Abdul Hamid, and it did not help that there was a striking contrast in the figure now cut by O'Conor and that cut by the German Ambassador and *doyen* of the diplomatic corps, Adolph Baron Marschall von Bieberstein. The latter, formerly German State Secretary for Foreign Affairs, was a large man in robust health and extremely able. Masterful in manner, he had established a commanding presence in Constantinople and was generally regarded as the outstanding ambassador in the city.[88] O'Conor, by contrast, whose health was clearly failing, was seen at least by one of

---

Tyrrell to O'Conor, 21 June 1907, OCON 6/1/64; 27 Sept. 1907, OCON 6/1/66; 28 Nov. and 10 Dec. 1907, OCON 6/1/67. O'Conor to Tyrrell, 26 Sept. 1907, OCON 6/1/66; and 28 Nov. 1907, OCON 6/1/67. Lamb to O'Conor, 1 Nov. 1907, OCON 6/1/67.

[87] CAC Cam., O'Conor to Douglas, 6 Oct. and 22 Dec. 1907, OCON 5/5/9.

[88] An almost awe-struck sketch of Baron Marschall was written by O'Conor's successor, TNA, Lowther to Grey, 30 Jan. 1910, FO371/1002.

his own staff as "dull, unimaginative and slightly depressed"—and a person whose charm was revealed only to "privileged friends".[89] Now believed by the Foreign Office to be living on borrowed time, he could not, however, bring himself fully to read the signs, the most obvious of which was Hardinge's decision in the spring of 1906 to impose Tilley on him as head of chancery without consultation.[90]

The Foreign Office had been particularly unimpressed by O'Conor's handling of the 3 per cent question, as noted above, and in early 1907 continued to think that he was not pushing the Turks hard enough on this. Fitzmaurice reported to George Lloyd that O'Conor had been instructed to tell them that if they did not fulfil the engagements they had undertaken in return for award of the 3 per cent, Britain might have to "concert about controlling the Customs". Having failed to communicate this threat, he had received "a scalding tel. from the F.O. that w[oul]d make any man of guts resign".[91]

Though Fitzmaurice seems to have succeeded in keeping on good terms with O'Conor, his knowledge of his declining stock in London made him correspondingly less concerned to conceal from others the "O'Conoritis"[92] from which he suffered. Indeed, he began to seed with increasing relish the clouds already gathering over 'Elchi's' head, as his frank and intimate letters to George Lloyd eloquently reveal.

In September 1906 Fitzmaurice complained to Lloyd of the burden imposed on the chancery by the chore of copying, ciphering and registering O'Conor's "needless selfpuffing" despatches and telegrams.[93] In February of the new year he remarked that it was a pity that Baron Marschall had been forced to take the lead in persuading Abdul Hamid to send into exile his favourite, the appalling bully, Fehim Pasha, noting that O'Conor's own intervention in the German Ambassador's support came only at the eleventh hour—and would not have come at all if he had not goaded him.[94] In an aside on another matter he cautioned

---

[89] MECA Oxf.: Richard Massie Graves, Draft of opening chapters of an autobiography, GB 165–0125.
[90] O'Conor had actually been informed of this decision in the spring, CAC Cam., Hardinge to O'Conor, 29 Mar. 1906, OCON 6/1/56. See also Tilley, *London to Tokyo*, p. 43.
[91] CAC Cam., Fitzmaurice to Lloyd, 12 Mar. 1907, GLLD 7/1.
[92] CAC Cam., Fitzmaurice to Lloyd, 11 May 1907, GLLD 7/1.
[93] CAC Cam., Fitzmaurice to Lloyd, 23 Sept. 1906, GLLD 7/1.
[94] CAC Cam., Fitzmaurice to Lloyd, 4 and 27 Feb. 1907, GLLD 7/1. This affair was well covered in *The Times*; see also Waugh, *Turkey*, p. 100. O'Conor also wrote on

that "Elchi's words are forked".[95] He went on in this vein: O'Conor had brought on Onik Effendi's death by refusing to give him a title; Weakley was not getting the recognition he deserved either;[96] "only weak rotters...cling on after their time"; "Turks are more reliable than some British ambassadors"; and so on.[97] In effect summing up his thoughts about O'Conor in late November 1907, he described him as "a snake" and asked Lloyd—now in London—to find out what his chances were of another five year term as ambassador. His own conclusion on this point was pretty unambiguous: "The beast *must* go."[98]

A few weeks after this Sir Edward Grey commenced a letter to O'Conor with the observation that "Things at Constantinople look very bad". He followed this with a list of objectives which the embassy had failed to achieve. He did not blame the ambassador directly but it must have made 'Elchi' a little uncomfortable.[99]

"Ireland is the bull's eye"

Nevertheless, at the beginning of 1908 'the beast' was still in place and Fitzmaurice found that he had something else about which to worry. This was the threat posed to his relationship with George Lloyd by the question of Ireland, on which to his mind his cherished friend had extremely unsubtle views. This appears to have been the only issue to have disturbed—and then but briefly—the convivial atmosphere of the Therapia *Bodega* in the 'red-letter' year of 1906–7. Unfortunately, while Lloyd was recovering from illness in London a throw-away remark made

it at some length, claiming that his action "clinched the matter", TNA, AR 1907, in O'Conor to Grey, 13 Jan. 1908, p. 36, FO195/2363.

[95] CAC Cam., Fitzmaurice to Lloyd, 27 Feb. 1907, GLLD 7/1.

[96] Weakley never did receive much recognition, despite the reputation he subsequently acquired as an expert on Mesopotamian oil. See Marian Kent, "Great Britain and the end of the Ottoman Empire, 1900–23", in Marian Kent (ed.), *The Great Powers and the End of the Ottoman Empire*, 2nd ed. (Cass: London, 1996), p. 175.

[97] CAC Cam., Fitzmaurice to Lloyd, 11 and 20 May, 15 Aug. 1907, GLLD 7/1.

[98] CAC Cam., Fitzmaurice to Lloyd, 26 Nov. 1907, GLLD 7/2.

[99] Grey to O'Conor, 17 Dec. 1907, *BD*, vol. 5, no. 174. Immediately on hearing of O'Conor's death shortly after this, Hardinge said that "It was evident to us for some time that the machine was worn out", TNA, Hardinge to Villiers, 20 Mar. 1908, FO800/24. In his memoirs he said: "I was glad that he never knew that his recall had been decided upon. He had done excellent service in the past, though he had not been a success at Constantinople", Lord Hardinge of Penshurst, *Old Diplomacy* (Murray: London, 1947), p. 151.

by Fitzmaurice in a February letter ("I pray Allah to keep you safe from fogs and heresy about Ireland!")[100] evidently provoked a particularly strong counter-blast. This in turn eventually led Fitzmaurice to make a clear and particularly interesting statement of his political faith, which as he began to develop it over several letters also illustrated perfectly the court jester manner that he frequently employed to defuse a tension with a person in a superior social or official position:

> I'm sorry to have drawn you over Ireland. I didn't mean to, but your fusillades and diatribes against a small part of the *United* Kingdom fill me with sadness mingled with compassion, showing me as they do that the flame of hatred and passion which flared up that never-to-be-forgotten night in the 'Bodega' when you launched out into scathing...and passionate denunciation of poor uneconomic Ireland has not been quenched by knowledge or dulled by time. But, Tilki, I'm full of hope—even confidence that as years roll by you will, like Chamberlain, see the error of your ways and be glad to settle the Irish question at a round table conference with Redmond or his successor. I fear you are now a real disruptionist and are quite capable of robbing Ireland of the regalia of St. Patrick...A decade hence you'll be sound on an Imperial question second only in importance to that of Tariff Reform and Preference. I suppose you poisoned and poured vitriol on to my good name with Austen Chamberlain—Alas! Alas! I must take a shop in the Bezistan [grand bazaar] and give up working for the Empire. I shall never go on leave to England again but shall take a German steamer to Southampton and Queenstown where with Turkish officers I shall reform the Royal Irish Gendarmerie and reform the judicial methods of Resident Magistrates drawing their inspiration from Dublin Castle. I had a long talk with Abdul Hamid some time ago about the state of Ireland. He has a scheme of reforms but that is another story, as Kipling says.[101]

This time the jest did not work. "I pass over your diatribes re. the Irish party as unworthy of notice", Fitzmaurice commented on George Lloyd's next letter. But suddenly they had other disagreements: Lloyd had refused Fitzmaurice's request for a copy of his report on the Persian Gulf, which produced a reaction of fury; while Lloyd, mistaking for indifference to the outcome the characteristically allegorical account of the candidates for the succession to O'Conor with which Fitzmaurice had sought to entertain him, thought this was prompted by his older friend's arrogant assumption that he could restore Britain's "fallen

---

[100] CAC Cam., Fitzmaurice to Lloyd, 9 Feb. 1908, GLLD 7/3.
[101] CAC Cam., Fitzmaurice to Lloyd, 3 Mar. 1908, GLLD 7/3.

glories" whoever was appointed. This in turn got under the skin of
Fitzmaurice though he quickly changed the tone. "[A] truce to my silly
raillery", he said, but ended nevertheless with a somewhat risky statement of his political principles, prompted by a question from George
Lloyd about his views on patriotism versus cosmopolitanism.

He had, he said, always been a free trader in theory but a tariff
reformer in practice. Similarly, he was a cosmopolitan in theory but in
practice cosmopolitanism was the outermost of a series of concentric
circles which commanded his support in increasing measure as they
shrank in size to the centre. "Ireland", he wrote, "is the Bull's Eye":

> It is a small green circle—the next a red British one—then comes an all
> red Imperially British circle and then a further English-speaking one—out-
> side of which is a European etc white man's circle and outside of that a
> Cosmopolitan multi-coloured (yellow, copper, black etc.).

Until the formation of the Anglo-Japanese alliance and Japan's victories
over Russia, he had hoped that his "distant theoretical Cosmopolitanism
would end at the white circle". He was now disoriented but finished by
saying that he clung "to as much patriotism as is included within the
English-speaking circle though there it is weak while it gets stronger
until I get back into my tiny cosmos inside my green inner circle!"[102]

The relations of Fitzmaurice with George Lloyd survived these differences. It was also fortunate for him that his views on Ireland were
not, of course, radically out of line with the policy of the new Liberal
government in London.

End of a winter nightmare

The invective against O'Conor in Fitzmaurice's letters to George Lloyd
reached a crescendo in the winter of 1907–8. At the same time he also
began to campaign for his old friend, Maurice de Bunsen, currently in
Madrid, to be the new ambassador.

One occasion for Fitzmaurice to revile O'Conor was provided by
Macedonia, on which the new chief dragoman took a more ruthless
view than the ambassador. Macedonian reform under Ottoman auspices
was impossible, Fitzmaurice believed, and by sticking its neck out on the

---

[102] CAC Cam., Fitzmaurice to Lloyd, 10 Apr. 1908, GLLD 7/3.

question Britain was gratuitously undermining its economic interests in Turkey. Since, however, there was a consensus at home on the present policy, the only solution was to see Macedonia "lopped off" from the Ottoman Empire, even though "terrible events" would occur in the process: "the decrees of fate must run their course", he said.[103] When, therefore, in February a scheme for judicial reforms collapsed, which he thought O'Conor had handled badly, Fitzmaurice was delighted. Announcing that he was to let his pen "distil black treason", he informed Lloyd that it was the ambassador's "biggest fiasco for which he ought to be sacked".[104]

Another opportunity for attack on O'Conor, and one that was more justified, was provided by the dreadful mix-up over the appointment of a replacement for Stephen Musurus Pasha, the Ottoman ambassador in London, who had died in December 1907. Despite his warnings, Fitzmaurice told Lloyd, the ambassador had "bungled horribly" the whole business, which was a view shared by the Foreign Office.[105] Now, therefore, claimed Fitzmaurice,

> ought to be the psychological moment for bringing big guns to bear on the citadel of O'C's mystification and incompetence.... For G's sake let's have someone that is normal and can think, speak, write and act straight here or else give up the struggle and sing "Hail Germania!" This is all fearful treason to my chief but it is not treason to the Empire or British interests.

Just in case his young friend had not got the point, in the morning Fitzmaurice returned to this letter, saying:

> It occurs to me that in what I may have written to you yesterday evening there may be a semblance of exaggeration about Elchi springing from my personal animus against him. *You* know from experience...how positive results have only been attained after an infinity of trouble and

---

[103] CAC Cam., Fitzmaurice to Lloyd, 10 Apr. 1908, GLLD 7/3. A little after he wrote this, Fitzmaurice claimed to have been successful in lowering the embassy's profile in the European campaign for Macedonian reform, CAC Cam., Fitzmaurice to Lloyd, 11 May 1908, GLLD 7/3.

[104] CAC Cam., Fitzmaurice to Lloyd, 9 Feb. 1908, GLLD 7/3. Of course, the policy was Grey's. The correspondence on this between Grey and O'Conor has been published in *BD*, vol. 5, ch. 36.

[105] On this interesting and rather complicated affair, prompted by Abdul Hamid's decision to appoint to London the first Ottoman ambassador to be a Moslem rather than a Greek Orthodox, see TNA, FO371/532 (Jan.–Mar. 1908), and Fitzmaurice to Tyrrell, 12 Apr. 1908, FO800/79; and CAC Cam., Fitzmaurice to Lloyd, 9 Feb. and 10 Apr. 1908, GLLD 7/3.

undoing his evil negative work—how when a question arises he refuses
to tackle it—wastes oceans of money on telegraphing etc until it beco-
mes so envenomed and entangled that wild horses have to be employed
to get it out of the bog into which his funk, insincerity and distorted
methods have let it slip. How he is totally devoid of any patriotic or
broader feeling than that of a contemptible instinct of preserving his
wretched shrivelled-up self by lies and posing to the F.O. as working to
further British commercial interests about which he does not care a 2d
damn as long as he can hoodwink you—me—Brit merchants—the F.O.
etc. Hence failure of oil—irrigation and everything else in Mesopotamia
which our policy of course also was jeopardizing for shadowy political
issues which have now too ended in naught. An Amb. gets £8000 personal
and a practical £13000 to £15000 for doing more than this—for being
positive—straight—guiding the F.O. in their necessary gropings and at
least *telling them the truth*.[106]

What Fitzmaurice had omitted from this diatribe in February 1908 was
that O'Conor's health had been in a state of collapse since the previous
October, though it was not publicly admitted by the embassy until early
in March. This meant that the ambassador could often not even go
through the motions of functioning properly until mid-day, which had
distorted Fitzmaurice's own pattern horribly and "trebled" his work,
he maintained; it was also "maddening and disgraceful from a British
interest point of view".[107] But it was soon to be over. On 19 March Sir
Nicholas O'Conor died, and Fitzmaurice grudgingly had to admit that
at least at the end he had done something for British interests: he had
indicated his wish to be buried in Turkey. Fitzmaurice milked this for
all it was worth. As soon as he heard the news, he told George Lloyd,
he had driven to the Palace to inform the sultan, where he had:

> …played on the piano by sending in a message that "Sir N. instead of
> being buried on Irish soil to which all Irish men were so attached had
> wished to take his last rest in the Crimean War Cemetery side by side
> with those who had fought and died for Islam". This touched the right
> cord in the Caliph's pianola—and a thrill went through the Vatican of
> Islam—the electric current doing a rapid circuit through the Capital. I
> drove on to the G.V.'s house and that of the Min. for F.A. and all Stam-
> boul soon knew that the Brit. Amb. had bequeathed his mortal remains
> to Islam. A. H. wired to the King his condolences which thus reached the
> golf links of Biarritz. Izzet was despatched to H.M.E. to consult with the
> Bashtilki as to the funeral arrangements. One saw that they were made

---

[106] CAC Cam., Fitzmaurice to Lloyd, 9 Feb. 1908, GLLD 7/3.
[107] CAC Cam., Fitzmaurice to Lloyd, 3 Mar. 1908, GLLD 7/3.

on a scale befitting a Brit. Elchi and of a nature to make Marschall's eyes turn green with jealousy. The Turks responded to the note struck and you have read the results in the papers.[108]

Though he found it horrible to relate, Fitzmaurice had to admit to George Lloyd that his spirits had been lifted enormously by the death of O'Conor:

Elchi's death—horribile dictu—was the end of a fearful nightmare which lasted the whole winter. I had to slave so hard to make good the wastage from his wasting life that it seemed to act parasitically in diminishing my vital forces. Now I am whole myself again and have seldom been better in my life.[109]

He was also energised by the need to secure a replacement for O'Conor, and his campaign for de Bunsen now went into high gear. However, it required delicacy since the names of more prominent figures whom he thought unsuited to the post—notably the permanent under-secretary's first cousin, Sir Arthur Hardinge, and Sir Arthur Nicolson—were already being bandied about.[110] A particularly alarming rumour was also circulating that Adam Block might be a candidate—"may Allah forfend!" he exclaimed to George Lloyd.[111]

Fitzmaurice's tactics in promoting de Bunsen were typically indirect. First he encouraged others to take the lead with the Foreign Office. Secondly, he stressed the qualities of the ideal candidate for Constantinople rather than naming him, though these of course amounted to a photofit of de Bunsen.[112] When he learned that the Foreign Office proposed to delay the new appointment until October or even November, leaving in charge in the interim George Barclay, a man he thought in any case too fussy,[113] he worried that the sultan would take this as an insult. Accordingly, he begged George Lloyd to drop a heavy hint to this effect in "the proper quarter" in the Foreign Office without letting its source be known.[114] However, sensing his growing influence and long

---

[108] CAC Cam., Fitzmaurice to Lloyd, 26 Mar. 1908, GLLD 7/3.
[109] CAC Cam., Fitzmaurice to Lloyd, 10 Apr. 1908, GLLD 7/3.
[110] Both already had experience of Constantinople and for Hardinge it was his "greatest ambition" to return as ambassador, Sir Arthur H. Hardinge, *A Diplomatist in the East* (Cape: London, 1928), p. 29.
[111] CAC Cam., Fitzmaurice to Lloyd, 11 May 1908, GLLD 7/3.
[112] CAC Cam., Fitzmaurice to Lloyd, 26 Mar. 1908, GLLD 7/3.
[113] See also MECA Oxf., Richard Massie Graves, Draft of opening chapters of an autobiography, GB 165–0125.
[114] CAC Cam., Fitzmaurice to Lloyd, 10 Apr. 1908, GLLD 7/3.

on good terms with William Tyrrell, now private secretary to Grey, in the end Fitzmaurice could not resist a direct intervention. Writing to Tyrrell on 12 April, in a letter deliberately padded out with other items of interest, he said on this subject, among other things, that:

> Sir W. White used to say that the Amb. here can only strive manfully to keep the boat of British prestige and interests from slipping down stream while any Ambassador who, spurred by ambition, attempts to play a special role and to achieve great results is doomed to failure and disappointment. Thus, until the Macedonian tangle is unravelled, the situation here would seem to demand a man who is not in a hurry to make a reputation, who is serious, level-headed, and sympathetic and who is consequently likely to impress the Sultan and inspire him with personal confidence. Such a man will ensure our at least holding our own in matters commercial and, possessing the confidence of the Turks in his judgment, goodwill and intentions, will be able to mitigate the untoward events certain to accompany the Macedonian *dénouement*, while, should the Sultan die within a few years and a change of régime with its attendant troubles supervene, a man of sound common sense will be a safe and invaluable guide. The next few years may see clouded times fraught with big events which one would not like to see spell disaster to British interests and prestige, and a safe man, possessed of judgment and tact, knowing the value of "festina lente" [making haste slowly], would seem preferable to a "strong" man or a genius.[115]

The Foreign Office, as we shall see, was moved in some degree in the direction desired by Fitzmaurice but before the new ambassador arrived a 'big event' duly intervened.

---

[115] TNA, Fitzmaurice to Tyrrell, 12 Apr. 1908, FO800/79.

ILLUSTRATIONS

1. First year Arts students (Royal University of Ireland), 1883: Fitzmaurice in the front row, third from right
   (*Blackrock College, Co. Dublin*)

2. Junior master: Fitzmaurice, 1887 *(Blackrock College, Co. Dublin)*

3. The quadrangle of the French College, Blackrock, Co. Dublin, today Blackrock College (*Blackrock College, Co. Dublin*)

4. "Elchi": Sir Nicholas O'Conor, the ambassador of whom Fitzmaurice wrote—he "warped my reason and shrivelled my heart" (*Elliott and Fry, Ltd.*)

5. The 'second' dragoman: Hugo Marinitch, and the dragomanate's Slave Department, about 1890 (*unknown photographer*)

6. "Breakfast at Therapia": George Lloyd, the honorary attaché who "redeemed" Fitzmaurice in the "red-letter year" 1906–7
(*The Papers of Lord Lloyd of Dolobran, Churchill Archives Centre, Churchill College, Cambridge*)

7. The "dangerous friend": Abdul Hamid II, August 1908 (*unknown photographer*)

8. "King Log": Kiamil Pasha, the grand vizier who was pro-English to the
point of "infatuation" (*unknown photographer*)

9. Fitzmaurice with musician, about 1906 (*The Papers of Lord Lloyd of Dolobran, Churchill Archives Centre, Churchill College, Cambridge*)

10. "The Generalissimo": Mahmud Shevket Pasha, the grand vizier at whose assassination in 1913 Fitzmaurice is alleged to have conspired (*unknown photographer*)

11. The "windbag and chatterbox": Hakki Pasha, the CUP representative in London who urged the recall of Fitzmaurice in 1913 (*unknown photographer*)

12. Living between two Germans: Fitzmaurice in Sofia, 1915, a cartoon drawn by Sir Mark Sykes (*Hull University Archives, with kind permission of Sir Tatton Sykes*)

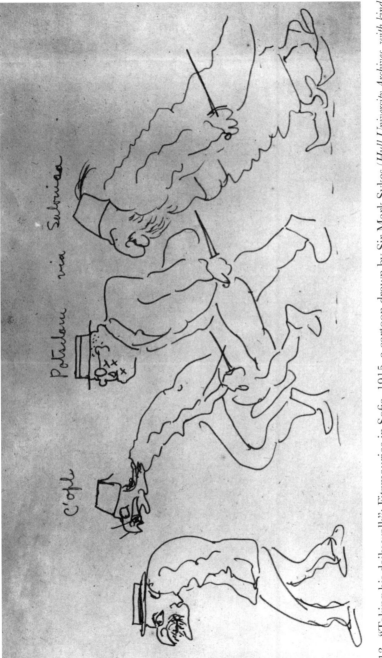

13. "Taking his daily walk": Fitzmaurice in Sofia, 1915, a cartoon drawn by Sir Mark Sykes (*Hull University Archives, with kind permission of Sir Tatton Sykes*)

CHAPTER FIVE

REVOLUTION, 1908

In early July 1908 a small element of the Turkish Third Army Corps in Macedonia mutinied. This action was inspired by a movement of exiles in Paris and elsewhere and included army officers, particularly in Salonica. They called themselves the 'Committee of Union and Progress' (CUP), better known as the 'Young Turks'. Moved by anger at the humiliation heaped on Turkey by the maladministration of the Hamidian regime, their immediate aim was the revival of the parliamentary constitution of 1876 and their long-term one to make the Ottoman Empire the equal of the other great powers—the "Japan of the Near East".[1] The uprising against Abdul Hamid in Macedonia quickly gathered strength, the *ulema* declined to stand in its way, and it was made clear to the sultan that he must either comply with the demands of the CUP or abdicate. On 23 July he gave in, replacing his most unpopular ministers with men known to favour constitutional government and promising a new era of enlightened rule with a resurrected parliament. Exploiting the considerable loyalty that remained to his office, he had preserved his formal position but that was all. Committee men were soon operating the main levers of power, albeit from behind the scenes.

The revolution of the Young Turks, which occurred without serious bloodshed, was welcomed in the capital by persons of all races and religions, to all of whom it promised equality as Ottoman subjects. It also took almost completely by surprise the entire Constantinople diplomatic corps, including Gerald Fitzmaurice. In view of his reputation for knowing everything that was going on, shoring up his position as well as developing a strategy for reacting to the revolution naturally became his immediate priorities. A solution to the second of these problems was not straightforward because it was an event about which he had very mixed feelings.

---

[1] Feroz Ahmad, "The Late Ottoman Empire", in Marian Kent (ed.), *The Great Powers and the End of the Ottoman Empire* (Allen & Unwin: London, 1984), p. 12.

Surprised

The British Embassy had been aware of mounting exasperation with Abdul Hamid's regime—even among Moslems—as early as January 1908.[2] Over the following months its consular outposts, especially in Macedonia, continued to report unrest, including a mutiny among reserve soldiers at Uskub and the likelihood of one among officers at Adrianople.[3] With this intelligence flooding in, it might be imagined that an expert on Turkey would have anticipated the start of the Young Turks' revolution in early July. However, in April Fitzmaurice had given William Tyrrell no more than a vaguely worded warning of possible trouble in "the next few years".[4] Furthermore, none of his six private letters written between 10 April and 8 July to George Lloyd, now in England recovering from the dysentery he had contracted in Iraq and mulling over the direction of his career, questioned the stability of the government. Indeed, Fitzmaurice was so unconcerned that on 9 June he told Lloyd that in September he would at last probably be able to take long overdue leave and return to England.[5]

There were of course extenuating circumstances, and these are well known: the widespread belief in Abdul Hamid's talent for suppressing opposition, the correspondingly tight secrecy of the Young Turks' organization, the suddenness of the uprising, and so on.[6] But there was more to it than this. Fitzmaurice had been permitted no leave from the over-stretched dragomanate since 1905, and at the beginning of June admitted privately that he felt "stale in body and mind".[7] In the months prior to the revolution he had also had an unusual number of distractions. These included O'Conor's death, his anxiety over his successor, and his resolve to impress whoever this might be by clearing

---

[2] TNA, AR 1907, p. 35, in O'Conor to Grey, 13 Jan. 1908, FO195/2363.

[3] TNA, Consular reports in FO195/2297.

[4] TNA, Fitzmaurice to Tyrrell, 12 Apr. 1908, FO800/79.

[5] CAC Cam., Fitzmaurice to Lloyd, 9 June 1908, GLLD 7/3.

[6] See for example Pears, *Forty Years in Constantinople*, ch. 16; Bernard Lewis, *The Emergence of Modern Turkey*, 2nd ed. (Oxford University Press: London, 1968), pp. 196–212 (incl. esp. note 2 on p. 211); Joseph Heller, *British Policy towards the Ottoman Empire, 1908–1914* (Frank Cass: London, 1983), pp. 6–11; and Feroz Ahmad, *The Young Turks: The Committee of Union and Progress in Turkish Politics, 1908–1914* (Clarendon Press: Oxford, 1969), pp. 2–7. For the British Embassy view, see TNA, AR 1908, 17 Feb. 1909, p. 2, FO371/768.

[7] CAC Cam., Fitzmaurice to Lloyd, 9 June 1908, GLLD 7/3.

away at the Palace as many as possible of the embassy's less important
cases before his arrival. There was also Barclay, the chargé d'affaires,
to tutor over the need to lower the British profile on Macedonia and
the Persian frontier question, and so let Russia draw more of Abdul
Hamid's fire—coaching which he thought was paying dividends. There
was a projected Blue Book on Armenia to water down,[8] and a final
distraction was the visit of the Duke of Saxe-Coburg in the critical first
week of July. "I have been meaning to write to you since the birthday
gazette but have been rushed over the Duke of Saxe Coburg's visit and
haven't had a moment to myself", Fitzmaurice opened an unusually
brief letter to Lloyd on 8 July.[9]

Tired and distracted, it is perhaps not surprising that Fitzmaurice
should have failed to anticipate a revolution hatched so secretively.
Nevertheless, he seems to have felt that his reputation for political
sagacity was now under threat and so took steps to shore it up. At the
end of July he claimed in a letter to George Lloyd that at the end of
the first week of the month he had warned Barclay that at any moment
he would "not be surprised to hear 101 guns pronouncing a Constitution",[10] and later repeated the same story to Tyrrell. For the latter's
benefit the wily dragoman also pressed into service a re-writing of the
history of his own opposition to the British campaign for reform in
Macedonia. Omitting to mention that he had previously objected to this
on grounds of futility and damage to commercial interests, Fitzmaurice
now asserted that his great fear about it had always been that it would
provoke a nationalist reaction that would sweep away Abdul Hamid.
He had "several times" told O'Conor as well as Barclay that this policy
was "insane" and implied heavily to Tyrrell that he had warned them
that "we were in the hour before the dawn of his [the Turk's] renewed
national existence".[11]

Whether because of footwork of this sort or not, Fitzmaurice's
reputation emerged unscathed from the Young Turks' revolution. On
one of the private letters that he was soon to be writing regularly to
Tyrrell, despatched in the following January, the latter minuted to Sir
Edward Grey: "It is worth your while to read this at your leisure. There

---

[8] CAC Cam., Fitzmaurice to Lloyd, 11 May 1908, GLLD 7/3.
[9] CAC Cam., Fitzmaurice to Lloyd, 8 July 1908, GLLD 7/3.
[10] CAC Cam., Fitzmaurice to Lloyd, 29 July 1908, GLLD 7/3.
[11] TNA, Fitzmaurice to Tyrrell, 25 Aug. 1908, FO800/79.

is nobody at our Embassy who is in such close touch with the Turks."[12] Years later, Dorina Lady Neave, at the time a great *belle* of the British community in Constantinople and niece of Adam Block, wrote of her old friend Fitzmaurice that "No British official gave a more emphatic warning to the Foreign Office in 1907 [sic] of the vigorous uprising of the virile Young Turk Party".[13]

Another new pupil

In early summer Fitzmaurice learned that Sir Gerard Lowther was to be the new British Ambassador in Constantinople. Lowther, who was 50 years old and currently minister at Tangier, had served as a second secretary at the embassy in Turkey in the late 1880s and been super-intendent of student interpreters when Fitzmaurice was at the school at Ortakeui. Aubrey Herbert thought him "an honourable English country gentleman, with the ability of his family, but with no knowl-edge of Turkey in revolution".[14] Valentine Chirol, who had excellent contacts with the Foreign Office, also privately doubted that his good qualities included the imagination needed to exploit Britain's current opportunity in Turkey.[15]

As for Fitzmaurice, he recalled Lowther as stout, placid and rather indolent, and wondered in a letter to George Lloyd whether the Foreign Office would "put enough pitch under his tail to keep him going for a decade in this capital". Nevertheless, he thought that he was a vast improvement on O'Conor: a straightforward, level-headed, no nonsense sort of person. He had known him fairly well, and thought that he would get on with him as well as any dragoman who had always to be correcting a chief who did not fully understand the Orient. Of course, he told Lloyd, he would have preferred de Bunsen, who was said to be weak but, he added prophetically, "you know how much the 'nameless', voiceless and impersonal Dragoman can influence and stiffen a man

---

[12] To which Grey added later "It would be worthwhile sending this to the Prime [Minister] and Lord Morley", TNA, 11 Jan. 1909, FO800/79.

[13] Dorina Lady Neave, *Romance of the Bosphorus* (Hutchinson: London, 1949), p. 153.

[14] Herbert, *Ben Kendim*, p. 271. See also Philip P. Graves, *Briton and Turk* (Hutchinson: London, 1941), p. 181.

[15] "[I]sn't he too John Bullish for a situation such as that in Turkey? I thought him so in Japan where he never understood or appreciated the people", CAC Cam., Chirol to Lloyd, circa Aug. 1908, GLLD 7/3.

with whom he is in thorough sympathy". With Lowther, he said, he would always have to wear a mask, "tho' not a thick one".[16]

Lowther's appointment commenced officially on 1 July but it was the end of the month before he arrived in Constantinople, where he received a rapturous popular welcome. This was in some measure because of Britain's close identification with liberal ideals but chiefly because the Young Turks wished to rejuvenate the British relationship as a counterweight to French and especially German influence in the Ottoman Empire—thereby giving themselves more room for manoeuvre.[17] Here was a huge opportunity for the new ambassador to re-establish British ascendancy at the Porte, and the Germans, who had invested so much in Abdul Hamid, were, as Fitzmaurice said, "sick unto death, flabbergasted and nonplussed".[18] Whether this opportunity could be seized, however, depended not only on the adroitness of the German response but on that of the Foreign Office in London. It also depended on Fitzmaurice, because Lowther soon fell under his spell.

Mixed feelings about the Young Turks

Only a year before the July revolution Britain had embarked on a new policy of great significance in the context of the European balance of power: friendship with Russia, a relationship given focus by the Anglo-Russian entente of 31 August 1907 and coloured by the convivial meeting between the British and Russian monarchs at Reval in June 1908. Since Turkey was Russia's traditional enemy, this inevitably reduced the warmth with which the British Foreign Secretary could welcome the victory of the Young Turks.[19] Sir Edward Grey was also anxious that a successful experiment with constitutional government in the Ottoman Empire, coupled with a new mood of national assertiveness, might encourage agitation for similar change among Britain's Moslem

---

[16] CAC Cam., Fitzmaurice to Lloyd, 3 June 1908, GLLD 7/3.

[17] Feroz Ahmad, "Great Britain's relations with the Young Turks, 1908–1914", *Middle Eastern Studies*, 2(4), July 1966, p. 307.

[18] CAC Cam., Fitzmaurice to Lloyd, 29 July 1908, GLLD 7/3.

[19] The Anglo-Russian entente had complicated Fitzmaurice's relations with the Porte before the revolution and led him to question its wisdom. Getting on to "non-nagging relations" with Russia was one thing; creating an entente with them was quite another. Hardinge, he thought, was going too far, CAC Cam., Fitzmaurice to Lloyd, 21 June 1908, GLLD 7/3.

subjects in Egypt and India.[20] Nevertheless, as a Liberal statesman he could hardly cold shoulder the liberal ideals of the Young Turks. In any case, if they were realized, they promised a solution to the perennial problem of the ill-treatment of Ottoman Christians and thus an end to the pressure on the European concert to intervene on their behalf. Nowhere did Grey look for more relief on this point than in Macedonia. Better prospects for British investments and commerce were also now in view. As a result, he gave a cautious welcome to the July revolution. Sympathy and encouragement were to be the watchwords, though it is noticeable that he told Lowther that Britain should only be ready to support "the better elements" among the Young Turks.[21] The foreign secretary's mixed feelings about them were shared by Fitzmaurice, though the chief dragoman added more negative ones and—as time wore on—tended to give these more emphasis.

In the hurried note that Fitzmaurice wrote to George Lloyd before setting out on 29 July to collect Lowther from Adrianople, he said that "We are now on the wave of a popular and nationalist movement which will have far reaching effects". It was not only the British position in Egypt and India that was in peril, he warned, but the entire system of European privileges in the Ottoman Empire.[22] In a much longer and more reflective letter written to Tyrrell after the dust had settled, he speculated on possible futures, about none of which was he optimistic. Either the Young Turks would be successful, in which case Britain could expect pressure from them in Aden and Cyprus as well as Egypt, and serious complications elsewhere. If they failed, which he evidently thought more likely, it would be because of the gigantic task that "the children"—as he now routinely described them in private—had set themselves. In their clumsy reforming zeal they would probably throw out the baby with the bathwater, including the caliphate itself, loyalty to which he believed was the only thing that held the diverse and ramshackle Ottoman Empire together.[23] The result would

---

[20] Ahmad, "Great Britain's relations with the Young Turks, 1908–1914", pp. 302–4; Heller, *British Policy towards the Ottoman Empire, 1908–1914*, pp. 10–12.

[21] TNA, Grey to Lowther, 23 Aug. 1908, FO800/79.

[22] CAC Cam., Fitzmaurice to Lloyd, 29 July 1908, GLLD 7/3.

[23] This point greatly impressed George Lloyd, who was now positioning himself for a career as a Conservative member of parliament. Indeed, he had already advanced it in the context of an extremely unflattering account of the Young Turks—redolent of Fitzmaurice's attitudes—in a speech to the Balkan Committee in London on 23 July. Lloyd counselled the Committee to reserve its support for a reform movement composed

merely be to provoke "a desperate internal struggle accompanied by disorders" and provide a perfect opportunity for external intervention, especially by Russia.[24]

There was also a more personal element to Fitzmaurice's deep reservations about the Young Turks. He had made a long and arduous career, at last at its pinnacle, in dealing with the 'Old Turk', many of whom, like the grand vizier, Ferid Pasha, he had grown to like and respect.[25] He could not be expected to regard their downfall with indifference. Nor could he be unmoved by the hostility of the Young Turks to the whole dragoman system itself, which they regarded as part and parcel of the old regime. Aubrey Herbert put this well:

> Now, in place of the old pashas, with their stately presence, their high honorifics, their venerable beards, he was called upon to meet a miscellany of Jews from Salonica, of Turkish Boulevardiers and moustachioed Syrians from Lausanne, who spoke to him, not in Turkish, but in the French of Pera. These men, who were now the chiefs of Turkey, had read Jean Jacques Rousseau, admired French novels, and considered an Official Interpreter to the Porte as a humiliation to their country. Othello's occupation was gone: Fitzmaurice's position remained, but its local and official seal had been lost in the Revolution. So complete a change of circumstance must have its influence upon any man.[26]

In his private letters, Fitzmaurice was willing to acknowledge these feelings. A month after the revolution he said to Tyrrell: "At moments I experience reactionary tendencies", adding that as one of the old regime he expected that soon he would have to "clear out and retire to some quiet Consulate to qualify for a pension".[27] His belief that Jews and Freemasons had great influence in the ranks of the Young Turks (see Ch. 6) did not endear them to the Roman Catholic in him either.

Shortly before the revolution the sultan had been most flattering towards Fitzmaurice and he had joked—or half joked—to George

of "true men" with indigenous origins who supported a "properly controlled Kalif", CAC Cam., Notes for Speech to Balkan Committee on the Revolutionary Rising in Turkey, July 23rd, 1908, GLLD 7/3.
[24] TNA, Fitzmaurice to Tyrrell, 25 Aug. 1908, FO800/79.
[25] At the time of the revolution Ferid, who had been grand vizier since 1903, believed that he was in personal danger. Despite the fact that he was pro-German, Fitzmaurice, responding to a plea from his son, swiftly intervened on his behalf, CAC Cam., Fitzmaurice to Lloyd, 29 July 1908, GLLD 7/3. Ferid managed to retain the confidence of the Committee and later reappeared as Minister of the Interior.
[26] Ben Kendim, p. 269.
[27] TNA, Fitzmaurice to Tyrrell, 25 Aug. 1908, FO800/79.

Lloyd that "Abdul and I are becoming dangerously friendly".[28] Nevertheless, he wept no tears over the contraction of his absolute power or the scattering of his more venal Palace acolytes. He had to admit, too, that the Young Turks had not surrendered to personal vindictiveness and revealed "a great sense of responsibility", a view shared by his friend Pat Ramsay.[29] Fitzmaurice was also delighted that the "footling reforms" in Macedonia had been swept away.[30] As for the discomfiture of the Germans in Constantinople and the soaring prestige of the British Embassy, this was of course a reversal of fortunes that he particularly savoured.

In early September George Lloyd returned for a short visit to Constantinople to see for himself what was going on, and was joined by his especially close Foreign Office friend, Sam Cockerell.[31] Discovering that the Young Turks had roots inside as well as outside the country,[32] Lloyd revised his opinion of the CUP and on his return to London announced in the *National Review* that on both moral and material grounds Britain should now give it wholehearted encouragement: the Liberal government was following the right course.[33] Fitzmaurice, who was deflated to see him leave so quickly,[34] congratulated him on his article and shared with him his delight over the list of recent gains for British interests in Turkey, chiefly commercial ones. "Even the German stronghold of the Army is yielding to gentle pressure", he told

---

[28] CAC Cam., Fitzmaurice to Lloyd, 3 June 1908, GLLD 7/3. Fitzmaurice's jesting manner and fondness for allegorical reasoning make it difficult now, as it was then, to be certain about his real feelings for Abdul Hamid when he came into regular contact with him as chief dragoman. The young Dorina Clifton believed that he "held a most sincere and respectful affection" for the sultan, who in return treated him as "a friend", Neave, *Romance of the Bosphorus*, p. 153. This is surely an exaggeration. However, Tilley, who admired Fitzmaurice, also believed that he "had a soft spot for the Sultan and thought better of him than most people". At the same time, though, he confessed to finding it sometimes "difficult to form any exact idea of his real meaning or his real belief", Tilley, *London to Tokyo*, p. 71. In retirement Fitzmaurice also told the Boland family (see Epilogue) that he got on "remarkably well" with the sultan, Bridget Boland, *At My Mother's Knee* (The Bodley Head: London, 1978), p. 71.

[29] TNA, Fitzmaurice to Tyrrell, 25 Aug. 1908, FO800/79; CAC Cam., Fitzmaurice to Lloyd, 13 Aug. 1908, GLLD 7/3.

[30] CAC Cam., Fitzmaurice to Lloyd, 29 July 1908, GLLD 7/3.

[31] S. P. Cockerell had been briefly in the Eastern Department in 1903.

[32] On his way home he actually interviewed members of the CUP in Salonica, C. F. Adam, *Life of Lord Lloyd* (Macmillan: London, 1948), pp. 46–7.

[33] G. Lloyd, "Some Aspects of the Reform Movement in Turkey", *National Review*, Nov. 1908.

[34] CAC Cam., Fitzmaurice to Lloyd, 7 Oct. 1908, GLLD 7/3.

him, "and an Englishman has got the contract for clothing the Turkish Tommy with 'Khakee'."[35] Of course, Fitzmaurice was more concerned with commercial than financial questions, and these advances were all very well. However, it was German *investment* in the Ottoman Empire, especially in the railways but in other public utilities as well, together with the enhanced political influence that this implied, that most worried the British.[36]

In Stamboul after dark for "King Log"

Encouraged by the silver linings to the cloud of revolution, and with the Foreign Office giving the Young Turks a cautious welcome, Fitzmaurice resolved to make the best of what he still feared would be a bad job. Under a blanket of official embassy non-intervention in Turkish politics, his strategy was now first to persuade Abdul Hamid to associate himself publicly with the revolution,[37] which was achieved without great difficulty; and secondly, to preserve the position of the new grand vizier, which was not.

The new grand vizier was the anglophile if octogenarian Kiamil Pasha. 'Ingliz Kiamil' was a liberal who was independent of the Palace and had been appointed with Committee support on the back of the new enthusiasm for Britain.[38] Fitzmaurice, who regarded him as pro-English to the point of infatuation,[39] became one of his intimates and thereby achieved a position of exceptional influence.[40] Arguing the importance of keeping an "old hand at the helm during the period of transition", and citing in support of this view the disasters that followed the too abrupt French Revolution, he urged that Kiamil should remain in office at least until after the first session of parliament.[41]

Fitzmaurice may have complained of feeling jaded before the revolution in July but its drama gave him a second wind. Aubrey

---

[35] CAC Cam., Fitzmaurice to Lloyd, 25 Nov. 1908, GLLD 7/3.
[36] I am grateful to Dr Keith Hamilton for reminding me of this.
[37] TNA, Fitzmaurice to Tyrrell, 25 Aug. 1908, FO800/79; CAC Cam., Fitzmaurice to Lloyd, 25 Nov. 1908, GLLD 7/3.
[38] Ahmad, *The Young Turks*, p. 27.
[39] TNA, Fitzmaurice to Tyrrell, 11 Jan. 1909, FO800/79.
[40] Aubrey Herbert observed that in Turkey Kiamil "was credited with no power of action apart from Fitzmaurice", *Ben Kendim*, p. 271.
[41] TNA, Fitzmaurice to Tyrrell, 25 Aug. and 30 Sept. 1908, FO800/79.

Herbert, who had also returned to obtain a first-hand view of events, described him as "still young, full of power and vigour".[42] Moreover, the dragomanate might have been creaking but at least in Andrew Ryan Fitzmaurice had an able and trustworthy number two, in fact the ideal number two: a man of intelligence if slow in speech, immensely knowledgeable in the working of the capitulations, modest, attentive to detail, and uncomplaining.[43] The dragomanate's workload had also been temporarily reduced, either because the new warmth for Britain reduced resistance to the cases it had to push or because, as with those concerning slaves, they had been made irrelevant by the revolution.[44] The net result was that Fitzmaurice had more time for the work he relished: political intrigue.

Kiamil Pasha needed Fitzmaurice when the revolution was rocked in early October by the Bulgarian declaration of independence, Austria's annexation of Bosnia and Herzegovina, and the unilateral declaration of the Cretans that they were annexed to Greece. These attempts to exploit Turkey's preoccupation with internal affairs bastinadoed the pride of the Young Turks and also created a delicate problem for Sir Edward Grey. The British foreign secretary did not wish to jeopardise Britain's newly restored influence in Constantinople by any hint of indifference to Turkish sensitivities. On the other hand, these events—especially the Bosnian crisis—were fraught with wide implications, including implications for Britain's new relationship with Russia. As a result, Grey was also anxious to avoid doing anything that would encourage Turkey to fight for its rights. Amicable settlement was thus very much the order of the day and in pursuit of this policy, which in the event proved successful, the first essential was to ensure a measured Turkish response. For securing this Fitzmaurice claimed some credit. He drove to Kiamil's house at the critical juncture and argued with him until four in the morning. Despite the fact that the grand vizier was "fearfully upset" and there was "wild talk of war", he told George Lloyd, it was finally decided that "the 'children' should bear up and show a manly restraint".[45] His influence with Kiamil appears to have been especially

---

[42] *Ben Kendim*, p. 268.
[43] Ryan, *The Last of the Dragomans*, Foreword by Sir Reader Bullard.
[44] Between July 1908 and February 1909 about one-third of the embassy's 120 cases had been resolved, TNA, AR 1908, in Lowther to Grey 17 Feb. 1909, FO195/2363, p. 72; Ryan, *The Last of the Dragomans*, p. 57.
[45] CAC Cam., Fitzmaurice to Lloyd, 7 Oct. 1908, GLLD 7/3.

significant in shaping Turkey's conciliatory policy towards Bulgaria, whose people he greatly admired.[46]

Fitzmaurice's support was needed again by Kiamil when Ferid attempted a come-back with German support in November. He had "sworn a nightly oath" to prevent this, at least while Baron Marschall remained in Constantinople, he told Lloyd in a letter at the end of the month. He had acted accordingly, "intriguing *frightfully*", and often finding himself in "quaint places in Stamboul after dark". In response to Ferid's spending on the press and attempts to "mine Kiamil's position", he said,

> I have counter-mined hard and Ferid is now dished and discredited.... Damn the beasts—their underhand intrigues actually encircled Lowther but this Tilki has burrowed low down and smashed the conspiracy I hope.

He was certainly concerned that the means he had used, which would not "bare the light of day", could be used to discredit him if discovered by the Germans but he consoled himself with the thought that they were justified by the ends achieved. There had at least been a superficial stability over the last three months when there might otherwise have been "several changes of ministry and corresponding chaos". Besides, while tiring, it had all been "splendid fun" and quite pushed out of his mind the pain in his left leg.[47]

At the end of November 1908 Fitzmaurice was cautiously optimistic about the way things were going. Kiamil had "shown real proofs of tilkihood by steering through foreign and internal shoals during the last three months under our guidance", he told George Lloyd, while the 'children' seemed willing to keep him, at least for the time being.[48] However, within days he had another battle on his hands.

Kiamil had begun to show impatience at the continuing attempts of the Committee to manipulate his government from behind the scenes, and in early December relations between them deteriorated. Whether

---

[46] Fitzmaurice spoke at this time as if he and Kiamil were joint rulers of Turkey: "...*we* are going to be merciful [to the Bulgarians]...as I said, *we* shan't be hard on the Bulgarians" [emphasis added], CAC Cam., Fitzmaurice to Lloyd, 10 Jan. 1909, GLLD 7/4. In return for financial compensation, Turkey finally acknowledged Bulgarian independence in the spring, though by this time Kiamil was no longer grand vizier. On British support for Turkey in this crisis, see Ahmad, *The Young Turks*, pp. 24–5.

[47] CAC Cam., Fitzmaurice to Lloyd, 25 Nov. 1908, GLLD 7/3.

[48] CAC Cam., Fitzmaurice to Lloyd, 25 Nov. 1908, GLLD 7/3.

at this point the CUP wanted to get rid of him or simply bring him to heel,[49] they attacked him in their press and Fitzmaurice saw this as the start of mortal combat. "Now Tilki", he wrote to Lloyd on the eve of the opening of parliament, "this was open war". Acting virtually as the grand vizier's chief of staff and campaign manager combined, he reported to Lloyd:

> I have worked some 12 to 15 hrs a day for the last 15 days—worked the press foreign and native—dived into all sorts of nests in Stamboul by night and early morning and have now the satisfaction of feeling that the Committee...has had a fall and chucked up the sponge for the present.[50]

There was still the risk of a vote against Kiamil in parliament on the following day but Fitzmaurice was fairly confident that it would not happen. Sounding for all the world like someone who had learned his trade as a Democratic Party boss in Chicago, he said that by virtue of most energetic "wire pulling" he had lined up for Kiamil all of the Arab deputies (about 30) and most of the Albanians (making a similar number), and predicted with certainty that the Greeks as well as many of the Anatolians would be "solid for him".[51]

He knew, of course, that a large majority of the deputies were pro-CUP—thanks in part to "anti-Christian gerrymandering" in the elections[52]—but banked on the Committee having been put into such a cautious frame of mind by the show of support for Kiamil over the previous fortnight that they would not risk forcing the issue. If they did, he had secured assurances that an adjournment would be moved by Kiamil's supporters on the grounds that about 40 members from distant provinces—where CUP support was weaker—had not yet been able to reach the capital. "The Sultan is quaking with nervousness", Fitzmaurice concluded this part of his letter to Lloyd, but had promised Kiamil that he would open parliament on the following day. Rumours abounded that Abdul would be shot or deposed, he said, and he would tell him the upshot the next night. "I must go to bed now", said Fitzmaurice, "being tired after a titanic struggle between two invisible forces".[53]

---

[49] Ahmad argues the latter; see *The Young Turks*, p. 32.
[50] CAC Cam., Fitzmaurice to Lloyd, 16 Dec. 1908, GLLD 7/3.
[51] CAC Cam., Fitzmaurice to Lloyd, 16 Dec. 1908, GLLD 7/3.
[52] TNA, Fitzmaurice to Tyrrell, 11 Jan. 1909, FO800/79.
[53] CAC Cam., Fitzmaurice to Lloyd, 16 Dec. 1908, GLLD 7/3.

As he had anticipated, Kiamil survived the opening of the first parliament of the revolution on 17 December; indeed, he survived it triumphantly. On the following day Fitzmaurice re-opened his letter to George Lloyd to relate the event, which he had witnessed from a seat "wedged in between the German Amb[assador] and his sausagey dragoman".[54] All of the deputies had behaved well and Abdul Hamid showed great composure. "He is certainly the best comedian in two continents", wrote an admiring Fitzmaurice, "and played his part perfectly".[55]

Had Fitzmaurice known he need not have written this letter, for only days later he had a delightful surprise when George Lloyd turned up unexpectedly in Constantinople and joined him in his hotel. He was en route back home, having had to abort a trip to India for party reasons.[56] This visit seems to have caused Lloyd to reconsider the Young Turks yet again. They had become "dictators" and he was enthusiastic for the hard line being taken with them by "the Sheikh"[57]—the name he and Cockerell now employed privately for Fitzmaurice—even if it risked placing great strain on Anglo-Turkish friendship.[58]

In January 1909 Kiamil received a further show of confidence from the popular chamber but the aged statesman's moment was soon to end. Alleging high-handed action in certain cabinet appointments in early February, the CUP whipped up hostility to him in parliament and secured his replacement by the more pliant Hussein Hilmi Pasha.[59] "Bad news", said Grey,[60] though private and public assurances were given that Turkish policy would remain pro-British.[61]

According to *The Times* correspondent in Constantinople, Philip Graves, neither the embassy generally nor the Foreign Office were particularly upset by the fall of Kiamil, since his bad relations with the CUP had made him something of a liability.[62] Fitzmaurice was less complacent. Writing once more to George Lloyd, whose political

---

[54] CAC Cam., Fitzmaurice to Lloyd, 19 Jan. 1909, GLLD 7/4.
[55] CAC Cam., Fitzmaurice to Lloyd, 18 Dec. 1908, GLLD 7/3.
[56] Adam, *Life of Lord Lloyd*, p. 47.
[57] Presumably because of his Yemen experience and his closeness to the Arab deputies in the Chamber.
[58] CAC Cam., Lloyd (Constantinople) to Cockerell, 28 Dec. 1908, GLLD 8/3.
[59] Ahmad, *The Young Turks*, pp. 33–6.
[60] TNA, min. of Grey, 15 Feb. 1909, FO371/760.
[61] *The Times*, 15 Feb. 1909; TNA, Lowther to Grey, 15 Feb. 1909, FO371/761.
[62] Graves, *Briton and Turk*, p. 126.

career now seemed launched and who remained eager for intelligence on Turkey,[63] he likened him to King Log in Aesop's fable of "The Frogs Desiring a King"—and the new cabinet to King Stork. As the frogs—who did not really need a government—had treated with contempt the log dropped by Jove into their swamp on their first request for a ruler, thereby getting instead a stork that gobbled them all up after they had demanded another, so in rejecting the cautious Kiamil the parliamentary deputies could look forward only to being polished off fairly quickly by the CUP's new cabinet. The same fate was in store for the Turkish people as a whole, 80 to 90 per cent of whom actually detested and dreaded the CUP, he claimed. Strongly nationalist and even fanatical, it was no better than the previous regime: a "secret ruling despotic force" with veiled anti-British sentiments to boot.[64]

Fitzmaurice no doubt exaggerated the popular hostility to the CUP but opposition forces—all dubbed 'reactionary' by the Committee—were certainly gathering, especially in the capital itself. Former office-holders and spies, soldiers who retained a fondness for absolutist government, constitutional purists, and others, not to mention Abdul Hamid himself, all had good reason to fear or hate the Committee; devout Moslems looked askance at its alleged domination by Jews, Freemasons, and assorted atheists.[65] Did Fitzmaurice actively support them, as has been frequently suggested?[66] Despite the ambassador's own *public* posture of non-intervention, the answer is: yes, though indirectly.

Fitzmaurice had never been squeamish about advocating the need for radical solutions—as for example in connection with Macedonia—and at this point he tilted decidedly in favour of eliminating the CUP. The hostility to it in his private correspondence increased, and his statement that the Turkish people were "looking to us to rid them of King Stork" suggests strongly the notion of a British obligation not to be shirked.[67] He was echoed almost verbatim in Lowther's despatches to

---

[63] Since his return from Turkey he had found his advice on events there much sought after in Whitehall, parliament and the press, and even at Windsor Castle. In the middle of January he was adopted as the parliamentary candidate of the West Staffordshire Conservative Association, Adam, *Life of Lord Lloyd*, p. 47.

[64] CAC Cam., Fitzmaurice to Lloyd, 25 Feb. 1909, GLLD 7/4.

[65] Ahmad, *The Young Turks*, pp. 42–3; Pears, *Forty Years in Constantinople*, pp. 257–9.

[66] See especially Ahmad, "Great Britain's relations with the Young Turks, 1908–1914", pp. 312–13.

[67] CAC Cam., Fitzmaurice to Lloyd, 25 Feb. 1909, GLLD 7/4.

the Foreign Office.[68] Given the constraints imposed upon it by Grey's policy of studied neutrality, however, the embassy could play no direct role in a *coup d'état*.[69] Nor was the embassy's secret service budget up to providing any significant subsidies to opposition newspapers like the *Levant Herald*,[70] though the press was the chief battleground between the Committee and its enemies.[71] Apart from inspiring articles in the press, therefore, which Fitzmaurice did as a matter of course,[72] another tactic was needed.

The best approach, Fitzmaurice believed, was to make the Committee-nominated cabinet unpopular by *causing* it to suffer policy disasters, for example on Crete. As he wrote to George Lloyd in late February: "We shan't get the odium now.... Even if Macedonia is lopped off, our position could almost stand the racket. This", he said, "is important."[73]

It can safely be assumed that Fitzmaurice converted the ambassador to this tactic because a week later echoes of it boomed in a despatch he wrote to Grey.[74] Lowther also adopted a "cold" attitude towards the Committee while keeping an open door to its opponents, notably the so-called Liberal Union. This gave them a green light,[75] though he warned Hardinge that "there will possibly be some shedding of blood".[76] As for Fitzmaurice, he told Lloyd of "growing chaos" in the country, claimed that the *Levant Herald*'s onslaught against the CUP was being supported by "thousands of Turks", and added: "We all wonder whether we are preparing some new neat little surprise for our friends in Europe who take an interest in our quaint doings".[77]

---

[68] Ahmad, "Great Britain's relations with the Young Turks, 1908–1914", pp. 311–12.

[69] Hardinge thought that, in any case, the CUP would "disappear in the not far distant future" without the need for a British push, TNA, Hardinge to Lowther, 23 Mar. 1909, FO800/193A.

[70] TNA, Lowther to Hardinge, 26 Feb. 1909, FO800/193B.

[71] F. McCullagh, "The Constantinople Mutiny of April 13th", *The Fortnightly Review*, 1 July 1909.

[72] CAC Cam., Fitzmaurice to Lloyd, 16 Dec. 1908, GLLD 7/3. Interestingly enough, his hand appears obvious in a letter signed simply "X" that was published in *The Times* on 16 Feb. 1909 under the heading "THE CRISIS IN TURKEY". This contained his pure gospel about the CUP, even using the allegory of "The Frogs Desiring a King", though this was garbled.

[73] CAC Cam., Fitzmaurice to Lloyd, 25 Feb. 1909, GLLD 7/4.

[74] This is quoted in Ahmad, *The Young Turks*, p. 37.

[75] Ahmad, *The Young Turks*, pp. 36–8.

[76] TNA, Lowther to Hardinge, 2 Mar. 1909, FO800/192.

[77] CAC Cam., Fitzmaurice to Lloyd, 6 Mar. 1909, GLLD 7/4.

Speaking of this time in his memoirs, Reader Bullard, the latest junior to join the dragomanate, described Fitzmaurice as "often being summoned out late for some crisis, never knowing when he would get back from his work or get a meal but keeping going with the aid of Garibaldi biscuits, which he carried in his pocket".[78] Clearly over-doing it, he became so incapacitated by illness that Lowther thought at one point that he would have to replace him.[79] This came at a critical juncture, as we shall see, and must have reduced his influence on events.

---

[78] Bullard, *The Camels Must Go*, p. 63.
[79] TNA, Lowther to Hardinge, 24 Mar. 1909, FO800/192.

CHAPTER SIX

"OLD REGIME THOUGH NOT REACTIONARY", 1909–11

The little—but hardly "neat"—surprise that had been foreshadowed by Fitzmaurice in his letter to George Lloyd on 6 March came a little over a month later, on Tuesday 13 April. A large-scale mutiny of troops in the capital, calling for the defence of the sacred law and the destruction of the Committee, wrecked the offices of the latter's mouthpieces in the press and turned out the government. However, the counter-revolution swiftly failed and Fitzmaurice's role in it led him to be charged with being a 'reactionary', called seriously into question his political judgement, and cost him some friends. This plunged him briefly into despair and it took much eloquence, Lowther's support, and the sympathy of George Lloyd to restore his spirits. Nevertheless, he was now a marked man as far as the Young Turks were concerned and, as a result, the exasperation with him of Sir Edward Grey began to mount. It is, therefore, remarkable testimony to his indispensability to the British Embassy in Constantinople, as well as to his ability to argue his corner, that he survived.

Discreet support for counter-revolution

Following the events of 13 April the CUP leaders, whose support in the capital was in fact slender, went into hiding, and—ironically enough—Fitzmaurice had that night to help save the life of Mahmud Muhtar Pasha, the one senior officer prepared to prolong the fight.[1] Thereafter his activities are relatively obscure because he had little time to write and afterwards remained tight-lipped about these events, even to George Lloyd. Nevertheless, it is clear that when he was not bustling in over-drive between the embassy, the Palace and the Porte, he was at the elbow of the ambassador, who had to take many difficult decisions quickly and whose telegraph traffic reached exceptional levels.

---

[1] GBP, *The Diaries*, 13 July 1909; and Pears, *Forty Years in Constantinople*, pp. 261–4.

After the scattering of the CUP, a stop-gap cabinet was formed by the Liberal Union until Kiamil could be reinstated.[2] The new cabinet insisted on its attachment to the Constitution and on 15 April requested British support. Grey at once said that Britain would continue to extend its "hearty sympathy" to any decent constitutional government in Turkey,[3] and this was all that Lowther and Fitzmaurice needed to hear. Seeing that the most serious threat to the counter-revolution would come from CUP-supporting officers of the Third Army Corps in Macedonia,[4] on the same day (15 April) the embassy lent its support to the counter-revolutionaries in the internal propaganda contest now launched. Ismail Kemal Bey, the newly elected president of the chamber, who was having some success in controlling events, claimed in his memoirs that this was done at his request.[5] Like the remaining deputies, who sent reassuring messages to their constituents, and the Porte, which sent them to the local authorities,[6] the embassy dispatched telegrams designed to soothe pro-constitution opinion. One was a circular message to consuls which said:

> Soldiers of army and religious element having demanded application of Sheri Law together with Constitution and dismissal of prominent Committee members of Cabinet and President of Chamber, Cabinet and President of Chamber resigned. Demonstrations of rejoicing lasted two days. Only a few accidental casualties. Capital now tranquil and new Govt. under Tewfik as Grand Vizier installed.[7]

The other telegram was more striking. It was marked "Confidential" and sent only to the consular officers in Salonica, Monastir, and Adrianople—the most likely sources of resistance to the counter-revolutionaries. It was also drafted in the unmistakeable hand of the master of the dark arts himself, Fitzmaurice. It read:

> Committees of Salonica Monastir and other places have telegraphed to Palace complaining of violation of Constitution and demanding reinstatement of Hilmi Pasha Cabinet and President of Chamber and

---

[2] Ahmad, *The Young Turks*, p. 43.

[3] TNA, Grey to Lowther, 15 Apr. 1909, FO371/770.

[4] TNA, Lowther to Lamb (Salonica), 15 Apr. 1909, FO195/2330.

[5] Sommerville Story (ed.), *The Memoirs of Ismail Kemal Bey* (Constable: London, 1920), p. 343.

[6] Story, *The Memoirs of Ismail Kemal Bey*, pp. 342–3; TNA, Lowther to FO, 16 Apr., FO371/770.

[7] TNA, Circular tel. to Consuls from Embassy, 15 April 1909, FO195/2314.

punishment of authors failing which the 3rd A[rmy]. C[orps]. will march on Capital.

Cabinet and President were not dismissed by Sultan but resigned in writing and with insistance [sic] and Constitution remains unimpaired.

You should judiciously and discretely[sic] exercise your influence in letting truth be known.[8]

On 17 April, after it became clear to the embassy that the Committee was preventing the government's own telegrams of reassurance from reaching Macedonia and that it may have overestimated the ease with which the threat from that quarter could be managed, it sent another telegram to the British consuls in the province. This urged them "discreetly and unofficially"—but too late—to encourage the "malcontents" in each district to send a small deputation to Constantinople to see for themselves that everything was all right.[9]

Meanwhile, the embassy was also trying to exploit British sea power, the diplomatic potential of which had been well appreciated by Fitzmaurice while he was in the Aden hinterland. Already at mid-day on 14 April Lowther had asked for warships to be made ready to proceed to Beirout, Smyrna and Salonica to protect British interests in the event of trouble spreading to the provinces.[10] London agreed and on 16 April, following news of massacres of Armenians at Adana, Lowther again emphasised the importance of having warships on hand, this time at Mersina and Athens.[11] However, on the very next day Lowther made a request for warships which had a more double-edged meaning.

As a result of consular telegrams from Macedonia, by 17 April the embassy had become aware of a growing suspicion—also taking hold in the capital—that Abdul Hamid was behind recent events: the Committee was winning the propaganda war. It also knew that a number

---

[8] TNA, Lowther to Consuls in Salonica, Monastir and Adrianople, 15 April 1909, FO195/2330, folio 384. The draft is of course initialled "G.L.". This text was also embodied, word for word, into a longer telegram sent to the consuls in Uskub and Serres on the following day, 16 April. In his "Britain and Ottoman domestic politics: from the Young Turk Revolution to the Counter-Revolution, 1908–9", *Middle Eastern Studies*, 37 (2), Apr. 2001, Hasan Unal overlooks the more important of these two telegrams, that is, the one drafted by Fitzmaurice and sent on 15 April.

[9] TNA, Lowther to Consuls in Salonica, Adrianople, Uscub, Monastir, and Serres, 17 Apr. 1909, FO195/2330. A. B. Geary, the acting vice-consul at Monastir, subsequently told Andrew Ryan that it was already too late for such a move so both he and Lamb ignored it, MECA Oxf., Geary to Ryan, 31 July 1909, Ryan Box IV, Item 8.

[10] TNA, Lowther to Grey, 14 Apr. 1909, FO371/770.

[11] TNA, Lowther to Grey, 16 Apr. 1909, FO371/770.

of Macedonian battalions were making for the capital. With the fate of the counter-revolution now in the balance, shortly after mid-day Lowther telegraphed to Grey that

> Several prominent Turks here are inclined to the view that people here may lose their belief that Great Britain takes an interest in the future of this country if we send no ships to these waters, the presence of which in the neighbourhood would tend greatly to improve the situation.

Lowther agreed with them and said that "some ships should be dispatched to Lemnos, whence they could be forwarded to places where a critical situation exists as occasion requires".[12]

The Foreign Office was clearly in two minds about how to respond to Lowther's new request. Grey was willing to meet it if British subjects were in real danger and sending warships to Lemnos was indeed the best way to protect them. On the other hand, encouraged by Louis Mallet, head of the Eastern Department, he recognized that the island's proximity to Constantinople meant that this could be widely seen as a political move.[13] As a result, Lowther received no immediate encouragement on this score and other remedies had to be considered by the embassy if the counter-revolution was to be saved.

The size of the avenging army from Macedonia, which was under the direction of the commander of the Third Army Corps, Mahmud Shevket Pasha, was swelling by the hour and approaching the walls of Constantinople. The government, which had fruitlessly sent one deputation to parley with it,[14] wished to send another and it was in the early evening of the same day that Lowther despatched his Lemnos telegram to London, that is 17 April, that the embassy played its last card—and took its greatest risk. It agreed to the request of the panic-stricken government that Fitzmaurice should accompany the deputation—more or less in the capacity of its spokesman—to argue with the 'Army of Deliverance'.

> Troops outside walls have consented to wait [Lowther cabled the Foreign Office], but if there is any attempt to attack them they will advance through town. Turkish Government are very anxious about situation, [and] consider that advance of troops would mean risk of a general massacre.

---

[12] TNA, Lowther to Grey, 17 Apr. 1909 (No. 127), FO371/770.
[13] TNA, mins. of Mallet and Grey, 17 Apr. 1909, FO371/770, folios 393–4.
[14] TNA, Lowther to Grey (No. 128), 5.20pm, 17 Apr. 1909, FO371/770.

At earnest request of Turkish Government, and in view of what I believe to be a very critical situation, I have authorized Mr. Fitzmaurice to accompany a deputation of Members of Parliament and Ulemas to the walls to try to convince Salonica troops that present Government are firm upholders of the Constitution.

Turkish Government believe that an independent authority, especially English, is more likely to influence these men than anything they can say.

I am fully aware of the danger of our immixtion in internal politics, but Rifaat Pasha assured me that it was unanimous wish of Cabinet that this effort should be made to save the situation, which was fraught with danger not only to Turkey but the whole of Europe.[15]

However, what might have been Fitzmaurice's finest hour never came. He set off to join the deputation but, on reaching Stamboul later the same evening, found that the government—allegedly now more confident of its success—had changed its mind about the advisability of including him.[16]

The deputation did no more than persuade the besieging Macedonian army to remain for the moment outside the city, and by 19 April the British Embassy had concluded that the game was lost. Lowther told the consuls in Macedonia to "let events take their course",[17] and shortly afterwards the 'deliverers' entered the capital, suppressed all opposition with little difficulty, and restored Hilmi Pasha to the grand vizierate. As for Abdul Hamid, he was deposed and replaced by his other-worldly younger brother, Reshad Effendi, who took the title Mohammed V. The new government was Committee-backed but senior military officers were henceforward to have a much more decisive impact on politics than hitherto; in fact, under Mahmud Shevket Pasha, the "Generalissimo", it was now in all but name a military dictatorship.[18]

"Poisoned arrows"

With the spectacular collapse of the counter-revolution, it was open season on the embassy and particularly on Fitzmaurice. At worst he

---

[15] TNA, Lowther to Grey (No. 129), 7.00pm, 17 Apr. 1909, FO371/770.

[16] TNA, Lowther to Grey (No. 131), 10.30pm, 17 Apr. 1909, FO371/770; and 20 Apr. 1909 (No. 287), FO371/771.

[17] TNA, Lowther to Consuls in Salonica, Serres, Uscub, Adrianople and Monastir, 19 Apr. 1909, FO195/2330.

[18] Ahmad, *The Young Turks*, p. 45ff.

was accused of being a 'reactionary' who had encouraged the Liberal Union not just out of misguided political principles but also in order to shore up his personal position. At best, he was charged with the greatest tactical sin of which a British diplomat could be guilty: backing the wrong horse. Miscalculating the balance of forces, he was charged with squandering the great opportunity provided by the July revolution to restore British prestige at Constantinople.

Prominent among the chorus of Fitzmaurice's critics was of course Sir Adam Block.[19] Others included H. F. B. Lynch and even consular colleagues. Among the latter were the consul-general, Harry Eyres, and William Heard, a friend of George Lloyd and until recently vice-consul in Diarbekir. Heard's particularly damaging allegation was that the counter-revolution had also provided the opportunity for the massacres of Armenians in eastern Anatolia, and that only the prompt action of the Macedonian army had prevented matters from getting much worse. He did not blame Fitzmaurice by name but this was not necessary.[20] Writing from Monastir, Arthur Geary told Ryan that he thought the rest of the diplomatic corps had also displayed a poor grasp of affairs during the counter-revolution but said "they had the sense to sit tight and await the course of events without giving themselves away...However", he asked rhetorically, "did H. E. and Fitzmaurice manage to make so awful a hash?"[21] Aubrey Herbert, who had hurried out to Constantinople on hearing of the counter-revolution, attacked him as well, and their friendship, already fraying, never fully recovered.[22] This was a bitter blow because Fitzmaurice and he had common friends, not the least George Lloyd and Gertrude Bell. To the former, Herbert, who had dinner with Fitzmaurice during his visit, admitted that he "had an extraordinary attraction" and "looks a long way ahead" but added that "in a few months he will need a friend more than ever he did".[23]

---

[19] Block, who aired his views to Gertrude Bell among others (GBP, *The Diaries*, 13/07/1909), was a supporter of the Young Turks and was a dangerous enemy because of his elevated status in the British community in Constantinople. To his position on the Debt he had added the presidency of the British Chamber of Commerce and had been knighted in 1907. He also had a private correspondence with Hardinge, now located in TNA, FO800/192.

[20] CAC Cam., Heard to Lloyd, 2 May 1909, GLLD 7/4.

[21] MECA Oxf., Geary to Ryan, 31 July 1909, Ryan Box IV, Item 8.

[22] FitzHerbert, *The Man Who Was Greenmantle*, pp. 86–7; CAC Cam., Fitzmaurice to Lloyd, 19 Jan. 1909, GLLD 7/4.

[23] CAC Cam., Herbert to Lloyd, 14 May 1909, GLLD 7/4.

These voices in Turkey swiftly produced strong echoes in London. As early as 20 April *The Times* published a thinly veiled attack on the role of the embassy from the Balkan Committee. Two days after this, Sir Edward Grey was forced to deny in the House of Commons that Britain had "in any way whatever given diplomatic support to the so-called Liberal Union in Turkey or criticised the action of the Committee of Union and Progress".[24] In the press, the widely read *Daily Mail* took up the story, and the upshot was that the Foreign Office itself joined in the chorus, albeit in more muted tones, as George Lloyd warned Fitzmaurice in early June. This "was only the overflow of what took place here on an accentuated scale", the chief dragoman replied.[25]

For Grey and Hardinge there was nothing for it but to re-emphasise that the only policy for Britain was to support the "best elements" of the CUP. Writing to Lowther on 1 May, the notoriously snobbish and condescending Hardinge said:

> Sir Edward has asked me to write you a few lines to ask you to impress upon Fitzmaurice, who naturally is regarded by the Turks as your "alter ego", and who is, as we know, an impressionable Irishman, that he should adopt a sympathetic attitude towards the Young Turks and be neither critical nor even impartial towards them. He should try to show them that we are friendly and sympathetic, and wish to help them. That is our feeling here, and the only practical line of policy to follow. Our only hope for a reformed Turkey rests now with the Young Turks, and if they do not meet with sympathy and cannot lean on us they will soon learn to lean on some other Power, and the splendid position which we had at Constantinople a few months ago will be lost.
>
> I am quite sure that on reflection you will see things as clearly as we do from here.[26]

A dispirited and sickly Fitzmaurice, his confidence in his own judgement badly shaken,[27] did not find the energy to write to George Lloyd about the failed counter-revolution until the end of May. Then, quoting melodramatically one of Omar Khayyam's quatrains in the *Rubaiyat*, he told him that:

> The Bash Tilki has gone and the fraternity has disappeared. "Tis but a tent where takes his one day's rest, a Sultan to the realm of death

---

[24] *Parl. Debs.*, 5th Ser. (Commons), vol. 3, 22 Apr. 1909, col. 1655.
[25] In a letter of 10 June, referred to in CAC Cam., Fitzmaurice to Lloyd, 26 June, 1909, GLLD 7/4.
[26] TNA, Hardinge to Lowther, 1 May 1909, FO800/193A.
[27] CAC Cam., Fitzmaurice to Lloyd, 8 Oct., 1909, GLLD 7/4.

addrest; The Sultan rises and the dark Ferrásh strikes, and prepares it
for another guest."[28]

In other words, Turkey's chief fox (Abdul Hamid) had gone. Was he—
the embassy's chief fox—to be next?[29] He had "been almost done to
death by the poisoned arrows of the ignorant and malicious ones" and
his spirit all but broken.[30] Though he claimed later that it was a joke,
it is half-believable that Fitzmaurice threatened to resign in the after-
math of the failed counter-revolution. It is wholly believable, as he also
claimed, that he asked Lowther for what he had insistently demanded
of O'Conor—release to the provinces. Once more he had Erzeroum
in mind and had some hope that Lowther would arrange it.[31]

Unfortunately for Fitzmaurice, Lowther—like his predecessor—
needed him too badly to allow him to spend the rest of his career
trout-fishing in Erzeroum.[32] At least this had a comforting corollary: the
ambassador could not afford to allow his chief dragoman to be made
a scapegoat for the fiasco of the counter-revolution. No doubt, too,
the role of Block in all this stiffened his response.[33] In replying to the
criticism of the embassy, Lowther pointed to its public even-handedness
and its good contacts with the "better elements" in the CUP.

> As to Fitzmaurice, who is indefatigable [Lowther told Hardinge], I am
> quite satisfied that he is in touch with all the various elements of the local
> political world, and that no Embassy, except perhaps the Russians, who
> have a Jew Dragoman in close touch with the Jew Committee of Union
> and Progress, is better informed than we are.

Thus he would not need the additional secret service money that Hardinge, implying that the embassy's information was poor, had earlier
offered him.[34] In any case, the ambassador remained convinced that

---

[28] CAC Cam., Fitzmaurice to Lloyd, 30 May, 1909, GLLD 7/4.

[29] Further on in this long letter he says: "Pat [Ramsay]wishes you were here to
finally dissolve tilkidom. It must be dissolved soon and the name buried under the
ruins of Abdul Hamid's régime."

[30] CAC Cam., Fitzmaurice to Lloyd, 26 June, 1909, GLLD 7/4.

[31] CAC Cam., Fitzmaurice to Lloyd, 26 June, 1909, GLLD 7/4.

[32] It is clear from Lowther's correspondence about Levant Service staffing questions
at this juncture, in which Erzeroum was mentioned, that the ambassador had not taken
Fitzmaurice's request seriously, TNA, Lowther to Montgomery, 21 June, and to Tyrrell,
15 Aug. 1909, FO800/193B.

[33] The ambassador had been converted to Fitzmaurice's view of Block quite early
on: "Block...as you know, is a regular bull in a china shop and frightfully unpopular
with the Turks", TNA, Lowther to Hardinge, 8 Dec. 1908, FO800/193B.

[34] TNA, Lowther to Hardinge, 6 July 1909, FO800/193B; for this offer, see Hardinge
to Lowther, 29 June 1909, FO800/193A.

Fitzmaurice's approach was the right one and continued to urge on the Foreign Office the need to be cautious about embracing the Committee too warmly.[35] The story of Fitzmaurice's successful midnight effort to save Mahmud Muhtar Pasha also helped, with even Block having to give him credit for this.[36] It was fortunate for the embassy, too, that despite the widespread rumours of its reactionary tendencies it had a temporary ally of convenience in an unlikely quarter: the CUP itself, which now displayed an unsentimental desire to maintain friendship with Britain as a counterpoise to German influence in what it now believed to be the too-powerful army.[37] All of this provided a good base from which Fitzmaurice could reply to his open critics in Constantinople and the "funny whisperings" in the Foreign Office.[38]

Fighting back

To anyone who would listen, Fitzmaurice insisted that the events of 13 April—as also the massacre of Armenians at Adana—represented the inevitable response of devout Moslems to the over-hasty actions and dictatorial methods of the Committee and *not* an attempt to restore the regime of Abdul Hamid. The sultan himself had nothing to do with the counter-revolution. It is true that "reactionary forces" got out of hand on 14 April, he conceded, but by the following day "they were all brought under control again and things were settling down smoothly".[39] The Constitution had *not* been in danger; the counter-revolution would simply have meant a return to a more moderate course. Furthermore, since the CUP had not learned much from the experience, "the Sheri" would react again, he predicted, and probably with more deadly effect. It might not be so violent but it might not need to be. This was because it was only distrust of Abdul Hamid that had held the CUP together: "Now that that asset of theirs is gone serious divergences are breaking out among them", he told George Lloyd.[40]

---

[35] TNA, Lowther to Grey, 12 May 1909, FO800/193B.

[36] GBP, *The Diaries*, 13 July 1909.

[37] Ahmad, "Great Britain's relations with the Young Turks, 1908–1914", pp. 316–17.

[38] CAC Cam., Fitzmaurice to Lloyd, 26 June, 1909, GLLD 7/4.

[39] Gertrude Bell's words, summarising his view, GBP, *The Diaries*, 5 July 1909.

[40] CAC Cam., Fitzmaurice to Lloyd, 30 May, 1909, GLLD 7/4. Fitzmaurice later told the historian, Harold Temperley, that he could not be absolutely certain that the sultan had no hand in inspiring the counter-revolution but it was still his "belief"

As to the specific charges against himself, Fitzmaurice answered these most systematically in his letters to George Lloyd, whose own letter to him of 10 June had been to him "a whiff of consolation and the breeze of life". A dragoman, he said, was expected to do the impossible, so he got no kudos when things went right and the whole blame when things seemed to have gone wrong. Had he underestimated the strength of the CUP? On the contrary, he claimed somewhat doubtfully, he had warned Lowther of Kiamil's imminent fall two weeks before it occurred and on the same occasion predicted that in two months Abdul Hamid himself would be a target.[41] Had he backed the wrong horse and jeopardised the British position at Constantinople? Certainly not, he replied. The embassy had *not* taken sides, despite being begged to do so by the counter-revolutionaries, though his argument rested on nothing but flat assertion and a slippery appeal to his young friend to wait patiently for the full story. In any case, he added more convincingly, recent events had not strengthened the German position in Turkey as much as some of the more panicky members of the British community believed; it had simply "brought to the surface the strong German leaven in the army". It was true that the Turks were "now silent under martial law and the terror of a vehmgericht which is secret except as to its sentences". Nevertheless, he still insisted, over 90 per cent of the Ottoman population preferred England and detested the CUP. Thus it remained a mistake for Britain to throw in its lot entirely with the Committee.[42]

Finally, was he "a reactionary at heart" and motivated chiefly by concern for his personal position? Only persons unaware of how long Fitzmaurice had been trying to escape the "Byzantine dungheap" of dragoman work could have believed this without qualification. To George Lloyd, who knew it well enough, he now elaborated. It was precisely because he hated the very idea of the post of dragoman, in which some unfortunate ended up the "plaything between two diametrically opposed mentalities", that he had always supported the

---

that he was innocent. Temperley, who was openly in awe of Fitzmaurice's knowledge, consequently supported this judgement in his "British policy towards parliamentary rule and constitutionalism in Turkey (1830–1914)", *Cambridge Historical Journal*, 4 (2), 1933, pp. 187–8.

[41] CAC Cam., Fitzmaurice to Lloyd, 26 June, 1909, GLLD 7/4.
[42] CAC Cam., Fitzmaurice to Lloyd, 30 May and 26 June, 1909, GLLD 7/4.

Constitution, which promised to abolish it. So much, he said, for being a reactionary.[43]

Of course, some of this must be taken with a pinch of salt because by this time Fitzmaurice's circumstances were far better than when he had been railing against his lot on returning from the Yemen frontier. Nevertheless, if dragomans were abolished because the Young Turks refused to deal with them he would either be released to a consulate or become in effect an oriental secretary. Either of these eventualities would have suited him. To the letter he wrote to George Lloyd on 26 June he added a postscript: "Excuse paper and pen. They are both old régime tho' not reactionary." This seems a fair summary of his attitude.

By this juncture Fitzmaurice seemed confident that he had shored up his position in Constantinople. Nevertheless, fighting back also meant confirming alliances in London. Here a key figure was, as usual, William Tyrrell. In his letter to Lloyd of 30 May Fitzmaurice had dropped a hint that his friend might take the necessary action, and it seems likely that he did.[44] A month later he wrote a private letter to Tyrrell himself, which was duly passed on to Sir Edward Grey: "the croakers are now silent or endeavouring to explain away their pessimistic state of panic", he told him.[45] When Gertrude Bell visited Constantinople for ten days in early July, Fitzmaurice made sure that he got to her before Block. She might have been a free trader but she went a long way to make up for this as far as Fitzmaurice was concerned by her hostility to the Suffragettes. More importantly, she had the ear of people such as Mallet, Chirol, and Tyrrell, and by now had a strong claim on being regarded as the central figure among British Arabists.[46] On four separate days between 5 and 11 July he spent hours with her, making sure that she had the correct version of events.[47] This she appeared to

---

[43] CAC Cam., Fitzmaurice to Lloyd, 26 June, 1909, GLLD 7/4.

[44] "Do you ever see W. Tyrrell? I never write to him. Give him my very best selams", CAC Cam., Fitzmaurice to Lloyd, 30 May 1909, GLLD 7/4. Among all of Fitzmaurice's letters to George Lloyd this is one of only two of which the latter had a typed copy made. It was also sanitized, and it is unlikely that Lloyd would have gone to this trouble if he had not wanted to circulate it to influential persons such as Tyrrell.

[45] TNA, Fitzmaurice to Tyrrell, 27 June 1909, FO800/79.

[46] Winstone, *Gertrude Bell*, p. 110.

[47] She must have taken some persuading that the sultan was not behind the counter-revolution and had not personally ordered the massacre of Armenians at the time, since she was a firm believer in his responsibility when writing to George Lloyd from Diarbekir on 3 June, CAC Cam., GLLD 7/4.

accept,[48] though by the last day he had clearly come close to boring
her with it: "We sat in the garden and talked till near midnight", she
recorded in her diary, "but Mr F[itzmaurice] said mainly the old things
about the Sultan etc."[49]

Unrepentant though they were about their role in the counter-revolution, Fitzmaurice and Lowther now had to make more of an effort
to court the Committee, their immediate aim being to encourage it to
emerge from the shadows and assume formal responsibility for government. This, Fitzmaurice hoped, would encourage moderation.[50] When
Djavid Bey, the CUP deputy for Salonica, for whose ability and sense of
responsibility he had a high opinion, was appointed to the key position
of Minister of Finance in June, he claimed it as a triumph.[51] In the following month a delegation of Ottoman deputies, including prominent
CUP members, visited Britain and—at Fitzmaurice's suggestion—was
shown hospitality by George Lloyd. Counting the mission a success and
telling Lloyd that "the children are alarmingly pro-English" despite their
dislike of Britain's position over Crete, he was by now in an altogether
happier frame of mind.[52] A lengthy visit to Constantinople by George
Lloyd in September and October completed his bliss, among other
things because his friend laid to rest the doubts he had been harbour-
ing about his role in recent events:

> You allude to the pleasure of your stay here [said Fitzmaurice, referring
> to a letter he had just received from Lloyd]. You will be still more pleased
> to hear how childishly delighted I was to have you come out and so to
> speak inspect our position and doings here and give us an approval as
> regards the British position. It bucked me up immensely for from what
> I told you you gleaned that one had a little shadow of doubt lurking in
> the folds of one's conscience as to whether baddish mistakes had not
> been made. I was much cheered by your verdict.[53]

---

[48] GBP, *The Letters*, Letter to her Mother, 7 July 1909 and *The Diaries*, 10 July
1909.
[49] GBP, *The Diaries*, 11 July 1909.
[50] CAC Cam., Fitzmaurice to Lloyd, 30 May 1909, GLLD 7/4.
[51] CAC Cam., Fitzmaurice to Lloyd, 29 June 1909, GLLD 7/4; see also TNA,
Fitzmaurice to Tyrrell, 27 June 1909, FO800/79.
[52] CAC Cam., Fitzmaurice to Lloyd, 4 Aug. 1909, GLLD 7/4; see also Fitzmaurice
to Lloyd, 28 July 1909, GLLD 7/4.
[53] CAC Cam., Fitzmaurice to Lloyd, 8 Oct. 1909, GLLD 7/4; also, Adam, *Life of
Lord Lloyd*, pp. 49–50.

Jews and Freemasons: smearing the CUP

The hostility of the Young Turks to dragomans in general relieved Fitzmaurice of some of his burden at the Porte. In June he noted that relations with the Ministry of Foreign Affairs were being conducted by senior members of the embassy's diplomatic staff and that now he only saw the grand vizier once a week.[54] It is true that he was still needed to push British cases at other ministries and was by no means excluded altogether from the MFA.[55] The revived parliament had also made the deputies a new focus of his attention. Nevertheless, by his own exceptional standards, he was relatively under-employed in what—under martial law—was a quiet period in Turkey. Since reference to the political 'undercurrents' of the Bosphorus, 'subterranean' goings on, and 'occult' influences had by this time become second nature to him, it is therefore not surprising that he should have taken this opportunity to brood on the deeper significance of recent developments. And what particularly gave focus to his thoughts was the striking improvement in relations between the World Zionist Organization and Turkey that had followed the Young Turks' revolution.

Encouraged by the CUP's rhetorical emphasis on religious and ethnic equality as well as by support from influential Ottoman Jews, the Zionists had played down any suggestion that they desired autonomy in Palestine but stepped up their pressure to persuade the Turks to lift restrictions on Jewish immigration. For their part the Turks, tempted by the prospect of major injections of Jewish capital, had hinted strongly at the possibility of concessions. The new emphasis on Turkish nationalism after the failed counter-revolution had certainly proved something of a dampener in Turkish-Zionist relations but not sufficient to discourage visits to Turkey in the summer of 1909 by the Zionist President, David Wolffsohn.[56] Since these coincided with the ministerial appointment of Djavid Bey, a 'crypto-Jew'[57] and Freemason, it is no wonder that Fitzmaurice's brooding should have been led to concentrate on the influence of Jews and Freemasons within the CUP, why

---

[54] CAC Cam., Fitzmaurice to Lloyd, 26 June 1909, GLLD 7/4.
[55] TNA, min. of Fitzmaurice, 24 Nov. 1909, FO195/2330.
[56] Isaiah Friedman, *Germany, Turkey, and Zionism, 1897–1918* (Clarendon Press: Oxford, 1977), pp. 138–49.
[57] A Dönmeh ('apostate'), who was nominally Moslem but really still Jewish, Friedman, *Germany, Turkey, and Zionism, 1897–1918*, p. 151, n. 67.

this should be of concern to Britain, and the Jewish question generally. Hitherto, reference to these groups had only occasionally—and then as asides—cropped up in his correspondence, though this was perhaps in part because of his need for circumspection on these subjects.

Influential members of the British colony in Constantinople, such as Sir Edwin Pears, were Masons.[58] So, too, was Aubrey Herbert[59]—and who was to say who else? Not so long ago a British ambassador had been the Master of the Constantinople off-shoot of the Grand Lodge of England (Oriental, No. 988) and District Grand Master of all of the English lodges in Turkey.[60] Above all, Fitzmaurice's most intimate friend, George Lloyd, was also a member of the 'craft'.[61] Some of his friends and allies were probably Jewish, too. Dudley Disraeli Braham, the former correspondent of *The Times* in Constantinople now working with Chirol in London, certainly was. Moreover, Lloyd's closest friend, Sam Cockerell, was sympathetic to the Jews[62]—if not necessarily a Zionist—and was on several occasions referred to by Fitzmaurice in his court jester manner as "the Yahudi".[63] In short, he had to tread warily.

Nevertheless, in the summer of 1909 Fitzmaurice began an investigation of these questions that was so detailed that he did not complete it until the following May,[64] though a short trailer for it appeared in the embassy's Annual Report published some months earlier.[65] When he emerged from "deep down in the bowels of the Earth",[66] his conclusions, which did not differ in general outline from views he had advanced to Tyrrell in June 1909,[67] were conveyed to Hardinge in the form of an exceptionally long private letter under Lowther's signature dated 29

---

[58] *Forty Years in Constantinople*, p. 259.

[59] Or at least he was by 1913, when he is revealed to be a member of the Crewkerne Lodge by documents in his private papers: SCA, DD/DRU/4/4.

[60] This was Sir Henry Bulwer (ambassador 1858–65), who became DGM in 1861 when the English lodges in Turkey were united, R. F. Gould, *The History of Freemasonry*, vol. VI (Caxton: London, ca. 1886). See also Muriel E. Chamberlain, "Bulwer, (William) Henry Lytton Earle, Baron Dalling and Bulwer (1801–1872)", *ODNB* [3935, accessed 3 May 2006], where Bulwer is described as "an active freemason".

[61] CAC Cam., Fitzmaurice to Lloyd, 3 June 1910, GLLD 7/4.

[62] CAC Cam., Lloyd to Cockerell, nd. (1911), GLLD 8/4.

[63] 'Love to S.P.C. I suppose he is still working hard in the cause of Zion', CAC Cam., Fitzmaurice to Lloyd, 25 Feb. 1909, GLLD 7/4.

[64] CAC Cam., Fitzmaurice to Lloyd, 3 June 1910, GLLD 7/4.

[65] TNA, AR 1909, 31 Jan. 1910, p. 6, FO195/2363.

[66] CAC Cam., Fitzmaurice to Lloyd, 27 May 1910, GLLD 7/4.

[67] TNA, Fitzmaurice to Tyrrell, 27 June 1909, FO800/79.

May 1910. These were such as to provoke the only sustained scholarly attention hitherto devoted to him, and that not favourable.[68]

The CUP, claimed Fitzmaurice, was dominated by Jews or crypto-Jews from Salonica who had exploited the secret procedures and capitulatory protection of an Italian Masonic lodge in that town to nurture their revolution. However, he went on to maintain that the Jewish Freemasons in the Committee had since created a grand lodge—the Grand Orient of Turkey—to bring under their control all of the lodges that had mushroomed throughout the Empire since the revolution and thereby consolidate their secret control over the Empire itself, including Egypt. Unlike the respectable lodges of England and Scotland, he maintained, the Grand Orient was not only political but atheistic, intolerant, intensely secretive, and unscrupulous in its methods. Its Grand Master was the minister of the interior, Talaat Bey, the shrewd and powerful former telegraph-operator who reminded a later American Ambassador of a party machine 'boss' in the United States.[69] Those behind the Grand Orient had probably themselves instigated the counter-revolution of 13 April, claimed Fitzmaurice, in order to provide an excuse for finally disposing of their enemies. The Jewish Masons had further underlined their true character by falsely claiming that Ottoman lodges were linked to English ones in order to increase their popularity in Turkey. Jewish ambitions in the Ottoman Empire would inevitably be pursued at the expense of the Armenians, Greeks and Arabs and it was in the interests of the Jews to keep alive the bad feeling between these groups and the Turks.

What were these Jewish ambitions? Why was the Jew seeking influence over the new government of the "pre-economic" Turk by lending him his "brains, business enterprise, his enormous influence in the press of Europe, and money"? The immediate object of the

---

[68] Elie Kedourie, "Young Turks, Freemasons and Jews", *Middle Eastern Studies*, 7 (1), Jan. 1971, pp. 90–104. This letter written by Fitzmaurice but signed by Lowther (and possibly tweaked by him) is to be found in the Lowther Papers, TNA, Lowther to Hardinge, FO800/193A. It is also usefully reproduced in full as an appendix to Kedourie's article. Kedourie was not certain of the authorship but rightly suspected the hand of Fitzmaurice. In fact, Fitzmaurice acknowledged authorship in the postscript to a letter to Tyrrell written a little earlier, even though he assumed at this point that Lowther would send it directly to Grey rather than Hardinge: "I am writing a longish private letter for Lowther to Grey on Freemasonry and the C.U.P. It will go in a day or two and you may find a thing or two of interest in it", TNA, FO800/79.
[69] Ambassador Henry Morgenthau, *Secrets of the Bosphorus*, 3rd ed. (Hutchinson: London, 1918), pp. 12–15.

exercise, claimed Fitzmaurice, was the capture of the Ottoman Empire for Jewish economic interests. Its ultimate purpose, however, was to facilitate acquisition of the Ottoman lands that were now regarded by international Jewry as the most desirable sites for the erection of a Jewish state: Palestine and, "as a sort of appanage", Mesopotamia. Abdul Hamid had been doomed as a result of his opposition to Zionist ambitions in Palestine.[70]

What were the implications of this Judeo-Masonic conspiracy for British policy? About the answer to this critical question Fitzmaurice seems to have been less sure, which is probably why his report carrying Lowther's signature ended with no policy recommendations of any moment. He had been hoping to return to England and discuss his conclusions with George Lloyd, among others, but this plan had to be shelved when—to his intense chagrin—Andrew Ryan had a nervous breakdown and was himself immediately ordered home by the embassy doctor.[71] To add to Fitzmaurice's distress, a proposed visit by George Lloyd to Constantinople, which he had seen as a "God sent compensation", fell through when at the last moment his friend diverted to Crete. He at once wrote to Lloyd, saying:

> I wanted to talk at you for 48 hrs as never I did before.... There are two or three points of 1st Cl[ass] importance on which I can't make up my mind and I so wanted to exchange thoughts with you.[72]

The only one of these points then mentioned by Fitzmaurice was Freemasonry. He did not mention that what was particularly exercising him was *Jewish* Freemasonry, and confined himself to asking Lloyd to use his influence to ensure that the English Grand Lodge followed the example of the Scottish one and refused recognition to the Grand Orient. He also gave no hint as to the nature of the uncertainties that were plaguing him, though it is not difficult to guess at what they were. How strenuously should Britain oppose the Judeo-Masonic conspiracy? What should be its attitude to Zionism?

Fitzmaurice believed that there were two reasons why it was in Britain's interests to work against Jewish influence over the Young Turk government. First, Jewish hostility to Russia meant that a Jewish-domi-

---

[70] Kedourie, "Young Turks, Freemasons and Jews", appendix; TNA, AR 1909, 31 Jan. 1910, p. 6, FO195/2363.

[71] Ryan, *The Last of the Dragomans*, pp. 69–70.

[72] CAC Cam., Fitzmaurice to Lloyd, 3 June 1910, GLLD 7/4.

nated Turkey was likely to be become more hostile to Britain because of the new Anglo-Russian entente. Secondly, in order to retain their hold over the Young Turks, the Jews would be forced to support their "national" and "Asiatic national" dreams, thereby imperilling British control in India and Egypt, and influence in Persia. On the other hand, Britain might obtain certain advantages from the domination of the Ottoman Empire by Jewish Masons. For one thing, knowledge of this would probably weaken considerably the impact of Pan-Islamic propaganda emanating from Constantinople among Indian Moslems. It would also turn—was already turning, he believed—the eyes of Ottoman Arabs to Cairo, thus evoking the distant possibility that the khediviate, under British auspices, would become a new power in the Near East.[73] Finally, Zionism itself possessed certain advantages to Gentiles and Fitzmaurice was beginning to emerge among its supporters.

In June 1909, as his epic investigation into Jewish Freemasonry was beginning, Fitzmaurice told Tyrrell that "the Jews are getting bold and openly talking of Zionism here".[74] Two days later he actually said to George Lloyd: "I am getting most keen on Zionism which is the great feature of our new life."[75] What his motives were he did not say but Gentile Zionism of a purely political kind was an established tradition in Britain and his own English hero, Joseph Chamberlain, had been located firmly within it.[76] Richard Graves, who had known Fitzmaurice when he was acting third dragoman in 1907 and thought him "powerful, tragic, ruthless and yet kind-hearted", years later speculated that he, too, was in this tradition. He thought it possible that Fitzmaurice had begun to think that the Jews would be "a lesser source of danger" to the world if they had a state of their own in Palestine rather than remain "a race of exiles with no loyalty to the countries of the diaspora and a special talent for acquiring money and power".[77] This is highly likely, as is the probability that, like Chamberlain and other British politicians after him, he also saw advantage in winning the gratitude of international Jewry by providing assistance to the realization of the Zionist dream.

---

[73] Kedourie, "Young Turks, Freemasons and Jews", appendix.
[74] TNA, Fitzmaurice to Tyrrell, 27 June 1909, FO800/79.
[75] CAC Cam., Fitzmaurice to Lloyd, 29 June 1909, GLLD 7/4.
[76] Christopher Sykes, *Two Studies in Virtue* (Collins: London, 1953), pp. 161–2. There was also a millennial tradition in Gentile Zionism.
[77] MECA Oxf., Graves Papers 1/1, 246a, 33a–b.

There were those at the time who thought that Fitzmaurice exaggerated the extent of Jewish influence over the Young Turks.[78] Much later, Bernard Lewis, the historian of Islam, drawing on the authority of the "voluminous Turkish literature on the Young Turks", more than agreed with them.[79] And the brilliant thinker and historian of the Middle East, Elie Kedourie, contemptuously described the conclusions of Fitzmaurice's investigation as "fustian fantasies".[80] No doubt he did exaggerate Jewish influence over the Young Turks; no doubt, too, he suggested a greater degree of Zionist conspiracy behind and Masonic collusion with them than actually existed. However, though his style may have been fustian, it does not follow that his exaggerations are evidence of "extremes of credulity"—or that they call into question his judgment on other aspects of Ottoman politics, as alleged by Kedourie.[81] For Fitzmaurice was not stupid; nor was he mad; and he was certainly not ill-informed.

It is in fact well established that Jews had been "streaming" into Masonic lodges in Europe since the late eighteenth century, chiefly as a means of gaining social acceptance.[82] It is also uncontroversial that Jews were extremely numerous in Salonica; that this was the well-spring of the CUP; that there were Jews in the Committee; that Freemasonry was popular in Turkey; and that Masonic lodges were used by the Committee to cloak the meetings of its members.[83] There were also serious people in Constantinople who substantially agreed with Fitzmaurice's analysis—or much of it.[84] In short, he did not make it *all* up, and it is a remarkable lapse on the part of such an eminent scholar as Kedourie to imply that he had. The real question is: Why did he exaggerate

---

[78] Adelson, *Mark Sykes*, p. 114; Herbert, *Ben Kendim*, p. 289.

[79] Lewis, *The Emergence of Modern Turkey*, pp. 211–12, n. 4. M. Şükrü Hanioğlu, who takes the subject of Freemasonry seriously but does not mention Jews at all, argues that the alliance between the Freemasons (where he sees Greek influence) and the Young Turks was a temporary marriage of convenience and that in fact they were following "divergent paths", *The Young Turks in Opposition* (Oxford University Press: London, 1995), p. 41.

[80] Kedourie, "Young Turks, Freemasons and Jews", p. 92.

[81] Kedourie, "Young Turks, Freemasons and Jews", p. 92.

[82] J. Katz, *Jews and Freemasons in Europe, 1723–1939*, trsl. from the Hebrew by L. Oschry (Harvard University Press: Cambridge, Mass., 1970).

[83] Masonic lodges were banned in the British Zone of occupied Germany after the Second World War precisely because, as secret societies, they could provide a cloak for hostile political activity; see papers in TNA, FO1049/379.

[84] For example, Graves, *Briton and Turk*, pp. 136–40; and Pears [himself a Mason, as he states in this book], *Forty Years in Constantinople*, pp. 258–9.

the role of Jewish Freemasons in the CUP both before and after the revolution of July 1908?

Due allowance must certainly be made for Fitzmaurice's lengthy education by a French Catholic order and his enduring attachment to Roman Catholicism. Since 1738, when Pope Clement XII had condemned Freemasonry as a threat to the true Christian faith, Roman Catholics had joined lodges only upon pain of excommunication. In 1910, as the *Catholic Encyclopedia*, which happened to be published in the same year, made clear, the position remained the same. Moreover, it was particularly in France, and particularly during the years when Fitzmaurice was at the French College, that Catholic writers began to popularise the connection between Freemasons and Jews, a group burdened to their minds with even more historical guilt. To this school of thought, it was generally the Jews in this 'diabolical pair' who gave the orders and the Freemasons who carried them out. By the 1880s the slogan 'Jews and Freemasons' had become a major feature of politics in France, and it is notorious that the connection was given prominence in the forged 'Protocols of the Elders of Zion' which were circulated by the Russian secret police in 1905.[85] There is no evidence that Fitzmaurice had read the works of the French writers but it would be astonishing if he had not picked up something of this outlook in his school and university days.

Pre-disposed by training and belief to attribute more influence to the Jews of Salonica than was warranted, Fitzmaurice—an instinctive propagandist—nevertheless had an obvious political motive for exaggerating their role. Anti-Semitism may not have been rife in Turkey but this did not mean that Jews were any more popular there than they were among the British governing classes.[86] So to foster with exhaustive detail the idea that the Young Turks had been captured by Jews employing as a cloak a particularly pernicious brand of Freemasonry and motivated by the true ambition of the Zionists to set up their own state in Palestine, was to blacken their reputation and weaken their position, which in some degree—by whispers in Constantinople as well as letters to London—there seems little doubt that Fitzmaurice did. That this also blackened the reputation of the German Embassy, since German Jews were a major force behind Zionism, was a bonus—and was well

---

[85] Katz, *Jews and Freemasons in Europe, 1723–1939*, chs. 10 and 11.
[86] Pears, *Forty Years in Constantinople*, p. 258.

understood by this embassy to be one of his motives.[87] Lowther was just the most obvious man to be persuaded.[88] Fitzmaurice's one-man smear campaign also promised to undermine the CUP's Pan-Islamic propaganda among Moslems in India, Egypt and elsewhere. By lending his authority to a particularly strong version of the Judeo-Masonic conspiracy theory Fitzmaurice may also have contributed to the belief in Jewish power that encouraged the British government to back Zionism in 1917. As we shall see in Chapter 9, during the Great War he also assisted that movement more directly.

Business as usual

By the summer of 1909 Fitzmaurice might have felt that he had fought off his enemies and substantially recovered his reputation but he remained exhausted and weak, and was "dying to get home".[89] Unfortunately for him, the CUP ministers had found that, confronted by the united hostility of the European embassies, they had to abandon their decision not to deal with dragomans.[90] The British dragomanate was also even more stretched than usual.[91] As a result, Fitzmaurice could not be spared and he had much to do besides writing his massive paper on Jews and Freemasons. With his health then steadily improving,[92] it was very much business as usual.

By the end of 1909, however, Fitzmaurice had another great interest: the General Election in Britain scheduled for January. His absorption in this was the greater because it was the first opportunity for George Lloyd

---

[87] Friedman, *Germany, Turkey, and Zionism, 1897–1918*, pp. 127–8, 151–3.

[88] When the Eastern Department in the FO finally got round to looking at AR 1909, Alwyn Parker drew attention in particular to "the paragraph on page 6 about Javid Bey" as the most interesting part of the whole 63-page document, TNA, min. of Parker, 2 May 1910, FO371/1002. This was what I referred to earlier in this section as the 'trailer' for Fitzmaurice's major report on Jews and Freemasons. See also Earl Winterton's account of his encounter with "the famous Mr. Fitzmaurice" during a visit to Constantinople in September 1910 in order to learn more about the CUP—"a spawn of Salonican Jews", *Pre-War* (Macmillan: London, 1932), pp. 184–9.

[89] TNA, Fitzmaurice to Tyrrell, 27 June 1909, FO800/79.

[90] TNA, Waugh to Chargé d'Affaires, 9 Dec. 1909, FO195/2316.

[91] In 1910, following his nervous breakdown in April, Andrew Ryan was absent for five months, TNA, FO371/1009.

[92] CAC Cam., Fitzmaurice to Lloyd, 26 Feb. and 15 Oct. 1910, GLLD 7/4.

to enter the House of Commons.[93] Having added 'Khakiism' (military conscription) to tariff reform and opposition to the Suffragettes to his remedies for imperial decline,[94] and joked that he and Lloyd should set up a "C.U.P. or Young England party",[95] Fitzmaurice cheered him on with another letter from Constantinople. The time had come, he said, that they used to talk about during all those evenings spent in the town *bodega* in 1906: the time to "throw off creeping senility born of success and luxury", rejuvenate the empire, and thereby give the lie to Lord Salisbury's pessimistic reflections on the fate of any imperial body dependent on sea power alone. He was quite absorbed by the political contest in Britain, he told his friend, and ended with a most flattering flourish:

> Its results will affect the world currents for long—perhaps for generations and perhaps for ever.... I'm for George Lloyd and not for Lloyd George. "What's in a name"? The fate of an Empire.[96]

The Conservatives lost the election of January 1910 but Lloyd himself was elected by a small majority. Any message of congratulation sent by Fitzmaurice has been lost but to Tyrrell he wrote:

> Personally I'm delighted at the result of the election which has been a set-back to socialist tendencies and a virtual victory for Tariff Reform...while the shrill voice of the suffragette has been hushed—I hope for many a long year. At times during recent years one felt anxious about the disintegrating forces at work at home but it is now certain that the saner and more virile spirit is not dead...I was glad of George Lloyd's victory at W. Stafford. He's of the right stuff and clean-cut. He ought to do well and good.[97]

Fitzmaurice's enthusiasm for George Lloyd's political prospects increased even further when at the end of 1910, with another general election in the offing, he learned that he had finally become "sane about Ireland", though he feared that his conversion might have come too late.[98]

During the remainder of 1910 and indeed until he finally went home on leave in the middle of 1911, Fitzmaurice enjoyed what for him was a period of relative calm. This was largely due to the fact that, Crete

---

[93] Charmley, *Lord Lloyd and the Decline of the British Empire*, p. 22.
[94] CAC Cam., Fitzmaurice to Lloyd, 8 Oct. 1909, GLLD 7/4.
[95] CAC Cam., Fitzmaurice to Lloyd, 8 Oct. 1909, GLLD 7/4.
[96] CAC Cam., Fitzmaurice to Lloyd, 17 Dec. 1909, GLLD 7/4.
[97] TNA, Fitzmaurice to Tyrrell, 14 Feb. 1910, FO800/79.
[98] CAC Cam., Fitzmaurice to Lloyd, 1 Dec. 1910, GLLD 7/4.

excepted, Turkey was beset by few problems abroad, while at home martial law remained in force and Mahmud Shevket Pasha ruled from behind the scenes with an iron hand. Fitzmaurice was also complacent to a degree about the turn of events. He had no "sentimental" objections to Shevket Pasha's dictatorship since it just meant that the Turks were obeying "natural instincts". It also meant that they had forfeited any "Constitutional" credentials with which to crave British indulgence on outstanding questions.[99] What was particularly gratifying to him, however, was that the CUP itself was now in a fix: still needing Britain as a counter to the deepening ties between the military and Germany while once more losing ground to the same conservative opposition that had provoked the counter-revolution in 1909. The opposition was crushed by Shevket Pasha in mid-1910 but re-appeared in such strength in early 1911 that the CUP seemed in danger of final collapse.[100]

Of course, what Fitzmaurice was not complacent about was the recovery in Constantinople of the position of Germany, where, he reminded George Lloyd, "the military magnet attracts and hypnotises Turkey's 5–6,000 German-trained officers".[101] It seems to have been this that was chiefly responsible for making him now more enthusiastic about the Anglo-Russian entente than he had been at the time of its announcement, even if it meant "a lot of squirming" for him at the Porte.[102] In November 1910, having referred to "the big world fight that is looming ahead", Fitzmaurice said to Lloyd, who had previously had reservations about Russia himself: "I'm glad you are reconciled to the Russian theory...it is better they should be with us than with Germany."[103] This sentiment was still comparatively rare among British officials serving in Turkey and Persia.

Grey exasperated

Fitzmaurice had hoped to be home for Christmas but once more his leave had to be postponed. Before he could get away he also had to suffer more attacks for his attitude towards the Young Turks. In early

[99] CAC Cam., Fitzmaurice to Lloyd, 27 July 1910, GLLD 7/4.
[100] Ahmad, *The Young Turks*, ch. 4.
[101] CAC Cam., Fitzmaurice to Lloyd, 15 Oct. 1910, GLLD 7/4.
[102] CAC Cam., Fitzmaurice to Lloyd, 17 Nov. 1910, GLLD 7/4.
[103] CAC Cam., Fitzmaurice to Lloyd, 17 Nov. 1910, GLLD 7/4.

March the government had been taxed by a non-CUP member in the Chamber of Deputies with the suggestion that it was supporting Zionism,[104] and there seems little doubt that the Committee believed this to be the fruit of Fitzmaurice's smear campaign. On 22 April 1911 Hussein Jahid, editor of the pro-CUP *Tanin*, the most influential newspaper in Turkey, launched an ironical attack on an unnamed dragoman which the cognoscenti knew full well to be Fitzmaurice:

> You meet with this dragoman friend everywhere...he is in newspaper offices until late at night. He is so fond of journalists that some nights he even visits them at their houses. And what a benevolent man he is, too! He says nothing to you but what is for the good and safety of your country. He is more anxious than you yourself at the disastrous state of the country. Oh, the Caliphate has no longer any influence in the land, religion has no restraint! Everything is going: the Government is encouraging Zionism, and wants to sell the country to the Jews! In the end, there won't be any country left, or any religion![105]

The attack was picked up by the Austrian press, which by and large shared Fitzmaurice's view of the Young Turks, and this attention made it newsworthy in *The Times* of London.[106]

Lowther once more sprang quickly to his chief dragoman's defence. This "malicious" article, he told Sir Arthur Nicolson, who had replaced Hardinge as permanent under-secretary, was full of "distorted versions of the truth" and provoked by the Committee's fear that Fitzmaurice "knows too much of their inner workings".[107] The ambassador followed this with a further letter covering an explanation of the press attack written by Fitzmaurice himself, which he unreservedly endorsed.

What was behind the article in *The Tanin*, claimed Fitzmaurice, was Committee resentment at his "recourse to unofficial sources" in order to discourage meddling in Egyptian affairs by the Grand Orient of Constantinople. This had recently appointed as its delegate in Egypt the Nationalist leader Mohammed Ferid, and the British Agency in Cairo had asked if the embassy could stop it. He was, he said, not surprised by the latest attacks because "the failure so far to bring the Egyptian lodges under the Grand Orient of Constantinople on the political theory that Egypt is an integral part of Turkey may be set down to

---

[104] TNA, Lowther to Grey, 4 and 7 Mar. 1911, FO371/1245.
[105] TNA, Lowther to Nicolson, 26 Apr. 1911, FO800/193B (annexed translation).
[106] *The Times*, 25 Apr. 1911.
[107] TNA, Lowther to Nicolson, 26 Apr. 1911, FO800/193B.

my action in the matter in the course of my duties". Lest the Foreign
Office should think that he did this sort of thing for idle amusement,
he had prefaced this observation with the reminder that two of the
victims of political assassinations since July 1908 had been Masonic
whistle blowers. "I have felt all along that my enquiries in the matter
were not free from danger", he remarked pointedly.[108]

Unfortunately for Fitzmaurice, no sooner had this episode died
down than Sir Edward Grey was exasperated by something else that
he learned about him. In a private interview with Sir R. F. Crawford,
the highly regarded British official successfully running the Turkish
Custom House, Grey learned that Fitzmaurice had told him that he
should consider leaving Turkey since Britain owed the present regime
no favours. The foreign secretary, who only at the end of February
had been obliged to state in the House of Commons that there was no
foundation for the impression "alleged to prevail in Turkey" that Britain
was unfriendly to the Young Turks, and had basked in the warmth of
Noel Buxton's approval as a result,[109] thus took it upon himself to write
privately to Lowther in the same vein that he had instructed Hardinge
to write to him two years earlier. He should be on his guard as to the
impressions that Fitzmaurice might be creating, he said, concluding:

> This isn't the first time that reports have reached me that the impression
> as produced from the Embassy was quite different from what was unders-
> tood to be the policy of H. M. Government. I was puzzled several times,
> especially in the early days of the new régime, by reports of this kind
> that were quite at variance with what you told me and what I wished,
> and I begin to think now that Fitzmaurice has perhaps been responsible
> for them.[110]

This letter produced a pained response from Lowther. "I beg you to
believe", he implored Grey by return, "that Fitzmaurice has in no way
been responsible for distorting the policy of H.M.G. here." He repeated
the explanation for the attacks on him already given to Nicolson, and
added that being a Roman Catholic was "an additional reason for the
'bogus' freemasons to attack him".[111]

---

[108] TNA, Secret memorandum by G. H. Fitzmaurice, 3 May 1911, encl. in Lowther
to Nicolson, 3 May 1911, FO800/193B.
[109] *Parl. Debs.*, 5th Ser. (Commons), vol. 22, 28 Feb. 1911, Oral Answers, col. 181
and 8 Mar. 1911, cols. 1328–9.
[110] TNA, Grey to Lowther, 15 May 1911, FO800/80.
[111] TNA, Lowther to Grey, 21 May 1911, FO800/193B.

By the late spring of 1911 Fitzmaurice could console himself with a number of thoughts. Lowther remained stout in his defence, and the embassy's Annual Report for 1910, sent to the Foreign Office in February, still reflected the dominance of his outlook: coolness to the spirit of the Young Turks, which was "merely nationalist and martial", and emphasis in particular on the controlling influence of Jewish Freemasons in their councils.[112] Even the Balkan Committee was by now, from time to time, peering over the top of the rose-tinted spectacles through which it had been inclined to view them.[113] Of great importance, too, Grey's powerful private secretary, William Tyrrell, remained a firm supporter and was still commending his private letters to Nicolson, R. P. Maxwell (the long-serving head of Eastern Department), and Grey himself.[114] As for George Lloyd, his carefully cultivated political protégé, he had become vocal in the House of Commons on the 'truth faith' (tariff reform), and on Near Eastern and foreign questions in general had gained the respect even of Noel Buxton.[115]

The fact remained, however, that Fitzmaurice had been attracting a fair degree of undesirable attention in Constantinople and the ripples of this were expanding. It was therefore as well that, finally, he should now be permitted leave, and just a few days after Lowther had written to Grey in his defence the ambassador wrote again recommending that he should have a full six months away.[116] There was no argument over this: "He has had no leave since January 1st 1906!" exclaimed Maxwell in a minute on this letter. So in June 1911 Fitzmaurice left Constantinople and Andrew Ryan became acting chief dragoman. It was actually to be a year before he returned to his Byzantine dungheap.

---

[112] TNA, AR 1910, in Lowther to Grey, 14 Feb. 1911, FO195/2363; see esp. pp. 3–5.

[113] Noel Buxton, "Young Turkey after Two Years", *The Nineteenth Century*, vol. LXIX, Mar. 1911.

[114] TNA, Fitzmaurice to Tyrrell, 1 Dec. 1910, 9 Feb. and 11 Mar. 1911, FO800/79 and 80.

[115] *Parl. Debs.*, 5th Ser. (Commons), vol. 22, 8 Mar. 1911, col. 1330.

[116] TNA, Lowther to Grey, 25 May 1911, FO371/249.

CHAPTER SEVEN

TROUBLESHOOTING IN TRIPOLI, 1911–12

Fitzmaurice appears to have stayed in London for most, if not all, of his first leave for five years. However, in late November 1911, well before this had run its course, he learned that instead of returning on schedule to Constantinople he was shortly to be sent instead to serve as acting consul-general in the Ottoman *vilayet* of Tripoli. Sam Cockerell, who lunched with him shortly after he received these instructions, mentioned the development in a letter to George Lloyd, who was honeymooning in Constantinople following his marriage earlier in the month.[1] The "Sheikh", he suspected, had mixed feelings about this posting: pleased with his "thrilling news" but upset at having to be "on the move again" before his leave was fully up.[2] Expecting to stay in Tripoli only for a short period, in fact Fitzmaurice remained until the middle of the following year. The reason for this was that this "African backwater", as he called it, had suddenly become a theatre of war between Turkey and Italy. Against a background of high international tension following the Agadir crisis, this led to fears of a general European conflagration. Fitzmaurice had been a storm crow for a while and some saw his arrival in Tripoli as a bad omen. It was, nevertheless, as a dove of peace that he was sent there.

The Italian invasion

Italy had long cast covetous eyes over the ramshackle Ottoman provinces of Tripolitania and Cyrenaica, only a short distance across the Mediterranean from Sicily, and the great powers had discreetly intimated that they were hers for the taking. Having failed to absorb them peacefully and been unsettled by the recent move of France on Morocco, in

---

[1] Fitzmaurice was presumably present at the wedding, though he was not sufficiently important to be included in the long list published in *The Times* on 14 November of those at the church. Cockerell was best man.

[2] CAC Cam., Cockerell to Lloyd, 30 Nov. 1911, GLLD 8/4.

September 1911 it finally steeled itself to seize them. The pretext for invasion was the claim that the local authorities had obstructed Italy's commercial interests and abused its dignity beyond further endurance. On 28 September an ultimatum was issued by Rome to Constantinople: surrender the provinces within 24 hours or be forced out. The Turks refused and a state of war between Italy and the Ottoman Empire was declared to exist on the following day.[3]

Italian designs on Tripoli had for some time placed Britain in an uncomfortable position. On the one hand, it had not wished to appear too complacent about them: this might inflame its Moslem subjects in India and elsewhere, as well as further weaken its position at Constantinople. On the other, and weighing more heavily, it had been anxious to avoid encouraging any Italian enthusiasm for participation in the Triple Alliance by a too vigorous opposition.[4] The upshot had been British support for Italian pressure on Turkey up to a naval demonstration—"the more usual method", observed Sir Edward Grey—but not as far as "outright and forcible annexation".[5] In the months preceding the crisis, Grey had clearly communicated his pro-Italian sympathies to Rome's ambassador in London,[6] and studiously avoided any promises of support to Turkey, for whose regime his enthusiasm was by now much reduced.[7]

When war broke out at the end of September 1911 there was, therefore, some dismay in the Foreign Office. The hostility of the British press to Italy was almost universal, and was soon being fuelled by accounts of Italian atrocities against civilians and the sufferings of

---

[3] On this crisis generally, see William C. Askew, *Europe and Italy's Acquisition of Libya 1911–1912* (Duke University Press: Durham, N.C., 1942); R. J. B. Bosworth, *Italy, the Least of the Great Powers: Italian foreign policy before the First World War* (Cambridge UP: Cambridge, 1979), chs. 5 and 6, and "Italy and the End of the Ottoman Empire", in Kent (ed.), *The Great Powers and the End of the Ottoman Empire*; C. J. Lowe, "Grey and the Tripoli War, 1911–1912", in F. H. Hinsley (ed.), *British Foreign Policy under Sir Edward Grey* (Cambridge University Press: Cambridge, 1977); and Eugene Staley, *War and the Private Investor* (Doubleday: New York, 1935), ch. 3. The contemporary overview of the British Ambassador in Rome can be found in his Annual Report on Italy for the Year 1911, reprinted in *BD*, 9 (1), pp. 259–62.

[4] However, it seems that Britain did *not* wish Italy formally to desert the Triple Alliance for fear that, against the background of a strengthening Franco-Russian combination, this would provoke Germany into war before things got worse for it. I am grateful to Dr. T. G. Otte for this observation.

[5] Grey to Rodd, 29 Sept. 1911, *BD*, 9 (1), p. 285.

[6] Grey to Rodd, *BD*, 9 (1): 28 July 1911 (p. 264); 19 Sept. 1911 (p. 274); and 27 Sept. 1911 (p. 281).

[7] Robbins, *Sir Edward Grey*, p. 265.

Maltese British subjects caught up in the fighting. These episodes were raised vigorously in the House of Commons and placed Grey on the defensive. British indulgence towards Rome was further tried when, at the beginning of November, and despite still having no control beyond the coastal towns occupied in early October,[8] it announced annexation: Tripoli was henceforth *Libia Italiana*. This proclamation not only ruled out any early negotiated settlement with the Turks but irritated Britain by terminating the capitulatory rights of its subjects in the province. In order to bring pressure on Turkey elsewhere, Italy also hinted at the possibility of taking the war to the Aegean, which carried a serious threat to Britain's Black Sea trade because of the fear that the Turks might defend the Dardanelles with mines. Grey, who was obviously quite fed up, told the British Ambassador in Rome, Sir Rennell Rodd, that for the moment he could not contemplate guaranteeing Tripoli to Italy even in return for an Italian undertaking to contract out of the Triple Alliance.[9]

Nevertheless, the Foreign Office, encouraged by Rodd, remained anxious to avoid alienating the Italians. As a result, Britain announced its neutrality in the conflict,[10] applied pressure to mute the anti-Italian tone of the press, and sought to persuade the Turks to acknowledge the occupation as a *fait accompli*. By the end of the year—with fears mounting of spring convulsions in the Balkans if the war was not concluded—it was transparent that Grey's policy was to see Italy quickly confirmed in its new possessions. However, he had no wish to be blamed for this in Constantinople, where a measure of sympathy for the Turkish point of view might exacerbate the discomfort of Germany, caught as it was between its friend and its ally. The foreign secretary insisted, therefore, that any mediation in the war should be a collective effort by the powers.[11]

---

[8] The local Senussi Arabs had sided with the Turks rather than risen against them; hence the Italians, whose military preparedness had in any case been poor, had run into stronger opposition than they had anticipated.

[9] Rodd to Grey, 25 Oct. 1911, *BD*, 9 (1), pp. 315–16, 322–3.

[10] In early November the British cabinet rebuffed a Turkish offer of alliance, Askew, *Europe and Italy's Acquisition of Libya*, p. 132.

[11] Min. of Grey, 27 Dec. 1911, and Grey to Buchanan, 29 Dec. 1911, *BD*, IX(I), pp. 352–3. On the broader background to Grey's attitude, see Lowe, "Grey and the Tripoli War, 1911–1912".

"We are not well served in Tripoli"

The diplomatic situation provoked by the war in Tripoli was thus extremely delicate for the British government. To make matters worse, the consul-general in Tripoli town since 1904,[12] Justin Alvarez, was causing problems. Alvarez had been one of the first student dragomans recruited into the Levant Service in 1877. Initially thought a bright prospect and intensely interested in Islamic culture, he was retained in the consular department of the British Embassy until 1890 and then given the consulate at Benghazi. In the meantime, however, he had acquired the reputation for being too bookish and even mentally unhinged. "Clearly mad", remarked Lord Salisbury, when informed of what the Foreign Office regarded as some particularly ludicrous misapprehension that Alvarez had formed about the prospect of an honour in 1898. He had also committed the great sin of acquiring a Levantine wife, and the even greater one of developing a style of hand-writing that was virtually illegible. He also still needed to be told by the Eastern Department how to number and reference his telegrams and despatches and how to use the cypher correctly.[13]

Alvarez might have been a close student of Islamic culture but this did not prevent him from being an enthusiast for the CUP.[14] As a result, he had got on well with the Turkish authorities in Tripoli and reacted badly to the Italian invasion. In particular, he was quick to give credence to the reports filed by war correspondents on alleged Italian atrocities. "I have reason to believe", he wrote on 27 October, "that since the events of the 23rd [a bloody engagement at Sciara Sciat], and the discovery that the Arabs are actively siding with the Turks against them, the Italians have lost their heads, and the soldiery have com-

---

[12] There was also a British consul in Benghazi in Cyrenaica.

[13] TNA, Salisbury to Layard, 19 Sept. 1878, FO78/2771, and FO to Alvarez, 18 and 20 Nov. 1911, FO371/1263; CAC Cam., O'Conor to Barrington, 12 Apr. 1899, OCON 4/1/17, and Barrington to O'Conor, 18 Apr. 1899, OCON 6/1/20. Alvarez's handwriting had particularly exercised Hardinge but the consul-general displayed great reluctance to use the type-writer that he was sent. Eventually he gave in and there was rejoicing in the Eastern Department when his first type-written despatch arrived in May 1909. He was, however, still prone to relapse into long-hand, TNA, FO371/775–9, 1012, 1238, 1010 and 1240.

[14] His comments on the "reactionaries", who were strong in Tripoli, were markedly hostile following the counter-revolution in April 1909, TNA, Alvarez despatches in FO371/774–6.

mitted atrocities unworthy of such a civilized nation."[15] This was not what the Foreign Office wanted to hear. Nor was it inclined to accept it at face value, especially after receiving a contradictory account from Rodd in Rome several days later.[16]

Worse was to come. On 17 November the Italian Ambassador in London complained to Sir Arthur Nicolson, the permanent under-secretary, that Alvarez, who, he insisted, suffered an anti-Italian bias, had admitted to Italian journalists that he had personally assisted in the despatch of the 'atrocity' reports. General Caneva, the commander of the Italian forces, had, said the ambassador, refused to allow this story to be telegraphed from Tripoli but he feared that it would leak out and make a bad impression in Italy.[17] Sure enough, three days later Rodd reported from Rome the story appearing under such headings as "Complicity of British Consul" or "Author of Infamous Reports is British Consul".[18] In reply to a demand for an explanation from Grey, on the same day Alvarez had dismissed the charges as "thundering lies".[19] Nevertheless, Vansittart, at this point a clerk in the Eastern Department, drew the moral: "Innocent or guilty Mr. Alvarez will in future be persona ingratissima to the Italians and his utility to us must suffer in consequence."[20]

At about the same time that it concluded that the objectivity of the reporting of Alvarez left much to be desired, the Foreign Office became irritated with his despatches for other reasons. For one thing there were not enough of them, though this was largely because, aware of his bias, the Italian military censors held them up. The pretext that they used to take this action was an alleged misunderstanding concerning their destination. Alvarez's cyphered cables, they claimed, were not being sent to the Foreign Office but to 'Prodrome, London', which they could only conclude was a private press agency. Since 'Prodrome' had been the telegraphic address of the Foreign Office since 1884, this naturally incensed the consul-general and elicited some sympathy for him among junior officers in the Eastern Department.[21] What none of

[15] TNA, Alvarez to Grey, 27 Oct. 1911, FO371/1256.
[16] TNA, Rodd to Grey, 6 Nov. 1911 (received 13 Nov.), FO371/1257.
[17] TNA, Nicolson to Grey, 17 Nov. 1911, FO371/1258.
[18] TNA, Rodd to Grey, 20 Nov. 1911, FO371/1258.
[19] TNA, Alvarez to FO, 20 Nov. 1911, FO371/1258.
[20] TNA, min. of Vansittart, 21 Nov. FO371/1258.
[21] TNA, Alvarez to Grey, 19 and 20 Nov. 1911, and mins. on Rodd to Grey, 20 Nov. 1911, FO371/1258.

them could forgive, however, was that when his telegrams did arrive they were thought to be superficial and hopelessly vague. After receiving a particularly vapid and badly corrupted message on 20 November, the official who superintended the Eastern Department, Louis Mallet, summed up a general feeling: "His telegrams are useless."[22]

The result of this state of communications with Tripoli was that Grey and his junior minister, F. D. Acland, were left floundering when pressed for information on the Italian invasion in the House of Commons. Furthermore, questions were starting to be asked by members about Alvarez himself, not least because of his suspiciously foreign-sounding surname. Was the secretary of state receiving proper reports from the consuls in Tripoli and, if not, would he take immediate steps to secure such reports?[23] Was Alvarez actually a British subject?[24] Was he not in reality a Spaniard? And, "in view of the present and probable future importance of this post", would not the secretary of state "consider the desirability of appointing thereto a British-born member of our Consular service with experience gained by actual service in some similar position in the Near East?"[25] Though Acland was able immediately to correct the misapprehensions behind the last question,[26] Nicolson, Mallet and Grey had all just about had enough. The last straw as far as the permanent under-secretary was concerned arrived in the shape of a telegram from Alvarez on 20 November. This contained the suggestion that the Tripoli question might be resolved by creation of an Italian protectorate under a Moslem prince. "We have not asked Mr Alvarez for his views as to possible bases for peace negotiations", minuted Nicolson, in the same breath observing that "[w]e are not well served at Tripoli". The private secretaries, he added, should see if there was "a suitable man ready to hand" to replace him.[27] A few days later Mallet said that "[t]he sooner Alvarez is superseded the better". For his part, Grey recorded that "The Italian Ambassador asked

---

[22] TNA, Alvarez to FO, 15 Nov. (delayed by censor), FO371/1258.
[23] *Parl. Debs.*, 5th Ser. (Commons), vol. XXX, 2 Nov. 1911, col. 983; 9 Nov. 1911, col. 1787; 13 Nov. 1911, col. 4.
[24] *Parl. Debs.*, 5th Ser. (Commons), vol. XXX, 7 Nov. 1911, col. 1453; 9 Nov. 1911, col. 1789.
[25] *Parl. Debs.*, 5th Ser. (Commons) vol. XXXII, 5 Dec. 1911, col. 1371.
[26] "He is a natural-born British subject…[who]…has served at various posts in the Near East and Mediterranean", *Parl. Debs.*, 5th Ser. (Commons), vol. XXXII, 5 Dec. 1911, col. 1371.
[27] TNA, min. of Nicolson on Alvarez to FO, 18 Nov. 1911, FO371/1258.

me privately yesterday whether we could not have a real Englishman as Consul at Tripoli. We ought", the foreign secretary concluded, "to have one now".[28] Ten days after this Alvarez demanded to know of Grey whether he had received an apology from General Caneva for stopping his telegrams to London. "I am not seeing him for the present", he added.[29] By this time the Foreign Office was in despair over Alvarez but his fate was already sealed: "He is to be relieved by Mr Fitzmaurice", said Grey.[30]

Since appeasing the Italians was the chief motive for removing Alvarez, replacing him with Fitzmaurice instead of with the experienced and capable vice-consul, Alfred Dickson,[31] was a shrewd move. For one thing, it was flattering because he was not just another consular officer but the holder of the most important position in the Levant Service. His reputation for toughness in dealing with the Turks was also no doubt reassuring. On top of this, he was a Catholic and spoke some Italian. His broad experience and strong grasp of commercial and financial as well as political questions also meant that he could converse as easily with representatives of the *Banco di Roma* as with other Italian officials and military officers. As for handling Alvarez, Fitzmaurice himself thought that it was an advantage that he and the consul-general were "old acquaintances".[32] Last but not least, he had for some time favoured the idea of bringing Italy into the Anglo-French camp.[33]

The idea of diverting Fitzmaurice to Tripoli originated in the fertile mind of William Tyrrell[34] but undoubtedly had strong support in the Eastern Department of the Foreign Office. The chief dragoman's admirers, such as Vansittart, must have emphasised his suitability for the task as a trouble-shooter, while those with reservations about his attitude to the CUP—including Grey himself—probably saw it at the least as a neat device for postponing his return to Constantinople. George Lloyd, for one, suspected this thinking, telling Cockerell that "I'm not sure that Tripoli is very good as an appointment for the Sheikh—they

---

[28] TNA, undated mins. on Rodd to Grey, 20 Nov. 1911, FO371/1258, probably written on 21 November.
[29] TNA, Alvarez to Grey, 1 Dec. 1911, FO371/1258.
[30] TNA, min. on Alvarez to Grey, 1 Dec. 1911, FO371/1258.
[31] Dickson had been vice-consul at Tripoli for thirty years and frequently acting consul-general.
[32] TNA, Fitzmaurice to Tyrrell, 6 Jan. 1912, FO800/80.
[33] TNA, Fitzmaurice to Tyrrell, 9 Feb. 1911, p. 10, FO800/80.
[34] TNA, Lowther to Tyrrell, 20 Mar. 1912, FO800/193B.

may try and keep him there".[35] Cockerell had reservations of a different nature. It would be a "tricky job" for him, he suggested, since "masterly inactivity", which it seemed was what was required of the British Consul-General in Tripoli, was not exactly his style.[36] Predictably enough, it was Lowther who made a noise of his disapproval, as is clear from a slightly strained private letter that he wrote to Tyrrell in the following spring. It was a mystery to him, he said, why Dickson could not have been left in charge.[37] However, though he probably suspected that he was to be deprived of the services of his chief dragoman for considerably longer than he had anticipated, there was nothing that the ambassador could do about it. In December Fitzmaurice left England for Tripoli.

Unwelcome guest at the consulate-general

After being five days "tempest-tossed" at sea, Fitzmaurice arrived in Tripoli town on Christmas Day. No doubt the words of Aubrey Herbert's maiden speech in the House of Commons, given on 14 December, were still ringing in his ears. He would have winced at the reference to the "fine experiment" of the Young Turks' revolution, to which British policy was alleged to have been "stonily indifferent". On the other hand, he would have taken consolation from his former friend's advertisement of the catastrophic implications for European peace of a continuation of the Italo-Turkish conflict, for this also advertised the importance of his mission.[38]

Fitzmaurice's arrival in Tripoli aroused predictable curiosity, both at the time and later. He told Tyrrell that it had caused some press comment, "partly traceable" to one of his arch-rivals, Paul Weitz, the Constantinople correspondent of the *Frankfurter Zeitung* and influential long-time adviser to the German Embassy.[39] Later, Harold Temperley recorded that a distinguished American diplomat had once discussed with him "with some alarm, in New York, what the British Government

---

[35] CAC Cam., Lloyd to Cockerell, nd, GLLD 8/3.
[36] CAC Cam., Cockerell to Lloyd, 30 Nov. 1911, GLLD 8/4.
[37] TNA, Lowther to Tyrrell, 20 Mar. 1912, FO800/193B.
[38] *Parl. Debs.*, 5th Ser. (Commons), vol. XXXII, 14 Dec. 1911, cols. 2563–9.
[39] Morgenthau, *Secrets of the Bosphorus*, p. 18.

really meant by dispatching him to Tripoli as Consul-General during the Italo-Turkish War".[40]

As for Alvarez and his wife—"very highly strung to put it mildly"—Fitzmaurice found them living virtually as recluses, and they gave him a less than seasonal reception.[41] Alvarez had been instructed to take leave and hand over to him on 1 January, the issue of his transfer to a new post to be discussed when he returned home. However, using the excuse that after 20 years' residence in Africa he and his wife could not face a northern climate in winter, he soon made it clear that he was not going to be prised out quickly.

Despite his cool reception and his agreement with the Foreign Office that Alvarez had handled the Italians badly, Fitzmaurice was initially disposed to make excuses for the consul-general's behaviour. He even took steps to nurture his professional rehabilitation, though this was no doubt in part because he saw this as a means of keeping his own stay in Tripoli a brief one; it may have been a provincial post but it was not exactly the sort for which he was looking. Since Alvarez was an orientalist, he told Tyrrell in early January, it was a "natural impulse" for him to side with the Turks, while his other-worldly preoccupation with his books had made him easy prey for those in London and elsewhere who had been trying to make England seem anti-Italian. The consul-general, wrote Fitzmaurice, had been "the victim of a political wirepulling". Now, however, matters stood differently. A spirited resistance to the Italian invasion had been made by the Turks and, with the war in stalemate and now less newsworthy, Tripoli had "already dropped back into its proper side-tracked obscurity". Moreover, Alvarez now saw things less emotionally, both he and his wife spoke Italian well, and neither really had the bias of which they had been accused. As a result, concluded Fitzmaurice, there was no reason why he should not remain in his post if it proved too difficult to transfer him—as he wished—to another consulate-general where his specialist knowledge would not be wasted.

Unfortunately, Alvarez had latched on to an official telegram in which he was referred to as still the "titular" of the post, and a month later, when Fitzmaurice next wrote to Tyrrell, he was still refusing to depart

---

[40] *The Times*, 30 Mar. 1939 [obituary notice on Fitzmaurice].

[41] Unless otherwise stated, the following account is based on the letters that Fitzmaurice wrote to Tyrrell from Tripoli on 6 Jan., 12 Feb. and 5 June 1912, TNA, FO800/80.

on leave. Insisting that he remained consul-general and that Fitzmaurice, who was ten years his junior in the Levant Service, was merely a sort of personal assistant, he insisted on carrying on much as usual. He kept control of the post's archives, met all visitors, and had all of the mail except that bearing Fitzmaurice's name brought to him first.

> The result [Fitzmaurice told Tyrrell] is that foreign colleagues, Italians and others are naturally somewhat puzzled at this apparent game of Box and Cox, and some of the Italians who imagined my coming here was meant to make good Alvarez's connection with the virulent anti-Italian campaign of certain 'British' journalists in October and November last, are now at a loss to understand how Alvarez remains on…and are beginning to suspect that I am really here on some other and special mission which their imagination figures out in various forms. My ingenuity in devising answers to constant queries as to why Alvarez has not yet left, when he is going etc etc has been well nigh exhausted.

His sympathy for Alvarez now completely dried up, Fitzmaurice had warned him that his attitude was likely to be construed as insubordination and damage his career. But, he told Tyrrell, "he has shown himself as obstinate as a Spanish mule and generally runs away when one tries to speak to him in a friendly way". He was also fearful of being "drastic" with him because this could hardly pass unnoticed in such a provincial setting as Tripoli and would be a serious embarrassment. He thus urged Tyrrell to remind Alvarez by telegraph of his obligation to leave without further delay. "I could then, if necessary, put the screw on a bit and ensure his departure", Fitzmaurice added. As for his own position, he could remain on until after the Italian advance into the interior—expected "within a fortnight or so"—when the atmosphere of Tripoli town would return to something resembling normality. At this point, the capable vice-consul, Dickson, could take charge and he could return to Constantinople. The Foreign Office ignored the latter hints but must at least have acted on Fitzmaurice's advice in regard to Alvarez in this letter to Tyrrell of 12 February, for it could not have been long after this that he finally left.[42]

---

[42] Alvarez was next given charge of the consulate at Trebizond but in January 1913 was forced to retire altogether "on the grounds of mental deterioration", TNA, FO to Treasury, 5 Mar. 1913; also Cartwright to Upcott, 2 Apr. 1913, T1/11526.

Soothing the Italians and reporting the "war"

Having adopted an attitude of friendly neutrality towards the Italians on his arrival, Fitzmaurice appears to have had little difficulty in restoring harmonious relations with the occupying authorities. "My coming here has helped to dissipate the clouds from the Italian point of view", he told Tyrrell in early January. In addition to soothing the Italians at every subsequent opportunity, he occupied himself with claims for losses suffered by British subjects and especially with writing terse and somewhat sardonic despatches on the desultory progress of the Italian occupation.

Fitzmaurice formed a low opinion of the abilities of the Italians as colonial administrators:

> Since my arrival here I have had cordial relations with all sorts and conditions of Italians.... I move about a good deal on horseback and on foot and have met a great number of generals, officers and deputies, of whom some thirty have visited this place. They are pleasant, but one's general impression is that they are narrow and small instead of being big and broad. The Arabs loathe them and would prefer the French or British. More than centuries separate the Roman with his Pax Romana and the modern Italian, as governors and administrators of alien races.[43]

He also had little good to say about the military campaign.

In the middle of January he undertook an intelligence-gathering round trip by steamer to Tobruk, taking in Benghazi—where communications with the British Consul had been disrupted—and Derna.[44] He noted the "customary reckless bravery" of the Turco-Arab forces, and in a second well appreciated despatch of 29 January carefully analysed the "negative, slow and costly course" adopted by the Italians. This consisted of "keeping within their trenches and relying almost entirely on their vastly superior artillery". In view of their "dread of another Adowa" this "Fabian policy" was understandable, he maintained, and in the long run would probably prove wise. However, in the short run it emboldened their enemies, demoralized their own troops, and was

---

[43] TNA, Fitzmaurice to Tyrrell, 12 Feb. 1912, FO800/80.
[44] TNA, Fitzmaurice to Grey, 29 Jan. 1912 (No. 3 Political), FO371/1530.

damaging to European prestige throughout north and west Africa.[45] To convey his contempt for these tactics, whenever Fitzmaurice used the word 'war' in these despatches he invariably placed it in inverted commas. On the other hand he sprang to the defence of the moral conduct of the Italian soldiers.

In late January and again in March, having made discreet inquiries to avoid giving offence to the occupying authorities, Fitzmaurice had dismissed Turkish charges that the Italians had fired on Red Crescent hospital tents and personnel.[46] Then, following a freshly launched campaign in the British press, on 15 April he sent a despatch to the Foreign Office about the atrocities alleged to have been committed by the Italians in late October of the previous year. In its attention to detail, careful reference to sources, and measured tone, it was reminiscent of his despatches on the Armenian massacres in 1896. He reckoned that the Arab casualties had been nearer to 400 than the 4000 claimed by one British journalist and implicitly endorsed by Alvarez. They had in any case occurred chiefly because the Italians had been "maddened" by the barbarous mutilations of their dead and wounded by Arab friendlies attacking them in the rear. The Italians, he noted, had probably suffered more casualties than the Arabs but concealed this for fear of the public reaction in Italy. Finally, in apportioning blame, Fitzmaurice once more took the opportunity to plunge his knife into the Young Turks. The Italians may have lost their heads to some extent and the Arabs had behaved as one would expect of an ignorant and fanatical people whose land had been invaded by infidels. But, he argued,

> the primary responsibility would [seem to] lie with the Young Turk leaders here, who, knowing the almost mathematical result of inciting the Moslem Arabs to start a religious war, deliberately stirred up their fanaticism and launched them against the Italians. This departure from the rules of civilised warfare was the work, too, of Young Turks who professed to discard and reprobate the theocratic methods of the old régime in Turkey and to have become constitutional in the western sense. It is perhaps worth noting that... [t]he orders to resist à outrance were sent from Salonica....[47]

---

[45] TNA, Fitzmaurice to Grey, 29 Jan. 1912 (No. 2 Political), FO371/1530; other military despatches by Fitzmaurice are located in FO371/1526. See also Bosworth, *Italy, the Least of the Great Powers*, pp. 166–7.

[46] TNA, Fitzmaurice to Grey, 30 Jan. and 20 Mar. 1912, FO371/1528.

[47] TNA, Fitzmaurice to Grey, 15 Apr. 1912, FO371/1537.

This despatch evidently did Fitzmaurice a lot of good in the Foreign Office. "The number of Arabs killed... has evidently been grossly exaggerated", minuted Vansittart on it. "I wish we could publish this", added a colleague. "It would not please the Young Turks" was all that Maxwell could say but Mallet said that "It completely exonerates the Italian troops".

Fitzmaurice had not been long in Tripoli before concluding that the Italians ought to be waging what would later be called a 'hearts and minds' operation to win over the Arabs, while concentrating their military attacks only on the Turks and their more fanatical Arab allies. By late February he was beginning to see signs that this was being done and that it was paying off. He also drew the moral that the weak response to the Italian attack among Moslems in Egypt, India and elsewhere was beginning to show that Pan-Islamism as a political force was something of a myth.[48]

Despite the better tactics observed by Fitzmaurice in late February, the Italians were unable to bring off the definitive defeat of their Turco-Arab opponents. As a result, under pressure from the powers to bring the affair to an end, especially after it widened the conflict to the Dodecanese and the Dardanelles, Italy was soon exploring the possibility of a negotiated settlement with Turkey. Talks began at unofficial level in July and eventually bore fruit in October 1912 at Lausanne, where Turkey—now reeling from the assault of the Balkan League—had no alternative but to confirm Italy's acquisitions. However, Fitzmaurice's return to Constantinople did not need to wait on this. "I came here before my leave was finished", he wrote to Tyrrell in early June, "but the man who has been doing my work in Cons[tantino]ple is I hear seedy and I understand Lowther wants me to return without dallying". He was intrigued to see what Constantinople would feel like without Baron Marschall, who had finally left the German Embassy.[49] Back at the British Embassy in the middle of the following month, he was thus in ample time to have a hand in the further contraction of the Ottoman Empire which followed the outbreak of war in the Balkans.

---

[48] TNA, Fitzmaurice to Grey, 22 Feb. 1912, FO371/1534.
[49] TNA, Fitzmaurice to Tyrrell, 5 June 1912, FO800/80. Lowther had complained of Fitzmaurice's delayed return in his own letter to Tyrrell of 20 Mar. 1912, FO800/193B.

CHAPTER EIGHT

RETREAT FROM CONSTANTINOPLE, 1912–14

Fitzmaurice resumed his duties in the dragomanate on 18 July 1912,[1] shortly after the embassy had moved to its summer quarters at Therapia. These were not quite as spacious as usual since the ambassador's house and the chancery had been burned down in the previous winter, and Sir Gerard Lowther had just gone on a cure to Marienbad partly in order to relieve pressure on the remaining accommodation.[2] In his absence, the able and experienced counsellor, Charles Marling, was once more in charge. The head of chancery was now George Kidston, only recently promoted first secretary and just arrived from St. Petersburg. The military attaché was Colonel Gerald Tyrrell, who was energetic, politically sophisticated and had considerable experience of the Ottoman Empire.[3]

Andrew Ryan, who had been acting for Fitzmaurice, welcomed him back with great relief. This was chiefly because his previous experience of dealing with political matters had been virtually non-existent,[4] but also because he was anxious to obtain his blessing for a memorandum that he had prepared on the low morale of the Levant Service and what might be done to improve it.[5] However, other events soon began

---

[1] He had stopped over at Malta where he had talked to the governor-general, General Sir Leslie Rundle, TNA, Fitzmaurice to Tyrrell, 3 June 1913, FO800/80.

[2] Lowther lost a great deal of uninsured property in this fire and the Treasury refused to compensate him for it. The FO was not impressed by his attitude in this matter, or in the rather querulous way he handled the question of what alternative arrangements were to be made for this summer; see papers in TNA, FO371/1263 and FO371/1483.

[3] Gerald Tyrrell had been military vice-consul at Van for four years and then employed with the Macedonian Gendarmerie for eighteen months before being appointed to the embassy at the end of 1909.

[4] Bullard, *The Camels Must Go*, p. 64. The diffident but honest Ryan said later that "I was quite incapable of filling the shoes of a man so remarkable for his knowledge of all things Turkish and for his grasp of Eastern politics", MECA Oxf., Memories of Twenty-Five Years Service GB 165–0248 Box 3 3/3.

[5] MECA Oxf., Untitled [The grievances of the Levant Consular Service], June 1912, incl. Ryan to Eyres, 25 June 1912, DS42.3GY, Ryan Box 4/1.

to command their attention: first the eclipse of the CUP following a mutiny in the army, and then the outbreak of the first Balkan War.

"A flicker in the Turkish candle"?

The grip of the CUP on the Turkish government had been weakening for some time, a tendency increased by deepening internal divisions.[6] It was now being blamed for failing to repulse the Italians in Tripoli; there was also trouble in Albania and some of the other provinces; and the economy was ailing. With constitutional opposition impossible, the unrest that was mounting began to look for a lead from the so-called 'Saviour Officers', who were connected to the Liberal Union and flexing their muscles just at the point that Fitzmaurice returned to Constantinople.[7] Following threatening moves orchestrated by this group, on 17 July the CUP government resigned, shortly to be replaced by one dominated by Liberal Union supporters. By the end of October, the aged Kiamil Pasha was once more grand vizier, a development which further poisoned relations between the new government and the CUP. Fitzmaurice, who had returned in the midst of these events, observed them with great satisfaction. Writing to Tyrrell a few days after Kiamil's return, he said that:

> Recent events in Turkey have, I fancy, again proved the wisdom of our not committing ourselves too closely to any one faction (Committee or other) in Turkey. We are free at a juncture when to have got entangled might have proved more than embarrassing....

The corollary, of course, was that Britain should not rush to embrace the new government either. Fitzmaurice had no illusions about the CUP; it was down but not out. Kiamil's latest grand vizierate might be just another "flicker in the Turkish candle".[8]

---

[6] Background developments in this Chapter are based chiefly on Lewis, *The Emergence of Modern Turkey*, pp. 220–4; and Ahmad, *The Young Turks*, ch. V.

[7] As early as the end of April Colonel Tyrrell had been visited by a young officer who told him that a majority of officers favoured replacing the CUP-run government by one pursuing an "English policy", TNA, G. E. Tyrrell to Lowther, 27 Apr. 1912, FO371/1486.

[8] TNA, Fitzmaurice to Tyrrell, 2 Nov. 1912, FO800/80.

Good offices in the first Balkan War

This letter to Tyrrell was written against the background of an equally dramatic development: the attack on Turkey in mid-October of the Balkan League (Bulgaria, Greece, and Serbia). Britain declared its neutrality in this conflict as well but public opinion was wholly behind the Balkan states. On the battlefield matters also went badly for Turkey. By the beginning of November its troops had already fallen back to the Chatalja lines only a few miles outside Constantinople, into which Turkish refugees were streaming.

Fitzmaurice had long admired the Bulgarians, and he was not alone; among the British, they were the most popular of the Balkan tribes.[9] With the prospect that a campaign spearheaded by them was now to resolve some of the most intractable problems of the region, especially Macedonia and Crete, it is understandable that he was almost light-headed at what seemed to the embassy to be the imminent sight of their troops on the streets of the capital.[10] On 4 November, with warships of the powers arriving to reassure their nationals, Lowther—doubtlessly accompanied by Fitzmaurice—met Gabriel Effendi, the minister of foreign affairs. The same night the ambassador reported on the meeting in a long telegram to the Foreign Office drafted—like most if not all of his important messages at this critical juncture[11]—in Fitzmaurice's unmistakeable hand.[12] The minister was not as pessimistic as some about the Bulgarians reaching the capital but if they did then the government and the sultan would have to leave, possibly for Broussa.

---

[9] Compton Mackenzie, *First Athenian Memories* (Cassell: London, 1931), p. 298. "I have called them the Japs of the Balcans", he said, "and think they may one day be the nucleus of something big", CAC Cam., Fitzmaurice to Lloyd, 10 Jan. 1909, GLLD 7/4. Over the next year he drafted numerous despatches for Lowther that minimised their responsibility for the many and varied atrocities that occurred in the fighting, apprehensive that the exaggerations of Turkish propaganda would inflame Moslem fanaticism: for example, TNA, Lowther to Grey, 13 Feb. 1913, FO195/2448 and 1 Aug. 1913, FO195/2453; and his min. on Lamb (Salonica) to Lowther, 22 Mar. 1913, discounting reports of forced conversions of Moslems to Christianity by the Bulgarians, FO195/2452.

[10] The AR 1912 said that "In the city itself the position was judged to be more precarious than more recent knowledge has shown", in Lowther to Grey, 13 Apr. 1913, TNA, FO881/10280.

[11] See TNA, FO195/2436 and 2437.

[12] TNA, FO195/2437, folios 280–2. The copy despatched to the FO was amended only slightly by Lowther, though a typical Fitzmaurice flourish ("Jacobin element of the committee") fell victim to Eastern Department editing before appearing in Confidential Print; see FO371/1504, folios 287 and 285 respectively.

This would reduce the city to "absolute anarchy" and, before order could be restored by the invaders, might well result in a "complete massacre of the Christians". Fanatical elements, enraged at the impending desecration of the caliphate's holy relics by infidels, would be at the forefront but the "Jacobin element of the committee would probably be the prime movers, their motto being 'committee shall succeed or destroy everything'". Gabriel Effendi himself thought that the powers should send more ships. As for Lowther, he considered that the Christian quarter of Pera might be offered more protection if the Bulgarians could be persuaded to enter from the east while naval guns were used to destroy the bridges connecting the quarter to Stamboul.

It was probably later that night, having seen off this telegram at 8.45 pm, that Fitzmaurice wrote his first letter for some time to George Lloyd.[13] Full of pathos and at times vainglorious, this message he described as a "last hurried note from Stamboul" and addressed it as from the "Ex-British Embassy, Constantinople". Invoking once more his favourite quatrain from the *Rubaiyat* of Omar Khayyam—"The Sultan rises and the dark ferrash strikes..." (see page 139 above), he sketched in even more lurid terms the end to which the city seemed doomed, thanks to the Committee. So as to avoid spreading panic, he said, he was maintaining a cheerful and confident face to those unfortunates who did not understand "the mysticism and psychology of the East retreating before the West". In reality, the fate of Peking following the Boxer uprising would probably pale in comparison to the fate of Constantinople and, the poor dragoman having to take his chances on the streets when others remained safe at home, his own end might well prove a "queer" one. If he could ever write again, he continued, it was unlikely that it would be from "Tzarigrad". Never mind. He felt that he had done his duty not only to Britain but to Turkey and Islam as well:

> In vain, it is true, and wittingly taking the line of greatest danger. Spirit lives or is reborn and it shall not all have been in vain from a British point of view. If I ever get the other side of the next few days events I shall write of the "decline and fall of the Ottoman State", otherwise turn down an empty glass—emptied to the memories of 1906.

The last line had introduced a slightly maudlin tone into this letter, and Fitzmaurice went on to complain gently that it was a long time since

---

[13] CAC Cam., Fitzmaurice to Lloyd, 4 Nov. 1912, GLLD 7/4.

he had received one from Lloyd. He also recalled the unsympathetic response he had met when trying recently to speak to him and Sam Cockerell about the great questions of the day. He signed himself "The ex-Sheikh (G.H.F.) and the ex-Wizard of Stamboul".

On the following day, 5 November, Fitzmaurice wrote in similar vein to William Tyrrell. Having crossed out 'Constantinople' on the letterhead of his embassy writing paper and inserted "Tzarigrad" in its place, he said:

> Swanlike, let me write you a last letter from Pekin before the Court and Porte flee bagless and baggageless (Gladstonese) to the shores of Asia...
>
> The drama of 1453 is being undone and one wonders whether St Sophia and the Seraglio treasures and the Relics of the prophet will survive this upheaval. The words Sultan, Grand Vizier, Grand Seigneur, Sublime Porte etc have lost their old connotation. The cobwebs of diplomacy and the formulas written in ink are replaced by tracings in blood on the map and framed.
>
> The Turkish Army rotted by C.U.P. doctrines and politics could not fight in the name of Djavid Bey instead of the Padishah and collapsed before the avenging Bulgar and the armies of the new Great Power—the "United States of the Balcans", which are undoubtedly the right horse besides being the favourites of the Gladstonian tradition.... I presume Ferdy, the bold bad man of Bulgaria, as I styled him in the 1897 Jubilee procession, will come in here and dictate the terms of peace.... The Committee of Union and Progress brought about Union between Turkey's foes and disunion among her elements. Hence the decline and fall of the Ottoman Empire.... If a general massacre etc etc like Turner's picture in the National Gallery "Wind, Rain and Speed"[14] sweeps over Anatolia and Syria in an expiring spasm of Panislamism now for four years harnessed to the chariot of Panjudaism, the prairie fire may even reach Egypt....
>
> Good night—au revoir in this world or the next,
>
> yours ever
> G. H. Fitzmaurice[15]

In the event, the Turks held out on the Chatalja lines and Constantinople was spared the fate that Fitzmaurice had foreshadowed.

At this juncture, with Lowther's blessing but the Foreign Office in the dark, Fitzmaurice took it upon himself to promote *direct* negotiations between Turkey and the Balkan League, first for an armistice and then

---

[14] Correct title: "Rain, Steam and Speed".
[15] TNA, Fitzmaurice to Tyrrell, 5 Nov. 1912, FO800/80.

for a peace settlement.[16] Kiamil, now thought by Fitzmaurice to be in his dotage, had previously urged mediation by the powers but with no success. This suited Fitzmaurice because he believed firmly that there was nothing to mediate: Turkey had no alternative but to surrender everything in Europe—Constantinople apart—as quickly and gracefully as possible.[17] Its German-trained army had been "crumpled up", he said to Tyrrell a little later, and its cabinet, "suspended in mid-air like Mahomet's coffin, reposes on nothing". Besides, surrender of its European provinces was in Turkey's own interests since this would enable it to consolidate its position as an Asiatic power. As for the perennial anxiety that Britain must not desert Turkey in Europe in order to avoid trouble among the Moslems in India, this was an "exploded bogey".[18]

Throwing himself into his mission of good offices with his usual energy, Fitzmaurice first saw the Bulgarian Chief Dragoman, M. Popoff,[19] and then the Russian Ambassador, Mikhail Nikolaevich de Giers—both of whom naturally needed little persuading to his point of view. He next lobbied every important Turk he could find, including the Sheikh-ul-Islam; and having seen that the grand vizier himself was prepared, on 11 November Fitzmaurice accompanied Lowther to see him. Kiamil Pasha duly indicated his desire to find some way of communicating directly with King Ferdinand of Bulgaria, Fitzmaurice duly reminded him of Popoff's continued presence in the city—and on the following day direct communication was duly arranged.[20] On 3 December an armistice—albeit excluding Greece—was signed, and later in the month Turkish and Balkan League plenipotentiaries assembled in London.

Fitzmaurice had clearly played a vital role in launching this diplomacy, as Vansittart and—more guardedly—Maxwell acknowledged.[21]

---

[16] He also urged the Albanians to deal directly with the Balkan League (especially with the "practical minded" Bulgarians) rather than leave their fate to a conference, TNA, Fitzmaurice to Lowther, 21 Nov. 1912, FO371/1515.

[17] TNA, Fitzmaurice to Lowther, 23 Nov. 1912, FO195/2438. This long and important memorandum was sent by Lowther to the FO on 26 November and is reproduced in *BD*, 9 (1), pp. 210–13.

[18] TNA, Fitzmaurice to Tyrrell, 18 Dec. 1912 (also 6 Jan. 1913), FO800/80.

[19] Popoff had been granted the protection of the Russian Embassy following the closure of the Bulgarian Legation at the outbreak of war, being nominally responsible only for Bulgarian consular affairs. This is an early example of what later became known as an 'interests section'.

[20] Memorandum by Mr. Fitzmaurice, encl. in Lowther to Grey, 26 Nov. 1912, *BD*, 9 (1), pp. 210–13; also, TNA, Lowther to Grey, 11 Nov. 1912, FO371/1513.

[21] TNA, mins. on Lowther to Grey, 26 Nov. 1912, FO371/1516. These initial minutes are omitted from the edited version of this document reproduced in *BD*, 9 (1), pp. 210–13.

However, both Sir Edward Grey and Sir Arthur Nicolson were irritated that Lowther had not consulted them about this initiative and afraid that on several points of detail Fitzmaurice had raised unrealistic hopes on Turkey's part. Grey favoured direct negotiations at this stage[22] and both agreed that the intervention of the embassy had been "happy in its results".[23] Nevertheless, no doubt they also concluded that this episode was further evidence that Fitzmaurice needed to be kept on a tight leash.

Spectator

The London Conference had soon reached stalemate, with the Turks digging in their heels particularly deeply over the strategically and symbolically important city of Adrianople. It was against this background that in late January 1913 Kiamil Pasha's government was overthrown by CUP officers led by the ruthless and charismatic Enver Bey, one of the leaders of the 1908 revolution who in the following year had been military attaché in Berlin. This move was apparently prompted by the expectation that Kiamil was about to surrender Adrianople to Bulgaria after all. The fallen grand vizier was escorted to a khedivial liner by Fitzmaurice and thence into exile in Cairo.[24] He was replaced by Mahmud Shevket Pasha. The Turkish candle had indeed flickered again.

Unfortunately for the CUP, Turkish forces suffered fresh reverses following the resumption of fighting with the Balkan allies in early February, and Adrianople finally fell on 26 March. Fitzmaurice revelled in this achievement. He might have become a spectator but at least the show was worth watching. The "United States of the Balkans" was the seventh great power, he subsequently told Tyrrell more than once, and had "rendered us all great services". Nevertheless, he worried that with the centre of gravity of Balkan diplomacy remaining in London, "Dame Europe" was allowing Turkey to hide behind her skirts. This was preventing the radical solution demanded by the realities of power,

---

[22] TNA, min. of Grey on Lowther to Grey, 17 Nov. 1912, FO371/1514.
[23] Mins. by Nicolson and Grey on Lowther to Grey, 26 Nov. 1912, *BD*, 9 (1), pp. 210–13.
[24] Ahmad, *The Young Turks*, p. 119.

and was to blame for straining the nerves of the Balkan allies and eventually causing them to fall out among themselves.[25]

In February 1913 London rather than Constantinople also became the setting for a whole raft of negotiations on outstanding matters with Turkey, despite the fact that the CUP's leaders had no faith in their ambassador, Tewfik Pasha, who was a model Old Turk. To represent them in the talks with the Foreign Office they sent instead the former legal adviser to the Porte, later grand vizier, Hakki Pasha, though he was thought by Fitzmaurice to be a "windbag and chatterbox" and in negotiations a complete push-over.[26] The subjects under discussion included the Baghdad Railway and Persian Gulf, on which resolution was being sought simultaneously by the Porte chiefly because of its anxiety to clear away obstacles to British agreement to a further increase in customs duties. What is interesting is that it was unusual for London rather than Constantinople to be employed for negotiations of this kind. It was probably preferred by the Turks in order to by-pass the British Embassy, which of course they now regarded as irredeemably hostile.[27] Whatever the explanation, Fitzmaurice was reduced to the role of spectator in the key negotiations between Britain and Turkey in the first half of 1913, and his involvement in Turkish domestic politics was also much reduced—though he was clearly straining at the leash attached to him by Lowther on the instructions of the Foreign Office.

Having penned in March a raft of despatches for Lowther amounting to a particularly savage indictment of the Committee government's "reign of terror" at home and refusal to face facts abroad,[28] Fitzmaurice began to listen with more than mild interest to the ruminations in Cairo of his octogenarian old friend, Kiamil Pasha. This was because, under the benign gaze of the Khedive and the British Agent and Consul-General, now Lord Kitchener, Kiamil was giving it out that it was he who would be grand vizier once more following the revolution in Constantinople that he regarded as imminent. This was no wild fancy,[29] and Kitchener took it upon himself to inquire on his behalf whether Lowther thought it advisable for him to return.[30] However, having been

---

[25] TNA, Fitzmaurice to Tyrrell, 9 Apr. and 8 May 1913, FO800/80.
[26] TNA, Fitzmaurice to Tyrrell, 13 Feb. 1913, FO800/80.
[27] These negotiations in London went on for over a year, finally issuing in an Anglo-Turkish convention in 1914, which was, however, never ratified.
[28] TNA, Drafts for Lowther to Grey, 3, 12, and 15 Mar. 1913, FO195/2451.
[29] TNA, AR 1912, p. 17, in Lowther to Grey, 17 Apr. 1913, FO881/10280.
[30] TNA, Kitchener to Lowther, 7 Apr. 1913, FO195/2452.

warned off by Nicolson when he had proposed to intervene on Kiamil's behalf in January,[31] the ambassador adopted an amusingly high moral tone to Kitchener: he could not possibly respond to such a question about internal Turkish affairs.[32] Thus discouraged, and learning that the Committee was determined to obstruct his return to Constantinople, Kiamil apparently decided instead to head for Smyrna. Nevertheless, it was Lowther and Fitzmaurice who came to his aid when, on 28 May, he ended up in the capital anyway.[33] This was a particularly sensitive juncture since it had just become apparent that, following sudden pressure from Sir Edward Grey, the signing of a peace treaty in London was probably imminent.[34] This would signify formal acceptance by Turkey of its territorial losses to the Balkan League, and thus enable opposition officers to make their move without courting the charge of fostering disharmony at home in time of war. Lowther and Fitzmaurice may have concluded that, under the cloak of courtesy to the Grand Old Man of Turkey, it would be prudent to place a side bet on his return.

Having arrived at the home of his son, Kiamil was immediately placed under house arrest, refused all communication with the outside world, and commanded by Colonel Djemal Bey, the vain and impetuous military governor of the city, to depart at once on a vessel bound for Marseilles. On learning this, Lowther immediately sent Fitzmaurice to pay him his compliments. Accompanied by the chief dragoman of the French Embassy, he managed to get in to see him, though only after an initial rebuff had been overruled by an appeal to Mahmud Shevket Pasha. Djemal Bey—according to his own account—thereupon offered his resignation.[35]

Perhaps in part because of the interest shown in his welfare by the British and French Embassies, Kiamil was permitted to remain in the capital a few days longer and then proceed to Smyrna rather than somewhere in Europe.[36] But, though this just kept the old statesman

---

[31] Lowther to Grey, 16 Jan. 1913, *BD*, 9 (2), no. 513.

[32] TNA, Lowther to Kitchener, 8 Apr. 1913, FO195/2452.

[33] The French steamer on which he was travelling was prevented from calling at Smyrna because of the danger of mines in the harbour and was forced to proceed to Constantinople. This was no concocted pretext. See *The Times*, 26 and 27 May 1913, and the papers on the subject generally in TNA, FO371/1821.

[34] *The Times*, 28 May 1913.

[35] Djemal Pasha, *Memories of a Turkish Statesman, 1913–1919* (Hutchinson: London, 1922), pp. 29–34.

[36] Leaning chiefly on a Lowther despatch of 31 May, Ahmad gives sole responsibility for this to the British Embassy (*The Young Turks*, p. 129). This may be true but not on

in the game, by this time Fitzmaurice probably had few illusions about his chances of ever becoming grand vizier again. In Smyrna he was given protection by the British Consul-General but after a few days "hustled" out of there as well, according to Fitzmaurice.[37] He returned to his birthplace of Cyprus, where he died in November.

With the figurehead of the opposition safely out of the way, the government survived. However, the story was not yet finished. On 11 June the grand vizier, Mahmud Shevket Pasha, was assassinated by gunmen on his way to the Porte. Harold Nicolson, at this stage a third secretary in the embassy,[38] told his future wife that Shevket "was the Cromwell of the Revolution here and the effect of the murder is as though Roberts, Kitchener and Asquith were all murdered on the same day".[39] The embassy thought it was probably not a political action but a simple act of revenge by army elements for the killing of Nazim Pasha, the minister of war, at the time of the January coup. Nevertheless, it provided the Young Turks with just the excuse they needed to crush the opposition. It also gave them a stick with which to beat Fitzmaurice.

Fitzmaurice: "The embodiment of the devil"

After the assassination of the grand vizier, Lowther told Sir Arthur Nicolson that:

> It is impossible to say whether any of our respectable friends were knowingly connected with the plot, or whether they were only well-wishers. Anyhow some of them had given us a good deal of trouble, and are constantly asking for asylum *or something more* [emphasis added].[40]

---

the basis of this despatch, which shows only that the embassy made representations to the government *in order to gain access* to Kiamil: TNA, Lowther to Grey [drafted by Fitzmaurice], 31 May 1913, FO195/2452; as received in the FO, it is to be found in FO371/1822.

[37] TNA, min. of Fitzmaurice, 6 June 1913, on Cumberbatch to Lowther, 27 May 1913, FO195/2452.

[38] He was the son of the permanent under-secretary and later famous, among other things, for his writings on diplomacy. He had been given high marks by Fitzmaurice for the standard of colloquial Turkish he had achieved after only six months and with limited opportunities for practice, TNA, Marling to Grey, 7 Aug. 1912, FO371/1509.

[39] Quoted in James Lees-Milne, *Harold Nicolson: A biography, 1886–1929* (Hamish Hamilton: London, 1987), p. 59.

[40] TNA, Lowther to Nicolson, 19 June 1913, FO800/193B. Among the asylum-seekers were Abdul Hamid's fourth wife and small son, for whom, on Lowther's instruc-

There lay the rub. Opposition figures, including army officers, were constantly seeking embassy advice and support in overthrowing the CUP.[41] Aware of the risks and alert to Grey's policy on non-interference though he was, even the military attaché was later duped by an *agent provocateur* into making compromising contacts.[42] Moreover, on 13 June some persons suspected of responsibility for the murder of the grand vizier had been found in a house owned by a British Maltese enjoying capitulary rights.[43] With the ample evidence of Britain's continuing regard for Kiamil Pasha provided by the events of April and May, it was, therefore, not difficult for the CUP and the German Embassy—headed since the spring of 1912 by Baron von Wangenheim, who was hardly less formidable than Baron Marschall—to start a whispering campaign suggesting embassy involvement in the plotting.[44] Nor was it difficult for them to make Fitzmaurice the prime suspect. He might now have been on a leash but his reputation was so deeply imprinted on the mind of the Constantinople political class that no-one believed it.

As Fitzmaurice had told William Tyrrell at the end of the previous year, he had already been the subject of "mountains of fustian prose" written in Constantinople about his "supposed intrigues" against the CUP with the object of returning Kiamil to power.[45] So it is not really surprising that Djemal Bey, who had crossed swords with him again after the 13 June incident,[46] in his memoirs went so far as to allege that Fitzmaurice was "the embodiment of the devil" and "the real mastermind behind Mahmut Şevket Paşa's assassination".[47]

---

tions, in April Fitzmaurice had arranged with the government a house and an end to harassment, TNA, Lowther to Grey, 22 Apr. 1913, FO195/2452.

[41] TNA, Tyrrell to Lowther, 27 Apr. 1912. Over a year earlier Colonel Tyrrell had been sounded out on the idea of a *coup d'état* by one of the Saviour Officers—and been commended by Grey for throwing cold water on it. "[O]ur attitude cannot be other than that of a spectator", minuted Henry Norman of Eastern Department. See folios 552–5, FO371/1486.

[42] Graves, *Briton and Turk*, p. 178.

[43] TNA, Lowther to Grey, 13 June 1913 [draft by Fitzmaurice], FO195/2451; [received in FO] FO371/1826; and Lowther to Grey, 17 June 1913, FO371/1826.

[44] Graves, *Briton and Turk*, p. 178.

[45] TNA, Fitzmaurice to Tyrrell, 18 Dec. 1912, FO800/80.

[46] Djemal had been unrepentant when Fitzmaurice was sent by Lowther to take issue with him over the violation of domicile at the house of the British Maltese subject on 13 June, TNA, Lowther to Grey, 17 June 1913, FO371/1826.

[47] Quoted in Ahmad, "Great Britain's relations with the Young Turks, 1908–1914", p. 313. It is interesting that, as Ahmad notes, this line was omitted from the English translation of this book (*Memories of a Turkish Statesman, 1913–1919*), no doubt for excellent legal reasons. It is also instructive that although Ahmad gave an uncritical airing to Djemal's allegation in his 1966 article cited at the beginning of this note, there is no

This allegation is still apparently believed by some in Turkey today, though there is not a shred of evidence to support it, and it is in any case inherently implausible. Quite apart from the official leash now holding Fitzmaurice back, the Generalissimo had been thought by both the Foreign Office and the embassy to be a moderating influence on the extremists in the CUP. Lowther, who had found him straightforward and easy to deal with, told Nicolson shortly after the assassination that he was "the best we could hope for under the circumstances".[48]

Loss of a patron

Already in April 1913 Grey had decided that Lowther would have to be recalled from Constantinople, in the middle of May it was public knowledge, and in early July—five years after his first arrival—he left Constantinople for good.[49] The Foreign Office believed him to be "too much identified with the anti-Committee parties",[50] and indifferent health had not improved his temper. Despite his flying start in the pro-British atmosphere following the Young Turks' revolution in July 1908, he had allowed the German Embassy to recover its position. In short, like O'Conor, he was also seen as a failure.[51]

After a dinner at the embassy during a visit to Constantinople following the January coup, Aubrey Herbert had written of Fitzmaurice in his diary that "He cannot be loyal to any chief. He hates Lowther alive now, I believe, as much as he hates O'Connor[sic] dead".[52] If this was true it might be imagined that Fitzmaurice would have welcomed Lowther's recall as much as he had cheered the passing of his predecessor. The evidence on this point is not clear but it seems unlikely; he certainly did not agitate for it. Herbert was not exactly objective about

mention of it at all in his monograph published a few years later and now the standard work on the Young Turks in this period, *The Young Turks*, pp. 129–30.

[48] TNA, Lowther to Nicolson, 19 June 1913, FO800/193B. See also TNA, AR 1909, 31 Jan. 1910, p. 8, FO195/2363, where Lowther, while admitting that Shevket Pasha was at that time being easily manipulated by the younger CUP officers, nevertheless described his personality and character, and the manner in which he had implemented martial law, in sympathetic terms.

[49] TNA, Grey to Nicolson, 12 Apr. 1913, FO800/365; *The Times*, 15 May 1913. He retired formally very shortly afterwards and died on 5 April 1916, aged only 58.

[50] TNA, min. of Crowe for Grey, Sept. 1913, FO371/1845.

[51] Heller, *British Policy towards the Ottoman Empire, 1908–1914*, p. 101.

[52] SCA, The Diaries of Aubrey Herbert, 22 Feb. 1913, DD/HER/70/2.

Fitzmaurice,[53] while Lowther had invariably respected his advice and stood by him when he was attacked. For his part, in the freedom of his private letters to George Lloyd Fitzmaurice had not uttered a single word of criticism against Lowther once he had become ambassador. Of course, he is likely to have grown weary and resentful at the amount of time Lowther had been spending taking 'cures' in Marienbad, and also to have been aware that a chief in whom the Foreign Office had lost confidence was a liability to the embassy. In any event, the issue now was: who would replace him?

Fitzmaurice lost little time in writing to Tyrrell on the subject, taking it upon himself to give voice to the embassy's own opinion:

> Lowther's resignation came on us suddenly and we are naturally specu-
> lating as to his successor unless the Cons'ple Embassy is to be reduced
> to a legation! As long as the new Ambassador does not come from Sofia
> [Bax-Ironside] or Lisbon [Sir Arthur Hardinge], we don't mind whether
> our fate comes from Madrid [Maurice de Bunsen] or Tehran [Sir Walter
> Townley]. There are slight rumours that Sir A. Nicolson may come. It
> is almost too good to be true. As he knows first hand the Armenian and
> Asia Minor problems which are coming up for solution, he would be
> ideal....

He added that Kitchener was also being mentioned but poured cold water on the idea on familiar grounds: "He would be wanting to play a role—a fatal thing to try among our Bosphorous currents."[54]

What had not occurred to Fitzmaurice was that none of these candidates would be chosen. Instead, Grey surprised many people besides the chief dragoman by turning to the man who for the last five years had been the superintending assistant under-secretary of the Eastern Department. This was Sir Louis Mallet, and he was to prove Fitzmaurice's nemesis. However, he did not arrive until late October and in the meantime the embassy was left in the capable hands of Charles Marling.[55]

---

[53] During the same visit he wrote sweepingly to his brother that: "FitzMaurice loathes Turkey and after that England. He is the Irish Catholic of the really bitter Dillon-Lynch type, cunning as a weasel and as savage", FitzHerbert, *The Man Who Was Greenmantle*, p. 115.

[54] TNA, Fitzmaurice to Tyrrell, 3 June 1913, FO800/80.

[55] "Hospitable and kindly under a gruff manner, outstandingly able, Marling had courage, a dry, sometimes cynical humour, and wit as well; a temper that did not suffer fools gladly, an honest mind, and a charming wife", Graves, *Briton and Turk*, p. 158. Andrew Ryan said of Marling that "He had at times a biting and sarcastic tongue.

Armenia again

As foreshadowed on the day that Kiamil had landed at Constantinople, the Treaty of London had been signed at the end of May and Turkish humiliation in Europe was more or less complete. However, even before this the Balkan allies had started to fall out among themselves over the sharing of the territorial booty, and at the end of June 1913 the second Balkan War commenced with a vengeance. Exploiting this situation, the Turks regained Adrianople in late July. Once more Fitzmaurice was little more than a spectator to all this but perhaps it was just as well. This is because he was still regarded as the embassy's expert on the 'Armenian Question' and this was once more coming to the fore.

Ever since the Adana massacres in 1909, even pro-CUP Armenians had given up hope that the new regime would be any improvement on its Hamidian predecessor. Moreover, endorsement of the collapse of Turkish rule in Europe by the great powers had given the Armenians fresh hope that they, too, might win support for greater autonomy. Fears of the behaviour of returning Turkish troops—fed on accounts of Christian atrocities against Moslems—and of Kurds granted licence by the weakening of central authority, made the need for this seem more urgent than ever. Reports coming into the embassy from consular posts in eastern Anatolia in late 1912 and the first half of 1913 had documented dreadful incidents and a general rise in tension in the area.

Under pressure from the Armenians and no doubt calculating that this was essential if the 'consolidation in Asia' being urged on it was to be successful, at the end of 1912 Kiamil's cabinet had itself seemed seized with the need to introduce administrative reforms in eastern Anatolia. The idea eventually agreed was to divide the six *vilayets* into two groups and place each under the supervision of a commission composed of two Moslems, two Armenians, and three foreigners.[56] The president of each commission would be one of the foreigners and, according to Fitzmaurice, the minister of foreign affairs wished him to be the one for the commission that would run the *vilayets* of Erzeroum, Van and Bitlis. This had great appeal to him. As he told Tyrrell:

I never suffered from it, but it harmed him in his career", *The Last of the Dragomans*, p. 70.

[56] A full account of the situation at the time and of the details of this proposal (almost certainly drafted by Fitzmaurice) is provided in TNA, Lowther to Grey, 31 Dec. 1912, FO371/1773.

If the scheme matures and is *real* I shouldn't mind licking those Kurdish chiefs into order. I sh[oul]d do it in 15 months unless assassinated by them. Drat them! I know their kidney.[57]

The Committee coup of 23 January was naturally the end of the prospect of a new career for Fitzmaurice as a pro-consul in Armenia. However, he remained much interested in the region's problems. He intervened to secure an amnesty for the small number of Armenians who had deserted from the army during the recent fighting.[58] More significantly, it appears to have been he who was responsible for seeing that a large number of the consular reports arriving at the embassy that described attacks on Armenians were forwarded in full to the Foreign Office. By this means the embassy not only made available to it detailed information on an item likely to be moving up the European agenda but made the greatest possible impact on opinion in the Eastern Department, which for some years now had refused to take up the Armenian question with the Turks.[59] On one such report that arrived in early March Marling had written a rather perfunctory note but Fitzmaurice said:

> Now that the international phase of the Balcan settlement seems to be approaching, and the matter of the 61st Art. of the Treaty of Berlin may be forced on the attention of the "Réunion des Ambassadeurs", might it not be well to forward such despatches in extenso?

"Let it go", instructed Lowther, adding "Are there others awaiting?"[60]

Certainly some and probably most of the covering despatches on similar reports sent by Lowther to the Foreign Office over the following months were drafted by Fitzmaurice.[61] By this time, though, the embassy was pushing at an open door and Lowther was instructed to make protests at the Porte about the mounting disorder in the 'Kurdo-Armenian' provinces. An important reason for this, however, was that at least since January the Foreign Office had been alarmed by the

---

[57] TNA, Fitzmaurice to Tyrrell, 6 Jan. 1913, FO800/80.

[58] Using the argument that "while thousands of Moslems, Jews, Greeks etc had evaded military service, some 10,000 Armenian soldiers had shown great bravery" and taken "relatively very heavy" casualties, TNA, min. of Fitzmaurice, 25 Apr. 1913, on Fontana (Aleppo) to Lowther, 12 Apr. 1913, FO195/2450.

[59] Heller, *British Policy towards the Ottoman Empire, 1908–1914*, pp. 82–3.

[60] TNA, min. of Fitzmaurice, 14 Mar. 1913, on Despatch from Erzeroum, 1 Mar. 1913, folio 149, FO195/2449; also Lowther to Grey, 14 Mar. 1913, FO371/1800.

[61] See especially drafts in TNA, FO195/2449.

mounting risk that the Armenians would seek their salvation under the protective wing of a Russian mandate on the model of Austria's earlier role in Bosnia and Herzegovina. This inaugurated a debate in which Fitzmaurice found himself on the opposite side to Mallet.

Fitzmaurice, as we have seen, had long been a firm believer in the Anglo-Russian entente. By the spring of 1913 he thought this more valuable than ever, chiefly because of the growth of the influence at Constantinople and economic penetration in the Ottoman Empire of Germany, with whom he now believed war to be inevitable.[62] With Britain dropping to the position of "a second class Power" in Turkey, the extension of Russian influence into the six *vilayets* was to be welcomed.[63] In any case, he claimed, the Armenians in the Caucasus were now enjoying security and prosperity, which suggested that the Russians would also bring better conditions to their cousins in Turkey.[64] In short, a Russian mandate in eastern Anatolia served the cause of Armenian humanity as well as the European balance of power, and was "the only really radical solution" to the Armenian question.[65] As for the fear—encouraged by Germany—that it would provoke a scramble by the other powers that would result in the final disintegration of the Ottoman Empire, this was based on three misconceptions. The first was that eastern Anatolia was not already a Russian sphere of influence when in fact it was. The second was that the Armenians would be readily absorbed into Russia when in fact a secure and prosperous Armenian population would be resistant to this; here the case of Bulgaria was instructive. And the third misconception was that the granting of semi-autonomy to a remote province would be the thin end of the wedge of imperial disintegration, when in fact the opposite was more likely to be the case since it would defuse rebellion and reduce the drain on central government expenditure; here what was salutary was the recent history of the Yemen.[66]

---

[62] Bullard, *The Camels Must Go*, pp. 63–4.

[63] TNA, Fitzmaurice to Tyrrell, 8 May 1913, FO800/80.

[64] TNA, Lowther to Grey, 31 Dec. 1912, FO371/1773. The German Ambassador believed that the new Russian policy to "pamper" the Armenians was cynically designed to make them a willing "instrument of agitation" against the day of the liquidation of Turkey in Asia, Wangenheim to Bethman-Hollweg, 24 Feb. 1913, *GDD*, pp. 194–5. Fitzmaurice would not have disagreed.

[65] TNA, Fitzmaurice to Tyrrell, 8 May 1913, FO800/80.

[66] TNA, Fitzmaurice [Memorandum on Armenian Reform] to Marling, 10 Aug. 1913, FO371/1815. This was included in Marling to Grey, 27 Aug. 1913, FO371/1815, and reproduced in full in *BD*, 10 (1).

Of course, the sub-text of Fitzmaurice's insistence that facts must be faced was his view that the division of the rest of Asiatic Turkey into spheres of influence might as well be accepted: Mesopotamia for Britain, Syria for France, Adana and western Asia Minor for Germany. As Heller has pointed out, this was obviously implicit in the suggestion made by Lowther in early June that foreign advisers to assist in reform should be allocated on this basis.[67] It was also explicit in an article published by the social Darwinist, Sir Harry Johnston, in March, which much impressed Fitzmaurice.[68] Clearly, Fitzmaurice—like Johnston—thought the Ottoman Empire was doomed and that the trick was to manage the process.

The alternative position to this, of which the chief advocate in the Foreign Office was Sir Louis Mallet, was the traditional view that the Ottoman Empire *could* survive in Asia and that it was in Britain's interests that it *should*. If the Empire imploded as a result of a scramble for spheres of influence, the British position both in the Mediterranean and India would be imperilled—and a European war would be more or less inevitable.[69] Mallet, while a supporter of the entente with Russia,[70] also felt that the Russian Foreign Minister, Sergei Sazonov, might be sincere about promoting reform in the six *vilayets* but that the Russian military and local authorities were not. Indeed, he thought that they would be glad to see disorder continue in order to provide a pretext for intervention.[71] This also aligned him with the German position.[72]

The clash between these two points of view came fully to the surface in the debate provoked in late April when the Turkish government made a request for officials and gendarmes exclusively from Britain to assist with the administrative reform of the Armenian-populated *vilayets*.[73] Mallet and the Eastern Department thought that this presented a great opportunity and urged full and immediate compliance. Maxwell was

---

[67] TNA, Lowther to Grey, 6 June 1913, FO371/1814; and Heller, *British Policy towards the Ottoman Empire, 1908–1914*, p. 86.

[68] TNA, Fitzmaurice to Tyrrell, 8 May 1913, FO800/80. Though the details of Johnston's proposal were different: "The final solution of the Eastern question", *The Nineteenth Century and After*, 73 (433), Mar. 1913.

[69] Heller, *British Policy towards the Ottoman Empire, 1908–1914*, p. 87; and TNA, min. of Mallet on O'Beirne to Grey, 11 June 1913, FO371/1814.

[70] K. Neilson, *Britain and the Last Tsar: British Policy and Russia, 1894–1917* (Clarendon Press: Oxford, 1995), pp. 31–2.

[71] TNA, min. of Mallet, Buchanan to Grey, 1 July 1913, FO371/1814.

[72] TNA, min. of Mallet, Goschen to Grey, 2 July 1913, FO371/1814.

[73] Heller, *British Policy towards the Ottoman Empire, 1908–1914*, pp. 84–5.

alone in flagging the need to consider Russian interests but even he suggested merely that they should be informed as a matter of courtesy.[74] However, the pro-Russian permanent under-secretary, Sir Arthur Nicolson, emerged as a powerful ally of Fitzmaurice. He agreed with Mallet on the importance of maintaining the traditional policy towards Turkey but shared the chief dragoman's pessimism about the future of its empire as well as his belief in the need to nurture the Anglo-Russian entente. He also thought that Russian annexation of the six *vilayets* was in any case "but a question of time".[75]

Nicolson persuaded Grey to his point of view,[76] and as a result Britain adopted a more cautious response to the Turkish request: provision of advisers should be shared with the other powers, and particular care should be taken to carry Russia along.[77] When Russia strongly opposed the Turkish plan, and the embassy argued that it was merely a German-inspired ruse to create friction between St. Petersburg and London, the Foreign Office resolved to find a compromise. This was, after all, a period of *rapprochement* between the British and German governments, however shallow its foundations. No advisers should begin work until all (including Turkey) were agreed on a project of Armenian reform. Russia should be permitted to take the lead in discussion of this, which should be conducted between the ambassadors of the powers in Constantinople.[78]

At the insistence of the Russians and with the ready acquiescence of the embassy, in the middle of June the Triple Entente ambassadors in Constantinople secretly conferred on a joint proposal based on the scheme first put forward in 1895.[79] They then instructed Fitzmaurice and his "great friend"[80] the Russian Chief Dragoman, André Mandelstam, together with the second secretary at the French Embassy, the Comte de Saint-Quentin, to draw up a detailed draft.[81] When

---

[74] TNA, mins. on Turkish Emb. to FO, 24 Apr. 1913, FO371/1814.

[75] TNA, min. on Lowther to Grey, 31 Dec. 1912, FO371/1773.

[76] In public, Grey supported Mallet's position; in private, that of Fitzmaurice: Heller, *British Policy towards the Ottoman Empire, 1908–1914*, pp. 88–9.

[77] Heller, *British Policy towards the Ottoman Empire, 1908–1914*, pp. 85–7.

[78] TNA, Grey to Benckendorff, 18 June 1913; min. of Mallet, Marling to Grey, 2 July 1913; and Grey to Marling, 4 July, FO371/1814.

[79] TNA, Lowther to Grey, 18 June 1913, FO371/1814.

[80] The description provided by Hakki Pasha, leader of the Turkish delegation in London, in conversation with Mallet: TNA, min. of Mallet on Marling to Grey, 1 July 1913, FO371/1773.

[81] TNA, Lowther to Grey, 17 June 1913, FO371/1814.

completed this was presented as the 'Russian proposal', and became the basis of discussion of Armenian reform by all six ambassadors, or, to be more precise, by the sub-commission of their secretaries and dragomans.[82] This had eight meetings between 3 and 24 July and, though the second Balkan War was now raging, became Fitzmaurice's major preoccupation.

The essence of the Russian proposal was that the six *vilayets* should be treated as one province under a governor-general, for preference a European (understood to be a Russian)[83] nominated by the sultan with the assent of the powers.[84] This was supported by Fitzmaurice and Saint-Quentin. The Turks had countered with a variant of the scheme they had proposed in the previous December. This dealt with eastern Anatolia only as part of a scheme for all of the Asiatic provinces. The six *vilayets* would be divided into two sectors, each to have a European inspector-general appointed by Turkey and enjoying only limited powers.[85] These ideas were known to be anathema to the Armenians but were supported by the German, Austrian and Italian dragomans.

Unfortunately for Fitzmaurice, on 20 July, following six meetings of the sub-commission on Armenian reform but with no agreement yet reached, Adrianople was re-taken by the Turks. The boost to their pride consequent upon this naturally made them even less likely than before to admit the key principle of European executive control in eastern Anatolia. With the Triple Alliance ambassadors thus stiffened in their opposition to the 'Russian proposal', the difficulties of securing agreement in the sub-commission were magnified. This was the background against which, on 10 August, Fitzmaurice submitted to Marling a closely typed report on its proceedings covering 17 foolscap pages.[86]

Fitzmaurice's report was impressive in its command of the history of previous attempts at reform and the broad compass of the examples on which it drew—in the Balkans and Arabia—to support its conclusions.

---

[82] TNA, Lowther to Grey, 30 June 1913, FO371/1814. The 'Triple Alliance' representatives on the sub-commission were Panfili (Austria), Chabert (Italy), and Schoenberg (Germany).

[83] Min. of Mallet on Buchanan to Grey, 2 July 1913, *BD*, 10 (1), p. 472.

[84] TNA, Lowther to Grey, 17 June 1913, FO371/1814, in which the proposal was included in full.

[85] TNA, Marling to Grey, 2 and 3 July 1913, FO371/1814.

[86] TNA, Fitzmaurice [Memorandum on Armenian Reform] to Marling, 10 Aug. 1913, FO371/1815. This was included in Marling to Grey, 27 Aug. 1913, FO371/1815, and reproduced in full in *BD*, 10 (1).

However, it was weakened by the lame observation that a "special Russian preserve" in eastern Anatolia would only lead to partition of the Ottoman Empire if "some other power has territorial designs on Asiatic territory"—which, of course, it did. Fitzmaurice's memorandum also revealed how thoroughly dispirited he was. At the end he hazarded the suggestion that a compromise—two provinces but run by governors-general—was theoretically conceivable but obviously he did not think it practical diplomacy.[87] His real conclusion was that if Britain was unwilling to bring pressure to bear on Turkey "to apply a radical remedy to the Armenian question", then it should wash its hands of the matter altogether. "Half measures and palliatives" were likely to do more harm than good, and in the case of the particular idea that a few foreign gendarmerie officers should be sent to the region, this was a waste of time. The only real deterrent to massacres was the fear of Russian intervention. Marling, praising in his covering despatch the "great ability and perspicacity" with which Fitzmaurice had analysed the matter, agreed.[88]

In the Foreign Office, Sir Eyre Crowe, who, following the appointment of Mallet to Constantinople had been given oversight of the Eastern as well as the Western Department, was also unstinting in his praise for Fitzmaurice's memorandum. This was of significance because Crowe, who in work habits, apprehension of German ambitions, and certain other respects resembled Fitzmaurice, was highly influential in the Foreign Office and marked out as the next permanent under-secretary.[89] It was "an admirable paper", he said, "and brings out in strong relief the principal points on which the whole controversy hangs". He thought he should be "warmly thanked for his thoughtful and effective presentation of a very complicated problem". Clutching at the possibility of the compromise Fitzmaurice had floated, Crowe advised that the question should now be taken up directly between London and Berlin instead of in "the rather unwholesome atmosphere of Constantinople".

---

[87] He returned to this in a postscript written four days later, having learned that the German Embassy—in response to Armenian pressure—was now supporting a compromise along these lines. Fitzmaurice thought this promising but added that, should the Turks be allowed to get away with the re-occupation of Adrianople, it would be a dead letter.

[88] TNA, Marling to Grey, 27 Aug. 1913, FO371/1815.

[89] Sibyl Crowe and Edward Corp, *Our Ablest Public Servant: Sir Eyre Crowe, 1864–1925* (Merlin: Braunton, Devon, 1993), chs. 6 and 12; Steiner, *The Foreign Office and Foreign Policy, 1898–1914*, pp. 108–18.

Nicolson agreed with his comments on Fitzmaurice, but observed that since it had now been learned that direct talks were proceeding between the German and Russian ambassadors in Constantinople, it would be advisable to await their outcome.[90]

Fitzmaurice's formal role in the negotiations on Armenian reform had come to an end with the last meeting of the sub-commission on 24 July, though no doubt he continued to lobby for the Russian proposal. In the event, the Russian and German Embassies actually agreed a somewhat diluted version of it in late September. This was heartily supported by Grey, and the Russian Embassy took the lead in trying to get the Turks to accept it. However, as Fitzmaurice had anticipated, the failure of the powers to force them out of Adrianople and a mood of mounting resentment at foreign interference combined to make them resistant. His last recorded intervention in the affair was in early October and was designed to sabotage a Turkish suggestion that two British inspectors-general should be employed in the (bisected) six *vilayets*—and if necessary one over all of them. The posts were offered to Robert Graves and Sir Richard Crawford, both at the time advisers to the Turkish Ministry of Finance. The Foreign Office and embassy both believed that this was a mischievous proposal aimed at sowing distrust between Britain and Russia. Accordingly, Fitzmaurice joined with Marling in urging Graves and Crawford to decline their invitations, which they did.[91]

A much diluted formula was finally agreed in early February 1914, by which time—as it happened—Fitzmaurice's career in Constantinople was as dead as any hope for Armenian reform.

Did he fall or was he pushed?

In the interlude between the departure of Lowther at the beginning of July 1913 and the arrival of Mallet in late October, embracing as it did the outbreak of the second Balkan War and the start of intensive deliberations on Armenian reform, Fitzmaurice and Marling were

---

[90] TNA, mins. (September) on Marling to Grey, 27 Aug. 1913, FO371/1815. Grey's thanks were sent to Fitzmaurice via Marling on 2 October, *BD*, 10 (1), n. 28, p. 516.

[91] Graves, *Storm Centres of the Near East*, pp. 287–8. See also mins. of Crowe, Nicolson and Grey on Marling to Grey, 7 Oct. 1913; and Grey to Marling, 14 Oct. 1913, *BD*, 10 (1), pp. 519–20.

placed under intense pressure. The rest of the diplomatic staff were either lacking in experience of Turkey, or absent—or both.

The head of chancery, George Kidston, had only been in Constantinople for a year, while Esmond Ovey had been in post for an even shorter time. As for the third secretaries, Harold Nicolson seems to have been much preoccupied with his love affairs (not excluding the one with his wife) and in any case had just been granted two months' leave—he left Constantinople on 25 June; Edward Keeling had been required in the Foreign Office since early April and did not return until 7 September; while the young Lord Gerald Wellesley, the third son of the fourth Duke of Wellington, had been in Turkey only since the previous November, clearly had no calling to the Diplomatic Service, and after the war resigned in favour of architecture. In the dragomanate, the archivist, W. E. Fuller, had gone on leave at the same time as Nicolson. The only consolation on the staffing front was that the promising third dragoman, Reader Bullard, had returned from leave in April. But this was a small consolation because, like Wellesley, he was still well short of thirty years old and—in the nature of his post—had enjoyed no serious political work. Furthermore, there was no military attaché in the embassy.[92]

It is hardly surprising, therefore, that just two weeks after he had taken over from Lowther, Marling should have told Nicolson privately that he was "overwhelmed with work", and opened his next letter with the same lament.[93] As for Fitzmaurice, he had not only to cope with Armenian reform on top of his usual duties but also the complicated and sensitive question of the effects of the constantly shifting frontiers of the Ottoman Empire on the staffing requirements of the Levant Service.[94] Then the Aden frontier question raised its ugly head again.

---

[92] Colonel Reed, who had been added to the strength to enable the embassy to cope with the work generated by the first Balkan War, was permitted to return home when his mother died suddenly in early June. Tyrrell, who had been unwell and had had no leave for some time, had—on Lowther's recommendation—been granted four months' leave and left on 25 June. After a brief final spell at the embassy in the early winter he finally left on 9 December, though by this time his replacement was already in post, TNA, FO371/1821 and 1848.

[93] TNA, Marling to Nicolson, 19 July 1913, FO800/368; 1 Aug. 1913, FO800/369.

[94] Some posts had changed in importance and needed re-grading, while in a large number Slavonic or Arabic was now needed more than Turkish, TNA, Lowther to Grey, 24 June, and Mallet to Grey, 20 Dec. 1913 [Drafts by Fitzmaurice], FO195/2451.

As part of the long process of trying generally to tidy up with Hakki Pasha as many issues in Anglo-Turkish relations as possible, the unratified Aden frontier protocols appeared on the agenda in August 1913. A bad memory for Fitzmaurice was therefore revived when in November the Eastern Department asked him to advise on its proposal that the protocols of 1903 and 1904, as well as those of 1905, should be ratified. He endorsed this but it probably struck him as the final insult to his achievement on the Yemen frontier when it emerged that the originals of the documents that it had cost him so much to produce had been lost. India said that they had gone either to Constantinople or London but the Foreign Office Library could not find them; nor could the embassy. "Extraordinary!", exclaimed Grey. When instructed to ask the Porte whether it happened to have copies, a humiliated Fitzmaurice received the sort of reply that he anticipated: they could be in the Yemen, or may have been destroyed at Yildiz during the counter-revolution in April 1909. Fitzmaurice himself said that they had been sent to the Aden Resident. At least this was a revenge of sorts on his old enemy of the Yemen frontier, General Maitland.[95]

It is unfortunate that we lack the insight into Fitzmaurice's state of mind at this juncture that would have been provided by private letters. His most recent one to George Lloyd—in which there was a hint of coolness—had been written in November 1912 and, though he wrote one to Tyrrell in October 1913, it was brief and unrevealing.[96] It is, nevertheless, reasonable to infer that his spirits were low. He was in poor health again and had not had a day's leave for nearly two years. He remained bitter about his lack of recognition[97] and—if not at this point then not long after—bitter about his pay, complaining that he received less than the consuls-general in Salonica and Beirout.[98] Furthermore, in the second Balkan War the Balkan League, which he had anointed as the seventh great power, had disintegrated; his cherished Bulgarians

---

[95] The papers on the sorry business of the lost originals are located in TNA, FO195/2456 and FO371/1805 and 2110. The original draft by Fitzmaurice of Mallet's despatch to Grey of 21 Jan. 1914 (FO371/2110) is located in the embassy's records held in FO195/2456, folios 508–9.

[96] TNA, Fitzmaurice to Tyrrell, 4 Oct. 1913, FO800/80.

[97] TNA, Fitzmaurice to Tyrrell, 6 Jan. 1913, FO800/80.

[98] TNA, min. of Tilley, 21 Aug. 1914; George Clerk sympathised, saying that "The Chief Dragoman is in many ways the most important officer in the Levant Service", min., 24 Aug. 1914. His salary was eventually increased but he was not informed of this until September 1914, min. of Tilley, 2 Sept. 1914, FO371/2136. See also *FO List 1915*, p. 51.

had been routed;[99] and Adrianople had been regained by an Ottoman Empire whose eclipse he had claimed to be imminent. All the discussion of Armenian reform had failed to produce the radical measures he believed essential. The Germans had regained their ascendancy in Turkey—a point highlighted for the world to see by the appointment in October 1913 of the German general, Otto Liman von Sanders, with unprecedented powers to overhaul the Turkish military machine.[100] Worst of all, the CUP was more firmly in power than ever—and more determined than ever to get rid of him. It was also pushing at a door that was beginning to widen in London.

On returning to Turkey after the *coup d'état* in January and quickly making contact with the CUP leaders, Aubrey Herbert had confided to his diary: "Feeling growing stronger against Fitz M."[101] Two days later he had a heated argument with Fitzmaurice's friend, Philip Graves, *The Times* correspondent in Constantinople, who was also a thorn in the side of the regime:[102] "He said Committee had been trying to get rid of him and Fitzmaurice, and that I ought not to visit them. I said Fitzmaurice and he had been trying to get rid of the C[ommittee], it was only tit for tat."[103] To Mark Sykes he wrote: "Fitz will catch a cold whispering behind doors and die the death."[104] Then, following the Committee's fear of a *contre coup* at the end of May and the murder of Mahmud Shevket Pasha only days later, there had been the start of the whispering campaign that Fitzmaurice was behind it all.

In the middle of August, Alwyn Parker, the Foreign Office's expert on the Baghdad Railway and the assistant head of the Eastern Department responsible for the important negotiations in London with Hakki Pasha, took a particularly dim view of a telegram from Marling reflecting the

---

[99] All that he could salvage from this was the claim that the Bulgarians' willingness to settle quickly afterwards was further evidence of their "practical" character, TNA, Marling to Grey, 2 Oct. 1913 [Drafted by Fitzmaurice], FO195/2454.

[100] For a recent account of the British role in defusing the crisis that this provoked, see William Mulligan, "'We Can't be more Russian than the Russians': British policy during the Liman von Sanders crisis", *Diplomacy & Statecraft*, 17 (2), June 2006.

[101] SCA, The Diaries of Aubrey Herbert, 22 Feb. 1913, DD/HER/70/2.

[102] Writing to the permanent under-secretary a year later, Sir Louis Mallet observed: "I trust they will not arrest Graves who irritates them to madness by making the most of their follies and never patting them on the back when they do well", TNA, Mallet to Nicolson, 17 Feb. 1914, FO800/372.

[103] SCA, The Diaries of Aubrey Herbert, 24 Feb. 1913, DD/HER/70/2.

[104] FitzHerbert, *The Man Who Was Greenmantle*, p. 114.

views of Fitzmaurice and urging strong pressure to prise the Turks out of Adrianople. "I think the Embassy at Constantinople are totally out of touch with the Turkish Government", he remarked.[105] Charles Hardinge, by now Lord Hardinge of Penshurst and Viceroy of India, agreed, and told him that, had he remained at the Foreign Office, he would have brought Lowther home earlier, adding that "[f]rom what I hear the whole staff ought to be changed, as they are known to have an anti-Turkish bias, which they do not attempt to conceal".[106] The Eastern Department was not prepared to go quite this far but it is clear that, as far as Fitzmaurice was concerned, the writing was on the wall.

Hakki Pasha, the CUP's real representative in London, whose negotiations seemed to be heading for a successful conclusion, had been repeatedly urging Fitzmaurice's recall on Parker—and probably on anyone else who would listen.[107] It would be astonishing if the Germans had not been doing the same, for Wangenheim had no doubt that it was only Fitzmaurice who was standing in the way of a more supportive British attitude to German ambitions in Turkey. Lowther, he had told Berlin in April, was unwell and in consequence weak:

> He is not strong enough to free himself from the influence of his First Dragoman. As long as Fitzmaurice continues his career here it will be vain even to try for a rapprochement with England.[108]

A decision seems, therefore, to have been made in principle that Fitzmaurice would have to be moved from the embassy. However, this was to be delayed until he had helped Mallet to settle in and also, presumably, until a post on an equivalent salary could be found for him. This was the background against which Sir Louis Mallet arrived as the new ambassador on 24 October. He was brought as far as the Dardanelles on the warship, HMS *Black Prince*, a break with recent custom designed to impress and flatter the Turks and thereby underline the strength of the British desire to improve relations.[109] It was perhaps also designed to flatter Mallet, who had hoped to become permanent under-secretary but whose star had dimmed while Crowe's

---

[105] Mallet was also disparaging about this message, TNA, mins. on Marling to Grey, 15 Aug. 1913, FO371/1837.
[106] Quoted in Heller, *British Policy towards the Ottoman Empire, 1908–1914*, p. 101.
[107] TNA, private min. of Crowe to Nicolson, 26 Sept. 1913, FO371/1845.
[108] Wangenheim to Bethman-Hollweg, 24 Apr. 1913, *GDD*, pp. 240–1.
[109] TNA, min. of Crowe for Grey, Sept. 1913, FO371/1845.

had brightened; for Sir Louis, the Constantinople embassy was very much a 'second prize'.[110]

Mallet's arrival is unlikely to have lifted Fitzmaurice's spirits. He was clever and had a strong intellectual grasp of the problems he would confront, having been intimately involved in the wide-ranging negotiations with Hakki Pasha in London.[111] Grey at least also appears to have believed that his lack of experience of Constantinople meant that he had no prejudices about Turkey. However, he had hardly any diplomatic experience of any kind. According to Philip Graves, he was also effeminate, which was a characteristic unlikely to impress the Turks.[112] He had also taken the hardest line against Russia in the Armenian question and—though an official of established hostility to Germany[113]—shown a distinct sensitivity to Berlin's point of view on this issue. He had applauded the re-taking of Adrianople, and was determined to make a fresh start with the Young Turks.[114] On the face of it, Fitzmaurice did not fit into this plan. However, once Mallet had got to Constantinople things did not at first turn out quite as might have been expected.

By his own admission, Mallet found himself out of his depth in the alien environment of the capital of the Ottoman Empire. "I am the prey of every rumour and sometimes I really feel as if I was living in a totally different world from London", he confessed to Grey.[115] Fitzmaurice, who was a past master at humouring and dissembling his true feelings to his chiefs, represented the best life-belt to hand. Mallet, suffering also a more than usually useless diplomatic staff in the embassy, clutched at him with pathetic relief. On 30 October the novice ambassador was escorted by Fitzmaurice into the presence of the sultan and the grand vizier so that he might present his credentials,[116] and a few days later told Grey and Nicolson that he would write later about his

---

[110] Steiner, *The Foreign Office and Foreign Policy, 1898–1914*, p. 106. See also Crowe and Corp, *Our Ablest Public Servant*, pp. 99–102.

[111] Neilson, *Britain and the Last Tsar*, p. 31; Ahmad, "Great Britain's relations with the Young Turks, 1908–1914", p. 323; TNA, Nicolson to Mallet, 24 Nov. 1913, FO800/371.

[112] Graves, *Briton and Turk*, pp. 180–1.

[113] Steiner, *The Foreign Office and Foreign Policy, 1898–1914*, pp. 104–6.

[114] Heller, *British Policy towards the Ottoman Empire, 1908–1914*, pp. 101–3.

[115] TNA, Mallet to Grey, 2 Dec. 1913, FO800/80. At the end of this month he repeated the need for "a period of acclimatization", Mallet to Nicolson, 31 Dec. 1913, FO800/371.

[116] TNA, Mallet to Grey, 30 Oct. 1913, FO371/1847.

chief dragoman. In the meantime, he found the work "incessant" and Fitzmaurice indispensable. To Nicolson Mallet said that "It is quite clear to me that I can't do without Fitzmaurice who is my right hand. No one else knows anything". A few days later he said that he "is unrivalled in his own line and has an extraordinary position here";[117] on Arab questions in particular he could rely on no-one else.[118] To Grey, Mallet wrote even more enthusiastically about his chief dragoman, developing his theme to its logical conclusion:

> It is becoming every day clearer to me that I shall not be able to do without him. His knowledge is so extensive and his means of getting it so varied that he is indispensable. I do not believe that his presence here will injure any chance of getting into good relations with the Young Turks. On the contrary, it is more likely to help me.... I do not think they will press it [his recall], as he appears to be on excellent terms with all the prominent people.

Grey was thus asked "to defer any decision as to his removal for the present" and to conceal from the Turks—should they press again—that it was Mallet who had asked for him to stay.[119] This was a remarkable turnaround. Mallet was not ruling out that Fitzmaurice might need to be removed at some point but he was coming close to saying that he was indispensable *indefinitely*.

The Foreign Office was quick to appreciate Mallet's situation, the more so after the departure for good first of Marling only three weeks after his arrival[120] and then of his equally experienced military attaché, Colonel Tyrrell, just three weeks after that.[121] "I must say that you have some of the most complicated questions to deal with which I have ever had the pleasure of seeing", Nicolson wrote to him, adding that his wish to retain Fitzmaurice was quite understood and that it would

---

[117] TNA, Mallet to Nicolson, 4 and 16 Nov. 1913, FO800/371.
[118] TNA, min. of Mallet on Grey to Mallet, 6 Jan. 1914, and Mallet to Grey, 25 Jan. 1914 [drafted by Fitzmaurice], FO195/2456.
[119] TNA, Mallet to Grey, 4 Nov. 1913, FO800/80.
[120] TNA, Mallet to Grey, 7 and 19 Nov. 1913, FO371/1848.
[121] The CUP claim that Tyrrell was removed at the instigation of the Turkish government (Djemal Pasha, *Memories of a Turkish Statesman, 1913–1919*, p. 100) is without foundation, though it is possible, of course, that Mallet had flattered them that it had been. In fact, Tyrrell's appointment was scheduled to terminate at the end of 1913, which is why he had been anxious to take his accumulated four months' leave in the summer, TNA, Tyrrell to Lowther, 14 May 1913, FO371/1821. He left Constantinople on 9 December, "on the termination of his appointment", TNA, Mallet to Grey 16 Dec. 1913, FO371/1848.

"receive every possible consideration".[122] Having presumably discussed the matter with his permanent under-secretary, Grey then told the ambassador that "Fitzmaurice shall certainly not be disturbed as long as you wish to keep him".[123]

Nevertheless, it was not long before Mallet was beginning to qualify his initial enthusiasm for Fitzmaurice, whose personality was in any case so different from his own.[124] "I am much obliged to you for allowing me to keep Fitzmaurice", he told Grey on 2 December, "as I find him the most interesting member of the embassy and the most useful though he is certainly too prejudiced against the present régime and has not much constructive ability."[125] A week later, he added in a further letter that "…some people will tell you that Jews run this country—it is Fitzmaurice's idée fixe—but I cannot think it is true and wish it were".[126] In late January he mauled about and toned down a draft written for him by Fitzmaurice on the anti-Christian commercial boycott that was gathering pace in Turkey, striking out, for example, the chief dragoman's ritual reference to the fact that, as might be expected, the "Salonica Jews" were behind it all.[127]

By early December Mallet thought that he was at last beginning to master his post,[128] and it is probable that this made him feel less need for Fitzmaurice. The Porte was flattering him with long-practised expertise,[129] and the Foreign Office followed suit.[130] In early February his new counsellor, Henry Beaumont, arrived. By this time, too, Fitzmaurice's condition—mental and physical—had worsened, and this no doubt reduced his usefulness to the new ambassador.

[122] TNA, Nicolson to Mallet, 10 Nov. 1913, FO800/371.
[123] TNA, Grey to Mallet, 12 Nov. 1913, FO800/80.
[124] Andrew Ryan says merely that Fitzmaurice and Mallet did not prove "congenial to one another", *The Last of the Dragomans*, p. 86.
[125] TNA, Mallet to Grey, 2 Dec. 1913, FO800/80.
[126] TNA, Mallet to Grey, 9 Dec. 1913, FO800/80.
[127] TNA, Mallet to Grey, 27 Jan. 1914 [draft by Fitzmaurice], FO195/2458.
[128] On 2 December 1913 he had already told Grey: "I am gradually becoming more at home but the post is a very difficult one to fill properly unless one has been here for some time", TNA, FO800/80.
[129] As for example in the inspired article of welcome published in the *Tanin* on 1 November, a translation of which Mallet forwarded to the FO under a decidedly smug covering despatch, TNA, Mallet to Grey, 7 Nov. 1913, FO371/1847.
[130] "I fear that you are having an exceedingly difficult time at Constantinople, but we all admire the skill with which you deal with so many delicate questions", TNA, Nicolson to Mallet, 16 Feb. 1914, FO800/372.

The departure of his ally, Marling, had done nothing for Fitzmaurice's workload, and the fact that Mallet showed every sign of being captivated not only by the Young Turks—even his *bête noir*, Djemal Bey[131]—but also by the Germans can have done nothing for his mood. Mallet's line on Turkish procrastination over Armenian reform was that the powers should take what they could get "without resorting to threats";[132] and when they did, he claimed fatuously that the Armenian question was "solved at last".[133] As for the Liman von Sanders mission that so troubled the Russians, Mallet was disposed to minimise its practical significance while arguing logically enough that in effect it served Britain's interest since a revived Turkish Army was essential to the integrity of what was left of the Ottoman Empire.[134] Wangenheim reported that Mallet's "friendship for Germany is becoming more and more apparent",[135] and the British and German Embassies were now on "very friendly terms".[136] All of this must have made Fitzmaurice squirm with discomfort.

Overwork, poor health, disappointments, and the cumulative impact of the pressure on his position, finally began to take their toll. At the end of January 1914 Fitzmaurice began to show signs of severe nervous breakdown and placed himself in the care of the embassy doctor.[137] The Foreign Office, however, which had heard nothing from Mallet about Fitzmaurice since early December, appears to have had no inkling of this. Nor did it seem to have had any plan to recall him in the near

---

[131] TNA, Mallet to Grey, 30 Dec. 1913, FO371/2117. "Sir L. Mallet is evidently much impressed with the character of Jemal Bey", minuted Norman on this despatch, with not a little suggestion of distaste, "and, I gather, rather admires the Committee party in general."

[132] Mallet to Grey, 18 Nov. 1913, *BD*, 10 (1), p. 530.

[133] TNA, Mallet to Nicolson, 10 Feb. 1914, FO800/372. Nicolson had to caution him against over-optimism on this point, TNA, Nicolson to Mallet, 16 Feb. 1914, FO800/372.

[134] The evolution of Mallet's views on this mission can be followed in *BD*, 10 (1), ch. LXXXVII.

[135] Wangenheim to the German Foreign Office, 19 Dec. 1913, *GDD*, p. 214.

[136] Waugh, *Turkey*, p. 141. Close relations with the German Embassy continued almost until the outbreak of war; see Charles Lister, *Letters and Recollections, with a Memoir by His Father Lord Ribblesdale* (Fisher Unwin: London, 1917), chs. 4, 5 and 11.

[137] Dr Hawkins, the London doctor under whose care he was placed on his return to England, reported that "He was suffering from severe nervous breakdown and presented symptoms not only on the cerebral side but also vasomotor symptoms, mainly cardiac and gastric", medical certificate enclosed in TNA, Fitzmaurice to FO, 14 Sept. 1914. All of the correspondence on Fitzmaurice's sick leave, including the embassy doctor's original medical note, are located in FO371/2131.

future either because in a despatch from Grey that was not received by the embassy until 21 February he was asked to revise the protocols and maps of the draft convention on the Aden frontier that had just been initialled.[138]

Two days before this despatch was received, on 19 February, the embassy doctor had advised Fitzmaurice to apply for immediate sick leave, which was no doubt now seen by Mallet as an undisguised blessing. The ambassador, who had been receiving constant complaints from the grand vizier that embassy people had been "too free in their criticisms" of the regime, most recently in the case of the consul-general, Harry Eyres,[139] lost no time in acting. On the following day, 20 February, he cabled the news to the Foreign Office, asking for Fitzmaurice's leave to be sanctioned by telegraph. This was done immediately. On the day after this, the embassy hurriedly wrote privately to George Clerk, who had been a first secretary in Constantinople in 1911 and had just taken over from Maxwell as head of the Eastern Department, about Grey's request concerning Aden. He was advised that in Fitzmaurice's absence there was no-one in the embassy competent to deal with the question and that "after rest in England he may be well enough to deal with it there".[140] On 22 February, nicely confirming that these examinations were none too serious, the already "absent" Fitzmaurice tested George Kidston on his Turkish and found that—employing the usual ambivalent formula—he had achieved "a competent colloquial knowledge of the language for ordinary purposes".[141] It was his last recorded action at the embassy. Four days later, still only 48, and having handed over his charge temporarily to Andrew Ryan once more, he left Constantinople, never to return.

The official line on Fitzmaurice's departure, which was that "a serious and protracted illness" had alone forced him to go, was given out by Grey's parliamentary under-secretary in the House of Commons on 21 October 1915 amid the minor furore created by publication of Pears's allegations about the inadequacy of the embassy staff prior to

---

[138] TNA, Grey to Mallet, 16 Feb. 1914, FO195/2456.

[139] Mallet had been afraid that, regretfully, he would have to sacrifice Eyres to appease the Turks and serve as a warning to the rest of the staff, TNA, Mallet to Nicolson, 14 Jan. 1914, and Nicolson to Mallet, 19 Jan. 1914, FO800/372; see also FO195/2456.

[140] TNA. min. of Beaumont, n.d. but almost certainly 21 Feb. 1913, on Grey to Mallet, 16 Feb. 1913, FO195/2456.

[141] TNA, Fitzmaurice to Mallet, 22 Feb. 1914, FO371/2131.

the outbreak of war with Turkey almost a year earlier.[142] It was repeated in the memoirs of his colleagues in the dragomanate.[143] By contrast, the CUP line, naturally arguing *post hoc, ergo propter hoc*, and probably encouraged by hints from Mallet, was that it was their repeated demands for his recall that had finally got rid of him.[144] The reality, as usual, seems to have been more complicated but only—in this case—slightly more so. The official line was substantially true: Fitzmaurice was perhaps slightly more a victim of a fall than a push but pushing there was, and this certainly helped him on his way.

---

[142] *Parl. Debs.*, 5th Ser. (Commons), vol. LXXIV, cols. 1970–1. The allegations of Pears were contained in his book, *Forty Years in Constantinople*, pp. 344–7. See also Ryan, *The Last of the Dragomans*, pp. 109–10.

[143] Bullard, *The Camels Must Go*, p. 64; Ryan, *The Last of the Dragomans*, pp. 86, 109–10.

[144] Djemal Pasha, *Memories of a Turkish Statesman, 1913–1919*, p. 100.

CHAPTER NINE

POLITICAL WARFARE, 1914–21

Fitzmaurice arrived back in England on 2 March 1914, and appears to have made steady progress in recovering his health. By September his doctor noted that he had shown considerable improvement, though he had only seen him on a few occasions since his return so he may well have been fit enough to resume his duties some time before then.[1] Britain was by now at war with Germany, an eventuality which Fitzmaurice had always predicted. Had he gone back to the embassy he would have found his position immeasurably strengthened; indeed, already something of a legend, he would probably have received a hero's welcome.[2] Why, then, did he not return to Constantinople in September? Why, indeed, had he not returned earlier?

Mallet had gone home in late July, though because of the dangerous political situation his leave was cut short and he was back at his post by the middle of August. According to Sir Edwin Pears, who was well-informed, it was believed in Constantinople that Fitzmaurice had actually recovered by this time and was expected to reappear with the ambassador. When he did not, the gossip was that it was because of an intervention by the Turkish Ambassador in London.[3] Whether this account is accurate or not is still impossible to say but it is highly probable. Marmaduke Pickthall, an outspoken member of the pro-Turkish lobby in London, who was also well-informed, said that "the return of

---

[1] Dr Hawkins's medical certificate of 1 September 1914, enclosed in TNA, Fitzmaurice to Grey, 14 Sept. 1914, FO371/2131. All of the papers bearing on Fitzmaurice's sick leave are located in this document.

[2] "When Turkey came into the War against us", records Earl Winterton, "a cynical friend of mine said that if only ten years earlier we had taken all the other members of the British Embassy away from Constantinople and left only Fitzmaurice there, she would have been on the Allies' side in the War", *Pre-War*, p. 189. Captain Reginald ('Blinker') Hall, shortly to be appointed Director of Naval Intelligence, took a similar view, Adm. Sir William James, *The Eyes of the Navy: A Biographical Study of Admiral Sir Reginald Hall* (Methuen: London, 1955), p. 60.

[3] *Forty Years in Constantinople*, pp. 344–5. Others said it was "representations from Berlin", James, *The Eyes of the Navy*, p. 60.

Mr. Fitzmaurice to the British Embassy at so critical a juncture would have been regarded as no less than a hostile act".[4]

It is true that shortly after Mallet had returned to Constantinople Fitzmaurice made an application for an extension to his sick leave supported by his doctor, who said that he was still unable to stand any severe mental strain and that three months further rest was necessary to ensure "complete" recovery.[5] On 19 September this was granted. It might be imagined, therefore, that this squashes the argument that he was sufficiently better by the summer to have returned to Constantinople, with or without the ambassador. However, doctors usually advise more rest for a complete recovery than any hard-working person is likely to take. Besides, if his return had been blocked it is likely to have made him press for extended leave out of a combination of a deep sense of injustice and sheer bloody-mindedness. Fitzmaurice, who had shown himself quite tenacious in defence of his rights in the days of O'Conor, was already a cauldron bubbling with resentments, not the least over his salary.[6] He had also taken very little leave during his career and his last one, in 1911, had been curtailed by two weeks when he was ordered to Tripoli. This also gave him a very arguable case for postponement until the middle of September of the point at which he would have to go on to half-pay.[7] In short, the application for more sick leave does not prove that Fitzmaurice was any more 'seedy' in the summer of 1914 than he had been periodically over the years; it was not necessarily illness that prevented his return to Constantinople.

On 5 November Britain declared war on Turkey. Three days later, well before his extended leave was up, Fitzmaurice informed the Foreign Office that he was once more fit for duty. How could he resist the call? By siding with the Central Powers the Young Turks may well have acted in their country's best interests, for a policy of neutrality would probably have eventually resulted in what remained of the Ottoman Empire being divided into spheres of influence by a victorious Triple

---

[4] "In Defence of British Diplomacy", *The New Age*, 21 Oct. 1915, p. 590; see also Graves, *Briton and Turk*, p. 188.

[5] See n. 1 above.

[6] TNA, mins. of Tilley [by then Chief Clerk in the FO], 21 Aug. and 2 Sept. 1914, FO371/2136.

[7] TNA, min. of H. L. Sherwood [Chief Clerk's Department], 15 Sept. 1914, FO371/2131.

Entente.[8] But in doing so they had at last revealed the face Fitzmaurice had always insisted they wore in secret—and it was difficult for anyone to claim that it was he who had provoked them because he had not been in Turkey for ten months. He was vindicated on this score as well as in regard to Germany. At last the gloves were off and he could expect to be used by the British government for the work for which he had special talent: intelligence gathering and, above all, covert political manipulation in a hostile environment—political warfare. He was not disappointed, for he was soon attached to the Foreign Office on 'special service'[9] and found his energies directed first towards Turkish Arabia.

"An expert in questions relating to Arabs"

In September 1914 concern was beginning to stir in London and Cairo that Germany would encourage a Turkish attack on Egypt in the event that war should break out between Britain and Turkey. As a result, the Foreign Office had already tentatively begun to consider how this might be foiled by engineering an Arab revolt in the Ottoman Empire while not precipitating an Anglo-Turkish rupture by moving prematurely. Following a recommendation by Andrew Ryan, who described Fitzmaurice as "an expert in questions relating to Arabs",[10] in early October—though he was still supposed to be on sick leave—his observations on this question had already been invited by the Foreign Office. It was not the first time he had been asked to comment on it.

In early 1913, following a request from the War Office for advice on the possibility that the threat to Egypt from Turkey had been reduced by the latter's reverses in the Balkan War, Fitzmaurice had cautioned against complacency. Chauvinistically-inspired military adventures, encouraged by German officers, might be undertaken in the direction of the Egyptian frontier by any CUP government that lacked the restraint of an effective internal opposition, he said, even in the absence of war between Britain and Turkey. He had also indicated that the energy of such adventures might be dissipated if the Turks had to cope with the

---

[8] I am grateful to Dr Keith Hamilton for this point; Machiavelli would have agreed.

[9] TNA, min. of Sherwood, 16 Nov. 1914, FO371/2131.

[10] TNA, Memorandum [by Ryan], encl. with Mallet to Grey, 22 Sept. 1914, FO371/2140.

serious unrest in the Ottoman Arab world that they would be likely to provoke.[11] With Britain already at war with Germany and assuming war with Turkey as well, Fitzmaurice now threw all of his weight behind the idea that this should be deliberately stirred up:

> Up to the recapture by the Young Turks of Adrianople in July, 1913, the Arab nationalist movement for autonomy was distinct and strong. Should Turkey go to war with the Western liberal Powers (France and England) that movement, exceedingly embarrassing to the Turks, would probably revive, especially if aided by us from Koweit and by the French in Syria where the Christian Arabs (e.g. in the Lebanon) like other Christian elements in the Ottoman Empire, are strongly pro-Entente and Anti-German. The movement would be one of Arab "liberation from the Turkish yoke".

Bearing in mind that there was no love lost between the Sunni Turks and the Shias in the Bagdad region and Persia, he added that Mohammerah (today, Khorramshahr), near the head of the Persian Gulf, would be a good centre from which to work. As for Ryan's anxiety that a hornets' nest thus stirred up might lead to the stinging of Britain's interests in the region in the future, Fitzmaurice's reply was that this—as even that perennial conundrum, the future of the caliphate—was a "minor" consideration. In the event of war between Britain and Turkey, he said flatly, "it would be our objective, in a life and death struggle like the present, to render her innocuous by every means at our command".

If the issue of the Turkish "de facto" caliphate was not an immediate priority, neither would it be wise for an infidel power such as Britain to lend support to any "de jure" Arab candidate, such as the Imam of Yemen;[12] this, said Fitzmaurice, would be the kiss of death. Nevertheless, he had chafed so often at the restraint imposed by the fear that any hostility to Turkey would anger Moslem opinion in India and Egypt because the sultan was also the caliph that he said that Britain should not stand in the way of any attempt to destroy "the Turkish Vatican of Islam at Constantinople". It was, however, to the priority of an Arab revolt that he returned in his conclusion, and particularly to Syria:

---

[11] TNA, War Office to FO, 27 Feb. 1913; Lowther to Grey, 16 Mar. 1913 [drafted by Fitzmaurice]; and min. of Fitzmaurice, 16 Mar. 1913, FO195/2452.

[12] The Khedive of Egypt, who had often been mentioned before as a possible contender, had ruled himself out—and told Fitzmaurice so in person some time earlier, TNA, Memorandum by Fitzmaurice in Lowther to Grey, 4 Nov. 1912, FO371/1505.

Syria would perhaps afford the best field for promoting an anti-Turkish Arab movement but the *modus operandi* would depend on harmonizing the French and the Cairo points of view.[13]

Fitzmaurice's memorandum was well received in the Eastern Department. It was also approved by Nicolson and Grey, and without doubt was a major factor in galvanizing the Foreign Office into seeking cooperation with the French in Syria.[14] However, this was regarded as a project to be approached with care because it was believed that, while France had "earmarked" Syria, it was less popular there than Britain.[15] The India Office, which had deep reservations about an Arab caliphate and found cooperating with Egypt difficult enough without having to consider France as well, also had to be carried along with some difficulty.[16] As for Mallet, while there still seemed to him to be a chance of keeping Turkey out of the war, he was extremely nervous that the Turks would find out about these machinations and begged that no commitments should be made in writing.[17] When this consideration was made irrelevant by the outbreak of war between Britain and Turkey in early November, matters were further delayed by complications caused by the temporary removal of the French government to Bordeaux.[18] Nevertheless, the ground had been prepared by discussion of the subject between Sir Arthur Nicolson and the French Ambassador in London,[19] and at the end of December a minor conference between the British and the French on 'Moslem Matters' finally took place in Paris, the government having returned to the capital earlier in the month. The French were led by M. Gout, chairman of the Committee for Moslem Affairs at the Quai d'Orsay, and the British by Sir Henry McMahon. In view of his encouragement of such a meeting

---

[13] TNA, Memorandum by Mr Fitzmaurice, 11 Oct. 1914, FO371/2140.

[14] TNA, mins. by Oliphant, Clerk, Crowe and Nicolson, 9–14 Oct. 1914; and FO to IO, 16 Oct. 1914, FO371/2140. Fitzmaurice had agreed with Ryan that the Hejaz and the Yemen should be excluded from the sphere of British activities but Grey had accepted the view of Clerk that they could not be ignored entirely since the Turks were themselves stepping up their own activity there.

[15] TNA, min. of H. Nicolson, 13 Oct. 1913 and Mallet to Grey, 12 Oct. 1914, FO371/2140; G. Bell to Military Operations Directorate, 5 Sept. 1914, FO371/2141.

[16] TNA, IO to FO, 19 Oct. 1914, FO371/2140.

[17] TNA, Mallet to Grey, 28 Oct. 1914, FO371/2140; see also Heller, *British Policy towards the Ottoman Empire, 1908–1914*, p. 149.

[18] IOL, Bertie (Bordeaux) to FO, 2 Dec. 1914, L/P&S/11/85 (P4715/1914).

[19] TNA, Nicolson to Grey, 19 Oct. 1914, and Grey to Mallet, 20 Oct. 1914, FO371/2140.

and his acknowledged expertise, Fitzmaurice was chosen to support McMahon.[20] The third member of the British delegation—probably proposed by Fitzmaurice—was his old friend from the 'red letter year' of 1906–7 in Constantinople, Percy Loraine, now a second secretary at the Paris Embassy.[21]

McMahon, who was a little older than Fitzmaurice and had had a distinguished career in the India Political Department, had just been appointed the first British High Commissioner to Egypt.[22] He had been on leave in England when war broke out and was asked to take in the Paris meeting on his way to Cairo. Since he had no knowledge of the Middle East it was as well that Fitzmaurice was to hand. They appear to have got on well, and would not have been short of topics of conversation alongside their official agenda. Like Fitzmaurice, McMahon had been much involved in boundary demarcation. He was also an enthusiastic Freemason, though naturally of the proper English sort.[23]

The India Office remained deeply sceptical that, in view of the fact that the Moslem world was hardly homogenous, any common measures with France could be readily concerted. As a result, it had only agreed to the Paris meeting on the understanding that each government would retain the fullest liberty of action in its own sphere and that discussion should be confined to an exchange of views and joint examination of the special problems that each government faced in its Moslem dealings.[24] In short, it had agreed to the meeting on the understanding that it would be "quite academic".[25]

The Anglo-French Moslem Conference lasted for just two days (30–31 December) and did not alarm the India Office.[26] The French

---

[20] The IO had asked the FO to send someone with McMahon who was "intimately acquainted with Arabs", IOL, Holderness (IO) to Grey, 7 Dec. 1914, L/P&S/11/85 (P4715/1914).

[21] Waterfield, *Professional Diplomat*, pp. 32–3.

[22] This was the post to which that of 'Agent and Consul-General' had metamorphosed when Britain declared Egypt a protectorate following the outbreak of war with Turkey, an event which removed British concern for Turkish sensitivities on the point.

[23] T. R. Moreman, "McMahon, Sir (Arthur) Henry (1862–1949)", *ODNB* [34794, accessed 20 Jan. 2007].

[24] IOL, Holderness (IO) to Grey, 7 Dec. 1914, L/P&S/11/85 (P4715/1914).

[25] IOL, min. of Sir Thomas Holderness, permanent under-secretary at the IO, on S of S for India to Viceroy, 14 Dec. 1914, L/P&S/11/85 (P4715/1914).

[26] IOL, mins. of Holderness and Lord Crewe, 12 and 14 Jan. 1915, L/P&S/11/85 (P4715/1914).

barely mentioned Syria, and McMahon was caution personified. He emphasised the dangers of "indiscriminate" attempts to arouse the Arabs against the Turks, and elicited without difficulty French agreement that it was absolutely essential "to avoid anything savouring of Christian interference in the internal affairs of Islam", such as action in regard to the caliphate. The one positive note to emerge from the conference was agreement in principle to pool ideas and materials in anti-Turkish propaganda directed at the Moslem population. In the British suggestion that this should take the form of branding the Young Turks as "free-thinking internationals" masquerading as Moslems, the influence of Fitzmaurice is obviously apparent.

Fitzmaurice was possibly disappointed with the way in which the India Office had been permitted to dampen enthusiasm for the idea of Anglo-French collaboration to stir up the Arabs against the Turks, especially in Syria. On the other hand, he could have accompanied McMahon with no illusions about its prospects, and in his autumn memorandum had in any case suggested no more than that Paris and Cairo (and by implication London) should ensure that they were not at cross purposes in any independent action undertaken. To this extent the meeting seems to have served some purpose, as the India Office conceded.[27] What is likely to have encouraged him further, however, is the obvious resolve of the French to throw their weight behind a general anti-Turkish movement among the Arabs. He must have rejoiced even more when, as reported by McMahon, upon whom this left a strong impression, they revealed their preference for treating the war as "one against the Germans and German party in Turkey and not against Turkey as a country". McMahon continued:

> They contemplate the possibility and *even probability* of the early overthrow of the German war party in Turkey and of an appeal for peace from Turkey [emphasis added].[28]

The French were talking Fitzmaurice's language.

---

[27] IOL, Holderness to FO, 15 Jan. 1915, L/P&S/11/85 (P4715/1914).
[28] IOL, McMahon (Paris) to Grey, 1 Jan. 1915, L/P&S/11/85 (P4715/1914). This message contains McMahon's report on and 'Résumé' of the conference.

"The most important person in the Eastern Theatre of the War"

At almost exactly the same time that McMahon and Fitzmaurice
had been in Paris, key members of the recently formed British War
Council were coming to the conclusion that some way must be found
to break the stalemate on the Western front, and Sir Maurice Hankey,
the council's secretary, had urged an attack on Turkey. If successful,
he argued, in a memorandum which both captured and shaped the
drift of opinion, this would not only remove from the conflict one of
Germany's most important allies but open up the vital sea-route to
Russia. Furthermore, it would so impress the wavering neutral Balkan
states that they would sign up to the Entente. Winston Churchill, First
Lord of the Admiralty, who had long favoured an attack on the Dardanelles, thereafter brilliantly manoeuvred the government into support
for this policy. Following the meeting of the War Council on 28 January
1915 the die was cast and the bombardment of the outer defences of
the Dardanelles began on 19 February. By early March they had been
reduced and the Anglo-French fleet was able to enter the straits. The
inner forts were a different prospect but at this point there appears to
have been a widely shared opinion in Constantinople that it was just
a matter of time before the Allied fleet broke through and the CUP
were ousted by a war-weary population.[29] This prospect appears to
have unnerved some members of the Turkish government—though
not the resolutely pro-German Minister of War, Enver Pasha—and
secret peace feelers were put out.[30] It was against this background that
Fitzmaurice was sent into action.

The Director of the Naval Intelligence Department (NID) of the
Admiralty at this time was the recently appointed Captain Reginald
Hall. With the Secret Service still a relatively young plant and the Royal
Navy an arm of the services that might be sent anywhere, under the
energetic and notoriously independent-minded Hall, Naval Intelligence
obtained a much wider remit than its name implies.[31] Apprehensive
about the implications for the Navy of the intervention of Turkey in
the war and undoubtedly aware of the emerging consensus in government for an attack on it, Hall was anxious to have more agents

---

[29] Morgenthau, *Secrets of the Bosphorus*, pp. 128, 149.
[30] Robert Rhodes James, *Gallipoli* (Pimlico: London, 1999), pp. 14–48.
[31] Eunan O'Halpin, "Hall, Sir (William) Reginald (1870–1943)", *ODNB* [33657,
accessed 20 Jan. 2007].

in the eastern Mediterranean.[32] In early January 1915, therefore, he recruited G. Griffin Eady, a civil engineer who had worked on railway construction in Turkey and was reported to be on "friendly terms with many of the most influential Turks";[33] he had also acted intermittently as an adviser to both the Foreign Office and the War Office.[34] Asked who else could help them, Eady replied: Gerald Fitzmaurice, together with Edwin Whittall, head of the well known Anglo-Levantine trading house in Turkey, J. W. Whittall and Company.[35] Both were promptly enlisted, though Fitzmaurice was not formally transferred to NID until November and until then appears to have remained as much at the beck and call of Grey as of Hall.[36] He was one of many civilians and wounded officers with special knowledge and talents drafted into Naval Intelligence during the war but he was also one of the first.[37]

It is striking that after he had recruited his Turkish specialists, Hall's thoughts about the eastern Mediterranean seem swiftly to have turned from merely obtaining contacts in the area[38] towards a more radical

---

[32] James, *The Eyes of the Navy*, p. 60. Though vague at points, James's biography of Hall is actually an important primary source. He knew him intimately and must also have known Fitzmaurice, having himself been made a senior member of NID by Hall in May or June 1917, Paul Kennedy, "James, Sir William Milbourne (1881–1973)", rev., *ODNB*; online edn, Jan. 2007 [31283, accessed 20 Jan. 2007], and *The Navy List*, July 1917, p. 538. James also had access to Hall's incomplete and unpublished autobiography, CAC Cam.

[33] CAC Cam., Draft Chapters of Hall's Autobiography, Draft 'C', Chapter Seven, "Lord Fisher and Mr. Churchill" [hereafter 'Hall's Autobiography'], HALL 3/5. For his work in Turkey, Eady had been given a high class of the Order of the Medjidieh.

[34] Hall says that he was first introduced to Eady in December but he was not formally enlisted until 15 January 1915, when he was given the temporary rank of Commander in the RNVR. Later he served at Brindisi and was assistant naval attaché in Petrograd from 1 August 1916 until March 1917. Of course, it was not until he returned to England that his name first appeared under the heading of the NID in *The Navy List* (July 1917). See also *FO List 1918*; Cptn. G. R. G. Allen [Eady's son-in-law], "A Ghost from Gallipoli", *Journal of the Royal United Service Institute*, 108 (630), May 1963; *The Times* (obit.), 9 Feb. 1937; TNA, RNVR service record, ADM337/119.

[35] *The Times* (obit.), 6 Mar. 1953.

[36] CAC Cam., Hall's Autobiography, HALL 3/5. In view of the intense secrecy required by his work, it is not surprising that Fitzmaurice was not acknowledged to be a member of NID in *The Navy List* until the beginning of 1917, and his transfer to the Admiralty in November 1915 was not acknowledged by the *FO List* until 1920. Whittall, like Eady, was made a temporary Commander in the RNVR on 15 January; he did not resign this rank until 15 October 1917, TNA, RNVR service record, ADM337/119.

[37] The small number of others recruited at this juncture is listed by James in *The Eyes of the Navy*, p. 32. They included the historian, Algernon Cecil, and George Prothero, editor of the *Quarterly Review*.

[38] James, *The Eyes of the Navy*, p. 60.

plan. This was to try to persuade the Turks to break with Germany and allow the Allied warships a peaceful passage through the Dardanelles. To achieve this, he thought, there seemed to be only two alternatives:

> either to promote a revolution aimed against Enver Pasha and the Young Turk party which was then in power, or, what in the absence of a suitable leader seemed to be the better plan, to persuade the more reasonable members of Enver's party to make peace with ourselves.[39]

Why Hall's thoughts turned in this direction is not clear from his auto-biography or from the account provided by his biographer. Though a political operation of the first importance, he appears not to have been ordered to launch it either by his political chief, Churchill, or the First Sea Lord, Admiral Lord Fisher. Instead, he probably set it in motion because he was persuaded of its merits by Hankey,[40] and because it was urged on him by his new recruits. Eady had spoken to the grand vizier, Prince Said Halim, shortly before leaving Constantinople in September and seems to have been convinced that he was just one among the more important of those in the government who secretly wished for a break with Germany.[41] Whittall would certainly have agreed with him, though he was not optimistic about the success of the proposed operation.[42] As for Fitzmaurice, he had always maintained that the basis of CUP support was exceedingly narrow and—hot foot from the conference in Paris—no doubt told Hall that the French were of the same view. Hall, meanwhile, was the most recent man to have fallen hopelessly under his spell.[43] In any event, as he said in his unpublished memoir, "by the end of January all three of them were in the Balkans".

At this point events become predictably murky. Hall's autobiography is hopelessly vague, especially on dates, as is the version related by his biographer, while in the treatment of the episode offered by Captain Allen, which is based on the "brief account" provided in the diary of his tight-lipped father-in-law, Eady, there is no mention of Fitzmaurice at all. Nor is there any mention of him in a more recent treatment of

---

[39] CAC Cam., Hall's Autobiography, HALL 3/5.

[40] Stephen Roskill, *Hankey: Man of Secrets, vol. I, 1877–1918* (Collins: London, 1970), pp. 159–60.

[41] Allen, "A Ghost from Gallipoli", p. 137.

[42] Alan Judd, *The Quest for C: Sir Mansfield Cumming and the Founding of the British Secret Service* (HarperCollins: London, 1999), p. 309.

[43] The miracles that Hall believed Fitzmaurice would have achieved had he not left Constantinople in February 1914 are detailed by James, *The Eyes of the Navy*, pp. 60–1. James shared this view.

the affair, which also gives prominence to the role of the Secret Service at the expense of Naval Intelligence.[44] Moreover, here and there in these writings there are errors of fact, faulty transcriptions from Hall's unpublished autobiography, and major inconsistencies.[45]

According to Judd, Hall asked Mansfield Cumming, head of the Secret Service, to oversee the practical arrangements involved in sending the agents on their mission.[46] Eady and Whittall then made for Athens, where they arrived on 1 February and commenced a correspondence with the Grand Rabbi, "who was known to be well disposed".[47] As for Fitzmaurice, it seems that Hall's memory may have played a trick on him and that, as Allen and Judd imply, he had not accompanied Eady and Whittall to Athens.[48] This is because, according to Foreign Office records, it seems that he was still in London three weeks later, at which point only was he sent to the Balkans—and on the orders of Grey, not Hall or Cumming.

On 21 February, just after the first attack by the guns of the fleet on the Turkish forts at the mouth of the Dardanelles, Grey sent a personal telegram to Sir Henry Bax-Ironside, British Minister at Sofia:

> In view of the attack on the Dardanelles and probable developments I want Fitzmaurice to be on the spot in the Near East.
>
> I am therefore sending him to Sofia as attached to the Legation with the rank of First Secretary. But the title is nominal as he should go to wherever he can be of most use from time to time in getting information or utilizing his knowledge and experience of Balkan and especially Turkish affairs. When operations against the Dardanelles begin to be successful he may be able most usefully at Sofia to get into touch with the Turkish party at Constantinople who are anti-German and well-known to him.
>
> I have asked him to send me his views of the Balkan situation through you and through the Minister of the Legation wherever he may be, but have authorised him to communicate direct to the British Admiral at the Dardanelles any information or suggestions which his knowledge of

---

[44] Judd, *The Quest for C*, pp. 308–10. This book, apparently written by a former member of SIS, is based on exclusive access to Cumming's diary.

[45] Rhodes James's account in *Gallipoli* (pp. 48–9) is based on the contributions of James and Allen but does not wrestle with these problems.

[46] That is, "preparing codes, arranging communications, paying £500 into Eady's bank and 'suggesting a scheme for Dedeagatch', the town where they were to negotiate with the Turkish representatives", Judd, *The Quest for C*, p. 309.

[47] Allen, "A Ghost from Gallipoli", p. 137.

[48] As Geoffrey Miller noticed, Allen says this was an Eady-Whittall operation, while James says it was Eady-Fitzmaurice, *Straits: British Policy towards the Ottoman Empire and the Origins of the Dardanelles Campaign* (Hull University Press: Hull, 1997), ch. 30.

Turkish affairs may enable him to give when it is likely to be helpful in the naval and military operations there.[49]

Before this went out, George Clerk, now head of the War Department,[50] suggested to Grey that, if the attack on the Dardanelles was successful, Fitzmaurice should—with Churchill's agreement—accompany the admiral into the Sea of Marmora and up to Constantinople. "His knowledge of Turkish feeling and personalities", added Clerk, "will be invaluable in any parleys with the Turkish Government or local authorities, and he can put all communications into proper form". Grey at once agreed to this but told Clerk that in the meantime he should get on and send the telegram to Sofia since he wanted Fitzmaurice to have some *locus standi* there and did not want to delay his departure.[51]

Fitzmaurice was thus given a roving brief by Grey in effect to do whatever he thought best to advance the cause of the war against Turkey. Five days later, on 26 February, the foreign secretary told the War Council that "what we really relied on to open the Straits [not provoke, as Churchill argued, by forcing them] was a coup d'état in Constantinople".[52] It is not difficult, therefore, to imagine what he said to Fitzmaurice, who probably also received at least a hint from George Clerk that, with luck, he would shortly be sailing to the Golden Horn with the British admiral to negotiate the surrender of Constantinople. What a triumph this would have been for him: knighthood assured.

Presumably Fitzmaurice set off immediately, that is, on 21 or 22 February—but he did not arrive at the legation in Sofia until 4 April.[53] On leaving England he probably went more or less directly to join up with Eady and Whittall in Athens.[54] It is also possible that they all spent

---

[49] TNA, Grey to Bax-Ironside, 21 Feb. 1915, FO800/43. Of course, Grey could have meant that he was sending Fitzmaurice to Sofia from Athens or somewhere else but from the tone of this message and the subsequent minutes this seems very unlikely.

[50] Created in August 1914 by a merger of the Eastern and Western Departments.

[51] TNA, mins. of Clerk and Grey, 21 Feb. 1915, FO371/2253. See also Committee of Imperial Defence. The War. After the Dardanelles. The Next Step. Notes by the Secretary, 1 Mar. 1915, CAB42/2.

[52] TNA, War Council, Notes of a Meeting of, 26 Feb. 1915, CAB42/1. Later in this meeting, Lloyd George and Balfour argued that a special envoy should be sent to the Balkan states to bring them in on the side of the Entente. Grey parried this by informing the council that he had sent Fitzmaurice to Sofia. "A larger mission would probably lead to intrigue and difficulties", he added.

[53] TNA, Bax-Ironside to Grey, 4 Apr. 1915, FO371/2295. The military attaché at the legation confirms that this was when Fitzmaurice *first* arrived, Lt. Col. H. D. Napier, *The Experiences of a Military Attaché in the Balkans* (Drane's: London, 1924), p. 138.

[54] He was certainly there because subsequently he mentioned a stay at Athens with Major Samson on Admiralty work in a claim to the FO for expenses, TNA, Fitzmaurice

some time at Dedeagach (modern day Alexandroupoli), a Bulgarian port on the Aegean close to the Turkish frontier, mention of which begins to crop up in the various accounts of the last stage of these negotiations and which was considerably closer to the mouth of the Dardanelles.[55] There was also a Levant Service consular post at Dedeagach, where the vice-consul, Godefroy Badetti, was well thought of by Fitzmaurice.[56] Wherever the negotiators were chiefly based, Fitzmaurice probably took charge of the operation. There is a further clue that supports this.

As the difficulties confronting the fleet began to mount in early March, Hall pressed the negotiators to get a result. However, they found themselves confronting a huge difficulty: Constantinople had just been promised to Russia,[57] so they were not allowed to meet the Turkish demand that it should remain the Ottoman capital after they withdrew from the war.[58] Therefore, to lend them assistance, on his own initiative Hall told his negotiators that they could offer a bribe to the Turks of up to £4 millions. However, this was to be reduced progressively with each day's delay. Hall may be said to imply in his own account of the affair that this relatively sophisticated idea was his own[59] but he was in regular communication with Fitzmaurice and was not a professional negotiator. By contrast, Fitzmaurice had made his reputation as someone who knew how to deal with Turkish officials; moreover, he had boasted of his successful use of precisely this technique—the Sibylline books principle—during his negotiations on the Yemen frontier (see above p. 64). In short, giving the Turkish negotiators what today would be called 'a fading opportunity' bears all the hall-marks of Fitzmaurice.

---

to FO, 4 May 1915, FO371/2295. Samson had been consul at Adrianople right through the Balkan Wars and served in Military Intelligence during the war.

[55] In "A Ghost from Gallipoli" (p. 138), Allen says that it was not until 15 March that the negotiators landed at Dedeagach, where they had arranged to meet a Turkish emissary—"Believed to have been Talaat Pasha, but this is not definitely stated [in Eady's diary]". However, the fact that Allen describes Dedeagach as a "Turkish town" hardly inspires confidence.

[56] TNA, min. of Fitzmaurice (2/11/1913) on Badetti to Mallet, 23 Oct. 1913, FO195/2454.

[57] Winston S. Churchill, *The World Crisis, 1911–1918*, vol. I (Odhams Press: London, 1938), p. 618.

[58] CAC Cam., Hall's Autobiography, HALL 3/5; Allen, "A Ghost from Gallipoli", pp. 137–8.

[59] James says that "Hall telegraphed to the negotiators to say that henceforth each day's delay must inevitably bring with it a lowering of the subsidy...", *The Eyes of the Navy*, p. 62 but Hall himself says "we therefore telegraphed to say that henceforth...", CAC Cam., Hall's Autobiography, HALL 3/5. In other words, James jumps to the conclusion that Hall meant that he had telegraphed this to his negotiators, when in fact he could have meant that "we" the British had telegraphed this *to the Turks*.

As things turned out, of course, and whoever was responsible for it, the tactic did not work. The future of Constantinople appears to have been the sticking point. As Eady is reported to have said after the war was over, the Turkish negotiators "knew full well that signing away that city would also mean signing their own death warrants".[60] Enver had evidently discovered what was going on and may also have taken steps to sabotage the negotiations.[61] In any case, on 15 March Hall's own cryptographers intercepted a message from Berlin to Constantinople which suggested that the Turkish forts within the Dardanelles were running out of ammunition. On being told this, Churchill and Fisher were elated. Having been somewhat alarmed to learn for the first time that the negotiations might cost the government £4 millions, they ordered Hall to call them off and resolved to press on with all speed to force the Dardanelles. Hall records that after the failure of the great attack launched three days later, the Cabinet asked him "to spare no expense to win over the Turks" but by this time it was too late: Turkish belief in British good faith had been destroyed.[62]

At about this time, Lord Fisher, the First Sea Lord, who had been so opposed to Churchill's Dardanelles adventure and knew that Fitzmaurice was trying desperately to deliver a peaceful passage of the Dardanelles for his ships, minuted to his secretary:

> Tell W. R. Hall to find out from the Foreign Office by *11 a.m.* where Fitzmaurice is—he was last at Sofia—and what his orders are.
> He is now the most important person in the Eastern Theatre of the War but unfortunately this is not realised.[63]

Hall, who had been quick to assure Fisher that he at least realised this, implies that the First Sea Lord said this before the middle of March, though the reference to Sofia suggests that the observation was made afterwards. In any case, if he did make it before he probably still believed it afterwards—perhaps moreso, for Fitzmaurice did not give

[60] Allen, "A Ghost from Gallipoli", p. 138.
[61] Reporting in his memoirs on a conversation at the Dardanelles forts on 15 March with Enver Pasha, who had taken him there to convince him that they were impregnable, the American Ambassador said that "He showed great bitterness against the English; he accused them of attempting to bribe Turkish officials...", Morgenthau, *Secrets of the Bosphorus*, pp. 135–6.
[62] CAC Cam., Hall's Autobiography, HALL 3/5. This account is endorsed by Patrick Beesly in *Room 40: British Naval Intelligence 1914–18* (Hamish Hamilton: London, 1982), pp. 80–3, as well as in the other sources already cited.
[63] CAC Cam., Hall's Autobiography, HALL 3/5.

up and go home. Instead he established himself at the British Legation
in Sofia, as initially directed by Grey, and now spent his energies on
trying to persuade King Ferdinand's government in Bulgaria to join
the Entente and attack Turkey. This would not only assure the impossibility of Turkey being re-supplied overland by the Central Powers
but draw off Turkish forces from the Dardanelles, thereby providing
an alternative means of securing a peaceful passage for the fleet. This
was his next hopeless mission.

Bulgaria: "Hours mean Empires now"

The problems for the British in bringing over the Bulgarians were
enormous. They had lost some sympathy in Sofia as a result of their
attitude in the second Balkan War, and were in any case hardly a good
bet as an ally since at this point it looked as if they might lose the war
to Germany.[64] Moreover, like the Roumanians, the Bulgarians were
alarmed by the recently revealed prospect that, should the Entente
triumph in the great conflict in spite of everything, Russia would be
given Constantinople and the straits. As if all of this was not enough,
Bulgaria demanded as its price for joining the Entente, among other
things, the Macedonian territory recently seized from it by Serbia.
However, London was reluctant to press its Serbian ally to make this
sacrifice for the common interest, and Bax-Ironside was a keen supporter of this line.[65] And then, of course, the Germans—desperate to
enlist the Bulgarian army for an attack on Serbia and re-open the vital
supply route to their besieged Turkish ally—were bidding to bring King
Ferdinand and his government firmly over to their own side, despite the
misgivings of Austria about the implications of such a policy for its own
Balkan diplomacy. The Germans were also better placed to give the
Bulgarians what they wanted, especially of course in Macedonia.[66]

Nevertheless, the British had no option but to join the contest for
Bulgaria and, with matters now looking more problematical at the

---

[64] Napier, *The Experiences of a Military Attaché in the Balkans*, p. 109.
[65] On the background to this, see C. J. Lowe, "The failure of British diplomacy
in the Balkans, 1914–1916", *Canadian Journal of History*, 4 (1), 1969; and Napier, *The
Experiences of a Military Attaché in the Balkans*.
[66] Gerard E. Silberstein, "The Serbian campaign of 1915: its diplomatic background", *The American Historical Review*, 73 (1), Oct. 1967.

Dardanelles, the Foreign Office was at least beginning to look more sympathetically at its territorial demands. Fitzmaurice encouraged this unbending with great vigour, invoking once more his favourite Sibylline books principle to urge that an attempt should be made to bounce them into an alliance with an immediate offer of the uncontested zone; delay would only see their price go up.[67] However, when he arrived in Sofia on 4 April he still had only two assets. First, he carried his reputation for being a great admirer of the Bulgarians and the man who had gone to such lengths to prevent the European concert from denying them the full fruits of their victory in the first Balkan War. Secondly, he had the support of the legation's temporary military attaché, the experienced and forceful Colonel Henry Napier, who shared his views almost entirely and had, as a result, already come into conflict with Bax-Ironside.[68]

Napier's memoirs, which are based on a diary, are an important source for Fitzmaurice's views at this time. On 7 April, at a lunch with the legation staff, he records Fitzmaurice arguing in typically melodramatic but no doubt spell-binding fashion that the assault on the Dardanelles should be halted until Bulgaria had been brought into the war. Pressing forward the attack before then would be "a slow and lingering process" in the course of which the Turks would "destroy all the Embassies [in Constantinople] and St. Sophia and then sack the town". However, once they knew the Bulgars were on the way, said Fitzmaurice, they would have no time to do this "as they would be only thinking of how to save their own skins".[69]

Three days later, on 10 April, Grey's telegram came in indicating that Bulgaria was to be offered the 1912 line, including Monastir, though this had to be agreed with the Russians and the French. Napier says that both he and Fitzmaurice thought this ought to do the trick and, at the last minute, on 12 April, Fitzmaurice decided to hitch a ride with him to Lemnos in order to press his argument on the commanders of the British operation in the Dardanelles, Admiral de Robeck and General Sir Ian Hamilton. After a difficult drive to Dedeagach, they were specially picked up and taken to Lemnos by HMS *Agamemnon*, one of the last pre-*Dreadnought* battleships to be built and one of

---

[67] CAC Cam., Fitzmaurice to Lloyd, 5 Sept. 1915, GLLD 9/1/3.
[68] Napier, *The Experiences of a Military Attaché in the Balkans*, Preface and pp. 26–7.
[69] Napier, *The Experiences of a Military Attaché in the Balkans*, p. 142.

the most powerful under de Robeck's command. Napier thought that this "civility" was perhaps due to the fact that the admiral was an old friend of Fitzmaurice's, which was news to his biographer. He also thought it merely incidental good fortune that the battleship made an "immense impression" on Bulgarian officials at Dedeagach, who were shown over the ship and given a nine-gun salute.[70] However, Fitzmaurice had employed this sort of trick at Turba in 1905, and it seems likely that—desperate to find any lever to bring the Bulgarians into the Entente—he was behind its use now.

Despite this auspicious start, matters did not go so well for Fitzmaurice at Lemnos. Together with Napier, he was shown over the even more awesome super-dreadnought *Queen Elizabeth* and seems to have been introduced to everyone who mattered. Then on 16 April they were summoned to a conference with de Robeck and Hamilton. This was also attended, among others, by Captain Roger Keyes, the admiral's attack-minded chief of staff. Confronting the assembled commanders, Fitzmaurice argued that the offer of the 1912 line "coupled with a friendly demand from the Tzar of Russia for Bulgaria's acquiescence in a landing at Burgas" would probably soon bring the Bulgarians over to the Entente; until this happened, postponement of further operations at the Dardanelles was advisable.[71] Unfortunately, Napier, who had initially supported Fitzmaurice, then openly disagreed with him and their cause, though probably doomed anyway, foundered at once.

Burgas was a port with a fine harbour on Bulgaria's Black Sea coast and Napier knew that Fitzmaurice was not alone among Entente diplomats in supporting the idea of a Russian landing there. However, he also knew the Bulgarians to be very sensitive about Burgas and so argued that the British should only go this far if the other inducements (including the Enos-Midia line with Turkey) failed to bring them in. It is extraordinary that Fitzmaurice had not discussed the Burgas question with Napier before this conference and agreed the line they would take. He was clearly annoyed at the military attaché's intervention, and, as Napier somewhat ruefully notes, this

> gave Hamilton the opportunity to say it was quite clear that Bulgaria was not coming in until the Allies had done something in the direction of the

---

[70] Napier, *The Experiences of a Military Attaché in the Balkans*, pp. 146–7.
[71] Napier, *The Experiences of a Military Attaché in the Balkans*, p. 148; see also CAC Cam., de Robeck to Churchill, 17 Apr. 1915, CHAR 13/65.

Dardanelles, and that he was going ahead with his plans independently of the Balkan States and their affairs.

And that was that: "The conference terminated."[72]

De Robeck told Churchill that, in the absence of a guarantee of Bulgarian intervention, he "entirely concurred" with Hamilton. So did Churchill, who in reply added that the "Russians have several times proposed to land troops at Burgas, but we have always protested against any violations of Bulgarian neutrality even to force the hand of the Bulgarian government".[73] Once more Fitzmaurice had failed to persuade the British government to take radical action.

A little over a week later the ill-fated Allied landings took place on the Gallipoli Peninsula. Before long they were seriously checked, casualties of a completely unexpected size were suffered, and in May political convulsions were provoked in London. But at least at the end of the month the Entente finally agreed on the kind of territorial promises that could be made to Bulgaria and these were formally presented in Sofia by their representatives.[74] Fitzmaurice himself tried to sell the package to the minister of war, General Fitcheff, and Napier, who was present at their encounter, provides an illuminating account of his style. He "spent at least half an hour on trivialities as one would in dealing with an oriental in order to get him into an agreeable and receptive frame of mind", and so—though systematic in his subsequent presentation—talked for far longer than initially agreed. Both were exhausted by the end and "Fitcheff", says Napier, "was delighted when I at last dragged Fitzmaurice away". In any case, nothing, said the Bulgarian war minister, could be done without a Balkan alliance.[75] This pointed to the dilemma, as Napier was quick to grasp: Bulgaria would not come in without the other Balkan states but it would not come in, either, without the kind of territorial concessions at their expense which would only turn them against it.[76] The Central Powers, who had been moved to "near panic" on 1 June when they heard news of the Entente offer, quickly relaxed when it became apparent that it had been rejected.[77]

---

[72] Napier, *The Experiences of a Military Attaché in the Balkans*, pp. 148–9.
[73] CAC Cam., de Robeck to Churchill, 17 Apr. 1915 and Churchill to de Robeck, 17 Apr. 1915, CHAR 13/65.
[74] Napier, *The Experiences of a Military Attaché in the Balkans*, p. 158.
[75] Napier, *The Experiences of a Military Attaché in the Balkans*, p. 162.
[76] Napier, *The Experiences of a Military Attaché in the Balkans*, p. 162.
[77] Silberstein, "The Serbian campaign of 1915", p. 59.

Later in the month, with steadily rising temperatures making the suffering of the troops on Gallipoli much worse and the fleet still unable to contemplate attacking the forts at the Narrows without support from the army, in desperation Fitzmaurice was asked to try bribing King Ferdinand's ministers. He was authorised by Sir James Drummond, Grey's private secretary, to offer them £2.5 millions as a "free gift"—or for "any purposes" which he thought would ensure a Bulgarian attack on Turkey before the end of July.[78] This sum was equivalent to over 3.7 per cent of Bulgaria's total income and possibly to more than a quarter of its national budget.[79] Napier had for some time more or less given up on the Bulgarians and had had to be restrained by Fitzmaurice from telling the Foreign Office to give them a deadline.[80] Fitzmaurice, however, was also deeply pessimistic about his chances of bringing them over, even with the assistance of a great deal of money.[81]

It was at this juncture that he received a visit from his old friend Mark Sykes, now a baronet and lieutenant-colonel. Sykes had secured for himself a position in Intelligence at the War Office and was at the start of a six month tour on behalf of Kitchener that was to take him as far as India and make him even more seized with the need for active engagement in political warfare than he was already.[82] He was appalled at the confusion in British policy in the Balkans and recommended—too late as it turned out—the appointment of a 'high commissioner' in Sofia with whom alone the Foreign Office should communicate.[83] As to Fitzmaurice, he wrote to his wife that his Irish friend was anxious about the attentions he was receiving from German agents, illustrating his fears in a memorable cartoon in the letter.[84]

In fact, Fitzmaurice now feared even the possibility of assassination. Berlin, he warned the Foreign Office, "would shrink from nothing to prevent the opening of the Dardanelles and fall of Constantinople".[85] Drummond tried to encourage him by telling him that a Russian secret

---

[78] TNA, Drummond to Bax-Ironside ("following for Fitzmaurice from Drummond to be decyphered only by himself"), 25 and 30 June 1915, FO800/43.
[79] I am grateful for this calculation—"a tentative estimate by a roundabout route"—to the economic historian, Derek H. Aldcroft.
[80] Napier, *The Experiences of a Military Attaché in the Balkans*, pp. 159–61.
[81] TNA, Fitzmaurice to Drummond, 5 July 1915, FO800/43.
[82] Adelson, *Mark Sykes*, pp. 185–7, 193.
[83] HUA, Sykes to Fitzgerald (WO), 30 Jan. 1916, DDSY(2), 1/52.
[84] HUA, Sykes to Edith Sykes, 4 July 1916, DDSY(2), 1/2f/41.
[85] TNA, Fitzmaurice to Drummond, 1 Aug. 1915, FO800/43. This was probably not a figment of his imagination, FO to O'Beirne, 29 Sept. 1915, FO800/43.

agent had also been sent to Sofia with money in his pocket and that a request had been made that he should cooperate with him.[86] At least he now had the money with which to negotiate, together with the possibility of a collaborator. Further good news was that Bax-Ironside, who had all along been opposed in principle to trying to get Bulgaria to join the Entente, was to be recalled at once and replaced by the able and experienced Hugh O'Beirne, counsellor of embassy at Petrograd for nine years.[87] Fitzmaurice swung into action.

He approached King Ferdinand indirectly and also made strenuous efforts to buy those ministers not already under German influence. In late July he seemed to have made progress with some of them.[88] Both king and ministers, however, gave Fitzmaurice essentially the same reply: the money would be nice but what was really needed was an effective guarantee of the uncontested zone. Unfortunately for Fitzmaurice, when it became clear that Bulgaria was unlikely to come in before the next major offensive at the Dardanelles (scheduled for August), George Clerk for one was not in favour of more liberality: "If successful, we shall not want them so much; if we fail, nothing will bring them in".[89] Meanwhile, the Russian agent had given up and left some time ago,[90] and when Chirol turned up in Sofia on a semi-official mission to stiffen British diplomacy in the Balkans, he was as depressed as Fitzmaurice at the situation he found.[91]

In August, after the Entente had refined for the last time its territorial offer to Bulgaria and the Suvla Bay operation on Gallipoli had failed, Fitzmaurice was reduced to using his money in order to buy the Bulgarian corn harvest, partly to please the politically important peasantry and partly to prevent the Germans from buying it first.[92] To Napier's

---

[86] TNA, Drummond to Fitzmaurice, 12 July 1915, FO800/43.

[87] Napier, *The Experiences of a Military Attaché in the Balkans*, p. 167; Lowe, "The failure of British diplomacy in the Balkans", p. 88, n. 51. Hugh O'Beirne arrived on 7 July.

[88] In order to "reconstruct" the Cabinet, the President of the Chamber asked for £10,000 to be placed immediately in a London bank account as "earnest money", which was done, TNA, Fitzmaurice to Drummond, 28 July and Drummond to Fitzmaurice, 29 July, 1915, FO800/43.

[89] TNA, min. of Clerk on telegram from King's Messenger to D.M.O., 18 July 1915, FO371/2490. Clerk was also referring to Roumania.

[90] TNA, Fitzmaurice to Drummond, 19 July 1915, FO800/43.

[91] Valentine Chirol, *Fifty Years in a Changing World* (Cape: London, 1927), pp. 311–14; see also J. D. Gregory, *On the Edge of Diplomacy: Rambles and Reflections* (Hutchinson: London, 1928), pp. 107–9.

[92] TNA, FO Memorandum, 'Bulgarian Corn', 19 Aug. 1915, FO800/95; CAC Cam., Fitzmaurice to Lloyd, 5 Sept. 1915, GLLD 9/1/3.

regret, he was also trying now merely to keep Bulgaria neutral.[93] Amidst all this—astonishingly enough—he found time to conduct a reconnaissance mission behind Turkish lines across the middle of the Gallipoli peninsula, revealing laconically to George Lloyd that "I have been to Maidos and across to Kabatepe where I got arrested".[94]

When, despite intense Entente pressure, at the beginning of September Serbia formally made clear its refusal to make sufficient concessions to the Bulgarians, Fitzmaurice knew for certain that the game was lost. In fact, the Bulgarians had been involved in serious negotiations with the Germans, Austrians and Turks during most of August and on 6 September secretly signed agreements with all three by virtue of which they finally agreed to enter the war. They had thrown in their lot with the Central Powers and promised to commence military action against Serbia in 35 days' time.[95]

Had Fitzmaurice known that this was imminent he would not have been surprised, and only on the day before conveyed his feelings to George Lloyd, who had joined Army Intelligence in Cairo following the outbreak of war with Turkey but since the Gallipoli landings in April had also been serving on General Birdwood's staff with the ANZACs.[96] It was possibly the first letter that he had written to Lloyd since November 1912 and was the last, or at least the last to survive. It was full of anger at the "pig-headed and obdurate" Serbs, and even more at the "*superlative stupidities*" of British policy, including the inability of his masters to appreciate "the value of *time* in war" (emphasis in the original). So it was up to the soldiers and sailors now, he said: "For God's sake push ahead without losing a *second*. Hours mean Empires now."[97]

As for his own efforts, which included press work as well as harvest buying, Fitzmaurice could boast only that he was winning significant influence in the Bulgarian Chamber. Among other evidence of this, he told George Lloyd, was the fact that the vice-consul had recently uncovered a plot to assassinate him.[98] Despite the increasing concern for his safety prompted by this discovery, which was shared by

---

[93] Napier, *The Experiences of a Military Attaché in the Balkans*, p. 190.
[94] CAC Cam., Fitzmaurice to Lloyd, 5 Sept. 1915, GLLD 9/1/3. How this came about and how he extricated himself he does not say.
[95] Silberstein, "The Serbian campaign of 1915", p. 65.
[96] Charmley, *Lord Lloyd and the Decline of the British Empire*, pp. 38–49.
[97] CAC Cam., Fitzmaurice to Lloyd, 5 Sept. 1915, GLLD 9/1/3.
[98] CAC Cam., Fitzmaurice to Lloyd, 5 Sept. 1915, GLLD 9/1/3.

Chirol,[99] Fitzmaurice stayed in Sofia until the end, that is, until Bulgaria rejected a Russian ultimatum to march against Turkey or demobilize. He left with the rest of the legation staff on 8 October.[100] Shortly after this King Ferdinand's forces invaded Serbia, and in the middle of the month Britain declared war on Bulgaria.

From Sofia, Fitzmaurice travelled with his colleagues to Athens, where he arrived on 12 October. Here he found Major Samson still in charge of Military Intelligence but with the novelist, Compton Mackenzie, now on his staff; Edwin Whittall was there too.[101] There was similar work to be done here to what Fitzmaurice had been doing in Sofia: Greece was another neutral Balkan state leaning towards Germany that had if possible to be persuaded to join the Entente. However, while Napier remained in Athens, Fitzmaurice lingered for only about a week. This was more than long enough for Mackenzie, who thought that the presence of the Sofia legation staff merely advertised to the Greeks Britain's diplomatic defeat in Bulgaria. Fitzmaurice also resembled too much a "crafty old oriental" for his taste and, a Philhellene, Mackenzie took exception to a derogatory remark made by Fitzmaurice about the Greeks and disagreed with his ruthless view on the tactics to be employed to force them into the war—seizing Corfu and setting up a blockade. He was "genuinely shocked", says Mackenzie, when he learned that Grey had offered the Greeks the carrot—possession of Cyprus—rather than the stick:

> He sounded like an old-fashioned assistant-master who could not keep pace with the ideas of a faddy Head, and who thought that the school was going to the dogs through lack of discipline and excess of prizes.[102]

Classicist though he was, Mackenzie had evidently not heard of the Sibylline books principle. Nevertheless, he conceded that Fitzmaurice was "generous and equable under criticism" and they appear to have

---

[99] TNA, FO to O'Beirne (Sofia), 29 Sept. 1915, FO800/43. O'Beirne was authorised to order Fitzmaurice to leave, preferably for Athens, should he judge his life to be in real danger. See also H. V. F. Winstone, *The Illicit Adventure: The Story of Political and Military Intelligence in the Middle East from 1898 to 1926* (Cape: London, 1982), p. 182.

[100] Napier, *The Experiences of a Military Attaché in the Balkans*, p. 211.

[101] *The Times* (obit.), 6 Mar. 1953; Elliot (Athens) to FO, 11 Aug. 1915, FO371/2537.

[102] Mackenzie, *First Athenian Memories*, p. 237. Napier, however, agreed with Fitzmaurice, *The Experiences of a Military Attaché in the Balkans*, p. 214.

parted on reasonable terms.[103] Fitzmaurice duly returned to London, where he no doubt anticipated a warm reception.

In October the Turkish memoirs of Sir Edwin Pears had appeared and were attended with considerable publicity.[104] In the opinion of Sir Edwin, so inadequate was the British Embassy in the absence of Fitzmaurice that it was "nothing short of a national misfortune" that—though recovered from his illness at the beginning of 1914—he was not permitted to return. Not to put too fine a point on it, the government had conspired at an action that had contributed significantly to the outbreak of war between Britain and Turkey—with tragic results all now too obvious at the Dardanelles.[105] With the government forced to defend itself on this charge in the House of Commons,[106] the reputation of Fitzmaurice was enhanced and that of Mallet commensurately diminished.[107] Nor does Fitzmaurice's reputation appear to have been dented by his failure in Sofia, where the prospects for success had never been great and had visibly diminished as the year wore on. In his memoirs, published in 1925, even Grey admitted that "with the military situation as it was, neither threats nor promises on our part would influence Bulgaria's decision".[108]

The nearly man

In November 1915 Fitzmaurice was formally "loaned" to the Naval Intelligence Division and remained there until well after the end of the war. What did he do over the next few years in NID? On the slender evidence available,[109] it seems that he worked in the Admiralty in London for the whole time, probably engaged for the most part in evaluating raw intelligence and assisting with the cartography of the

---

[103] Mackenzie, *First Athenian Memories*, pp. 236–8.
[104] *The Standard*, 1 Oct. 1915; *The Daily Mail*, 14 Oct. 1915.
[105] *Forty Years in Constantinople*, pp. 344–5.
[106] *Parl. Debs.*, 5th Ser. (Commons), Vol. LXXIV, 21 Oct. cols. 1970–1.
[107] Mallet was not employed again either in the Diplomatic Service or the FO, except for a brief period in the latter in 1918 and on attachment to the British delegation at the peace conference in Paris. He retired in April 1920, *The Times* (obit.), 10 Aug. 1936.
[108] Grey, *Twenty-Five Years, 1892–1916*, vol. II, p. 225.
[109] Only five files bearing his name were created in the FO during this period and one of those has been weeded: TNA, FO: Card Index, 1910–1919, Research Enquiries Room.

Middle East which was now such an intelligence priority and for which his boundary work so well qualified him.[110] Mapping was also a special interest of Sir Mark Sykes, now a rising power in Middle East policy and with whose schemes Fitzmaurice was to become increasingly associated, probably at the cost of his friendship with George Lloyd, who had never got on with Sykes and now regarded him as his most serious rival.[111] There was, however, some variation in his diet, as for example when in January 1916 his old friend from the American Legation in Constantinople, Lloyd Griscom, turned up in London. Griscom, now working for a law firm, had the delicate task of representing the interests of the pro-German Chicago meat packing company, Sulzberger and Sons, whose cargoes had been seized on the high seas as contraband. To Griscom's astonishment, Fitzmaurice appeared at his room at the Ritz while he was unpacking, and they swapped stories. On returning to his room later, he found that his luggage had been "thoroughly ransacked".[112] There seems nevertheless to have been a constant feeling in the Foreign Office that Fitzmaurice's talents were being wasted at Admiralty Old Building because he was regularly considered for further duties abroad. For one reason or another, however, these ideas came to nothing. In the First World War Fitzmaurice was a nearly man.

For example, in December 1915 the ex-khedive of Egypt, Abbas Hilmi II, in exile in Switzerland, told Sir Evelyn Grant-Duff, the British Minister in Berne, that he had caught wind of a British plan to support an Arab revolt. In return for compensation for his loss of Egypt, he said, he would be willing to throw his great influence in the region behind this strategy, in which event he would need an "English Secretary" who could transmit cypher messages to the agency in Cairo. Fitzmaurice, he said, was the man he had in mind.[113] What Fitzmaurice's reaction was to this idea—if it was ever put to him and, if it was, if it was printable—we do not know but it did not come off.

It was probably in part because of Abbas Hilmi's request for Fitzmaurice of the previous December that in July 1916 his was the name proposed by the Foreign Office as the man to go to Switzerland to

---

[110] On this subject, see the valuable article by Michael Heffernan, "Geography, cartography and military intelligence: the Royal Geographical Society and the First World War", *Transactions of the Institute of British Geographers*, New Series, 21 (3), 1996.

[111] Charmley, *Lord Lloyd and the Decline of the British Empire*, pp. 55–6.

[112] Griscom, *Diplomatically Speaking*, pp. 354–63.

[113] TNA, Duff (Berne) to FO, 17 Dec. 1915, FO141/648.

negotiate the price of his formal abdication.[114] On this occasion Ronald Storrs was the ex-khedive's own first choice but he could not be spared by the Cairo Agency, which agreed that Fitzmaurice would be a "very suitable" substitute.[115] However, while saying he was willing to go if needs must, Fitzmaurice indicated the drawback to the plan:

> his personality was too well-known to the C.U.P. and Nationalist agents, of whom Switzerland is full [George Clerk reported him as saying], for either his presence there or his interviews with Abbas Hilmi to remain concealed, and that every sort of wild story would be set on foot.

Fitzmaurice suggested instead, Harry Boyle, who had been to Lord Cromer at the Cairo Agency what he had been to Sir Gerard Lowther and had been brought from retirement to work in Whitehall for Military Intelligence.[116] Clerk agreed with his reasoning but before he had made a firm recommendation received a message from Sir Henry McMahon which simplified matters.[117]

By this time the Arab revolt against Turkey, actively encouraged by Britain, had just been launched and on 10 July McMahon, whom—as will be recalled—Fitzmaurice had served in Paris at the end of 1914, cabled the Foreign Office as follows:

> If Mr Fitz-Maurice can be spared his services could be very usefully employed here in connection with Arab question.[118]

No doubt McMahon had in mind that he should join the under-staffed Arab Bureau, the work of which was also then particularly difficult.[119] This unit had been recently inspired by Sykes, and Fitzmaurice was among the small number of persons involved in its planning in London;[120] in fact, NID had a substantial interest in it.[121] This invitation

---

[114] FO: Card Index, 1910–1919, TNA Research Enquiries Room.

[115] TNA, FO to High Commissioner for Egypt, 28 June 1916, FO141/648: "If the latter [Storrs] is not available I would propose to send Mr. Fitzmaurice who knows ex-Khedive thoroughly." According to Aubrey Herbert, it was Reshid Bey, the old Kiamilist now in exile in Paris, who had stimulated the idea that it was Fitzmaurice who should go to Switzerland, HUA, Herbert to Sykes, 10 Oct. 1916, DDSY(2), 1/32.

[116] "Obituary. Mr. Harry Boyle: Cromer's 'Eminence Grise' in Egypt", *The Times*, 8 Apr. 1937.

[117] TNA, min. of Clerk, 2 July 1916, FO371/2773.

[118] TNA, McMahon to FO, 10 July 1916, FO371/2773.

[119] TNA, McMahon to Balfour, 20 Dec. 1916, FO371/3043.

[120] TNA, Sykes to Clerk, circa early May 1916, FO371/2771.

[121] TNA, Sykes to Clerk, May 1916, FO371/2771; Adelson, *Mark Sykes*, pp. 193–9; Bruce Westrate, *The Arab Bureau: British Policy in the Middle East, 1916–1920* (The Pennsylvania State University Press: Pennsylvania, 1992), p. 27ff.

clinched it for Clerk, who thought that Fitzmaurice "would be more usefully employed in Cairo than in the Ad[miral]ty", while Boyle should negotiate with Abbas Hilmi. This decision was promptly communicated to McMahon by Grey.[122] With bad blood between the English and the Irish caused by the Easter Rising in Ireland and the manner of its repression, not to mention the fact that the trial for treason of Sir Roger Casement was not making Irish consuls flavour of the season, perhaps it also seemed to them a good idea to get Fitzmaurice well out of harm's way at this moment—*moderate* Irish nationalist though he was known to be. Since the posting would also have meant working with other friends as well, notably George Lloyd, Philip Graves, Wyndham Deedes, and Gertrude Bell, it might be imagined that Fitzmaurice would have jumped at this chance. However, once more an idea for prising him out of the Admiralty Old Building died the death: for some reason he did not go.[123] There is no record in the Foreign Office papers that Hall was consulted—or Fitzmaurice himself, for that matter. Perhaps Hall had ideas of his own for him; perhaps he was struck down by one of his periodic bouts of ill-health; or perhaps he let it be known that he now saw more advantage in enlisting the Jews than the Arabs in support of the Entente.[124]

In 1918 Fitzmaurice was considered for what would have been one of his most challenging appointments of all: consul-general in Moscow, where revolution was in full swing and to which the Bolsheviks—fearing a German advance—had moved their government from St. Petersburg in March. The file on this subject has been weeded and all we are left with is a tantalizing Foreign Office Registry index card. This, dated simply "1918", says no more than "Fitzmaurice, Gerald Henry. Suggestion to appoint him Consul General at Moscow".

---

[122] TNA, Grey to McMahon, 12 July 1916, FO371/2773.

[123] Harry Boyle did not go to Switzerland either; it was Lord Acton who was eventually employed.

[124] It is possible, though unlikely, that T. E. Lawrence—who had reservations about Fitzmaurice (see Epilogue)—had a hand in this decision. I have seen no direct evidence of any personal contact between them, though it is quite probable that they met when both were in London at the end of 1914, Lawrence in the Geographical Section of the General Staff (working on a military map of Sinai) and Fitzmaurice in the FO. Be that as it may, Lawrence would have learned plenty about him from Aubrey Herbert, George Lloyd, and Philip Graves, with all of whom he worked later in Cairo Intelligence, Jeremy Wilson, *Lawrence of Arabia: The Authorised Biography of T. E. Lawrence* (Minerva: London, 1990), ch. 10.

The existing consul-general was the cautious, scholarly Oliver Wardrop, who had been in post only since the October Revolution of 1917, when he replaced the colourful Robert Bruce Lockhart. Lockhart himself had been sent back to Russia by Lloyd George in January 1918 in order to establish unofficial relations with the Bolsheviks, whose 'de facto' government Britain was refusing to recognise; so by March he was in Moscow together with Wardrop.[125] However, Lockhart was believed by some in London to be too sympathetic to the Bolsheviks and he had certainly been hostile to the plans for Allied intervention in north Russia and Siberia, which in early August came to fruition.[126] With an urgent need for a political warfare specialist in Moscow whose heart was really in the task of rallying the anti-Bolsheviks in support of the feeble Allied forces, it seems likely, therefore, that *in effect* it was Lockhart who was being considered for replacement by Fitzmaurice rather than Wardrop. In the event, Lockhart swung behind the Allied intervention but this only gave him a short stay of execution—and perhaps Fitzmaurice only a short extension of any suspense. For the intervention provoked the Bolsheviks into strong actions against the Allied communities, including their consular officers. On 9 August 1918 Wardrop hauled down his flag and handed over the protection of British interests to The Netherlands. As for Lockhart, he was charged by the Bolsheviks with counter-revolutionary activities following the near-successful attempt on Lenin's life at the end of the month and imprisoned until early October.[127] The fragile relations between Britain and Bolshevik Russia had fallen apart and there was no post left in Moscow to which any new British consular official could go. Nevertheless it is interesting that Fitzmaurice should have been considered for this position because it confirms that someone senior in the Foreign Office—probably Clerk or Oliphant—thought that he still had plenty of fight left in him. It also suggests that it may already have been decided that he was not to be sent back to Constantinople.

In early October 1918 there surfaced yet another idea for using Fitzmaurice's talents. The War Office wanted him to be political adviser

---

[125] R. H. Bruce Lockhart, *Memoirs of a British Agent* (Putnam: London and New York, 1932), pp. 191–5, 200–1, 242–7, 263.

[126] In March, it seems, he had almost been recalled, Lockhart, *Memoirs of a British Agent*, p. 290.

[127] On this whole episode, see Richard H. Ullman, *Anglo-Soviet Relations, 1917–1921: Intervention and the War* (Princeton University Press: Princeton, N.J., 1961), ch. 10. Wardrop was also unable to leave Moscow until 3 October, *FO List 1920*.

on Balkan affairs to General Bridges, who was to be sent on a mission to Bulgaria to represent British interests at the headquarters of the French *Armée d'Orient*. The recommendation probably came from Napier, who was also going, and Fitzmaurice was promised the temporary rank of Colonel.[128] However, Lord Robert Cecil, the junior minister at the Foreign Office, told Milner at the cabinet on 14 October that he thought this not a good idea since Fitzmaurice would be regarded as too pro-Bulgar. Sir Eyre Crowe was of the same opinion and Harry Lamb was sent instead.[129]

Helping the Zionists

Nearly being sent on so many important missions must—at least in a few of the cases concerned—have been frustrating for Fitzmaurice. Nevertheless, remaining in London during the war had its compensations, and one of them was the opportunity it provided him to assist in promoting Zionism, to which, as we have seen (p. 149 above), he had long been attracted. This idea had been gathering adherents in London as the benefits to the war effort of gaining the gratitude of American Jews, in particular, began to be understood.[130] In early 1916, however, there was still hesitation over Zionism in British government circles, not least because Jewry itself was divided on the question; the vital importance of keeping the Entente in good health also meant that French ambitions in regard to Palestine had to be taken into account. There was, therefore, much lobbying and intriguing to be done by those who wished to push Britain into taking a sufficiently supportive position on the issue to make an attractive deal with the Jews possible. It was the kind of operation that was meat and drink to Fitzmaurice.

Fitzmaurice clearly made it his business to keep in close contact with the leading London Zionists, including the president of the English Zionist Federation and fellow Admiralty employee, Chaim Weizmann.[131]

---

[128] TNA, Thwaites (War Office) to Lord Robert Cecil, 13 Oct. 1918, FO371/3159.

[129] TNA, mins. on Thwaites to Cecil, 13 Oct. 1918, FO371/3159.

[130] Isaiah Friedman, *The Question of Palestine: British-Jewish-Arab Relations: 1914–1918*, 2nd expanded ed. (Transaction: New Brunswick and London, 1992), chs. 4 and 5.

[131] Leonard Stein, *The Balfour Declaration* (Vallentine-Mitchell: London, 1961), p. 34, n. 121. In his memoirs Weizman does not mention Fitzmaurice, though he says that "There were, at that time, alike in the highest Government posts, and in those of

He was also to be seen "bustling in and out of Ministries and official places in those days".[132] In view of his considerable powers of persuasion and reputation for political sagacity on matters Eastern, therefore, it is not surprising that Fitzmaurice was responsible for some notable converts. These allegedly included two of the most intelligent and influential figures in the British Army: Sir Henry Wilson, who rose to be Chief of the Imperial General Staff in early 1918 and had a reputation for political intrigue; and Sir George Macdonogh, who had been Director of Military Intelligence since the beginning of 1916.[133] It is perhaps also not entirely coincidental that Fitzmaurice's two admirers in the Admiralty, Fisher and Hall, also came out for Zionism. Indeed, when in January 1916 the first draft of what became known as the 'Sykes-Picot agreement' on French and British spheres of influence in the Middle East was discussed in London, it was Hall who emphasised the need not to overlook Jewish aspirations in regard to Palestine.[134] In the Foreign Office, where sensitivity to French claims to Palestine was a constant obstacle to the Zionists, one of the earliest converts was the respected Hugh O'Beirne, who at the end of the following month claimed that the Jews might be made an attractive offer on Palestine as a *quid pro quo* for withdrawal of their support from the Young Turk government, "which would then automatically collapse". Friedman is right to suspect the influence of Fitzmaurice in this extravagant claim; he would have been entitled to be certain had he known how intimately

---

secondary importance, men with a real understanding... [of Zionism] ... I set myself to discovering these men.... Some of them I met in the course of my work at the Admiralty", *Trial and Error: The Autobiography of Chaim Weizmann* (Harper: New York, 1949), p. 179.

[132] Sykes, *Two Studies in Virtue*, p. 194.

[133] Sykes, *Two Studies in Virtue*, p. 194. Macdonogh had converted from Methodism to Roman Catholicism and so may have presented a slightly easier target for Fitzmaurice. By contrast, Wilson was a militant Ulster Unionist. Not surprisingly, the two did not get on: Ian F. W. Beckett, "Macdonogh, Sir George Mark Watson (1865–1942)", *ODNB* [38446, accessed 30 Nov. 2006] and Keith Jeffery, "Wilson, Sir Henry Hughes, baronet (1864–1922)", *ODNB* [36955, accessed 30 Nov 2006]. An equally well placed source, Samuel Landman, who was Secretary-General of the World Zionist Organization from 1917 until 1922, confirms that Macdonogh was "won over" by Fitzmaurice, "Balfour Declaration—Secret Facts Revealed", *World Jewry*, vol. 2, nos. 42–3, 11 Feb., 1 Mar. 1935. In his *Great Britain, the Jews and Palestine* (New Zionist Press: London, 1936), Landman placed Fitzmaurice in the "front rank" among the small number of "Englishmen of vision" who served the cause of Zionism.

[134] Adelson, *Mark Sykes*, pp. 201–2; Friedman, *The Question of Palestine*, p. 111. Naomi Shepherd also detects the influence of Fitzmaurice in Hall's view, *Ploughing Sand: British Rule in Palestine, 1917–1948* (John Murray: London, 1999), p. 9.

Fitzmaurice and O'Beirne had worked in Sofia only months earlier.
O'Beirne ended the minute in which he expressed this view by saying
that, on the practicalities of any scheme, "I would suggest that we
might consult Mr. Fitzmaurice".[135] The influence of these men was all
considerable but it was through his relationship with Mark Sykes that
Fitzmaurice probably made his biggest contribution to advancing the
cause of Zionism.

The reputation of Sykes as an expert on the Middle East had risen
following his negotiations with the French at the beginning of 1916, and
in June Hankey secured for him a desk in the Committee of Imperial
Defence Secretariat in Whitehall Gardens. In December, after the elevation to Number 10 of Lloyd George, who had the fullest confidence in
Sykes, he was appointed a political secretary to the War Cabinet with
responsibility for Middle Eastern affairs.[136] These were ideal positions
from which to project influence throughout the government machine,
and his role in helping to persuade the government to declare its support for Zionism in the Balfour Declaration of November 1917 is well
known.[137] How did Fitzmaurice fit into this activity?

Sykes not only respected Fitzmaurice but was fond of him. They
both attended mass at Westminster Cathedral and thought alike on
most subjects. Despite Sykes's 'Unionism', they even seemed to be in
basic agreement on Ireland. They both kept at arm's length the Turcophiles, whose number included Mallet, Block and Herbert and at the
beginning of 1914 had organized themselves in The Ottoman Association.[138] Sykes's views on Zionism—including suspicion of assimilated
Jews—were identical to those of Fitzmaurice.[139] Though he followed
Fitzmaurice into support for the movement rather than the other way

---

[135] TNA, min. of O'Beirne, 28 Feb. 1916, FO371/2671; Friedman, *The Question of Palestine*, pp. 53–5.

[136] Adelson, *Mark Sykes*, pp. 209, 215–16, 236; Friedman, *The Question of Palestine*, p. 125.

[137] Adelson, *Mark Sykes*, pp. 235, 242–4; Friedman, *The Question of Palestine*, chs. 8, 12, and pp. 277–8.

[138] Repeated attempts to persuade Sykes to join this lobby were made in 1914, HUA, DDSY(2), 1/25 and 1/26; the names of neither Sykes nor Fitzmaurice appear on the membership lists included in these files; see also Adelson, *Mark Sykes*, p. 211. Following the outbreak of the war, Block's financial and commercial expertise was employed in economic warfare, eventually as Controller of the Finance Section of the Ministry of Blockade from June 1916 until November 1918, when he returned to Constantinople.

[139] Adelson, *Mark Sykes*, p. 208.

round,[140] his well documented conversion in 1916–17 shows no trace of Fitzmaurice's influence.[141] What instead the latter appears to have done is to encourage, inform, advise, and assist him in the execution of his policy: 'dragoman' (once more) to Sykes's 'ambassador'. Such a person was the more essential to Sykes because the drawback to the freelance role that he so relished was that he had no ministry to provide him formally with this sort of back-up.

Sykes had returned to England not long after Fitzmaurice, at the beginning of December 1915, and they were soon in close touch. In a typically cryptic and wholly metaphorical letter received by Sykes while he was absorbing the mixed reaction to the memorandum he had just agreed with Picot, and which captures well their relationship, Fitzmaurice addressed him as his "Submarine", threw in a reference to the previous night's "periscope", and promised to tell him about another "excellent opportunity for launching a torpedo" when they next met.[142] Thereafter the evidence for Fitzmaurice's assistance to Sykes is compelling, though his role here was even more shadowy than it had been in Constantinople, and only glimpses of it can be seen.

On 30 October 1916, Fitzmaurice accompanied Sykes at his second interview with Aaron Aaronsohn, who was on a secret visit to London. Aaronsohn was a most important figure among the Palestinian Jews, a valuable source of intelligence to the British, and believed to have had "the decisive influence in Sykes's conversion to Zionism".[143] There is also testimony from two good sources that Fitzmaurice assisted Sykes in encouraging the temporary but important rapprochement between the Zionists and the Holy See that commenced with the visit to Rome in April 1917 of Nahum Sokolow, a leading member of the executive of the World Zionist Organization and close collaborator of Chaim Weizmann in London.[144] From Sykes's appointments diary for

---

[140] c.f. Sykes, *Two Studies in Virtue*, p. 194.

[141] Friedman, *The Question of Palestine*, pp. 112–24; Adelson, *Mark Sykes*, chs. 11–12.

[142] HUA, Fitzmaurice to Sykes, 12 Jan. 1916, DDSY(2), 1/30.

[143] Friedman, *The Question of Palestine*, p. 122.

[144] The evidence is, however, vague on the details of Fitzmaurice's involvement. Christopher Sykes says simply that "he travelled to Rome for the purpose" but does not say when. He also emphasises the role of his father and makes no mention of Fitzmaurice in connection with Sokolow's satisfactory interviews at the Vatican, including one with the Pope himself, *Two Studies in Virtue*, p. 194. The more fully documented accounts of Sokolow's mission provided by both Friedman (*The Question of Palestine*, pp. 151–5), and Stein (*The Balfour Declaration*, pp. 404–8) follow the same line. However, Landman says

16 November, shortly after the agreement of the War Cabinet to the Balfour Declaration, we see Fitzmaurice meeting him in company with Sokolow.[145] Perhaps most interestingly of all, in view of his involvement in the attempt to buy Turkey out of the war during the Dardanelles operation, Fitzmaurice was now firmly aligned with Sykes and the Zionists in their successful bid to block attempts to make a separate peace between Britain and Turkey in the second half of 1917.[146]

The idea of a separate peace, which alarmed the Zionists because of its implications for Palestine, was supported by the British Turcophiles and the Americans, who sent former US Ambassador to Turkey, Henry Morgenthau, on a special mission to further the project. Its support by Adam Block—railed against by Weizmann as "a renegade Jew of Galician origin, who would do all he could to prevent the realization of a British protectorate of Palestine"[147]—would probably have been sufficient in itself to put Fitzmaurice on the other side. As it was, he did not need this sort of encouragement. However, in an undated letter to Sykes, written either in late 1917 or the beginning of 1918, it was not the risk of separate peace negotiations to Zionism that he emphasised but to the bonds between Britain and Russia, which, he believed, Germany hoped would be loosened by a falling out over some Near Eastern question:

> Therefore [he continued] the Allies—on the principle of the bundle of faggots—must keep absolutely locked together until the Mephistopheles workings on the German Faust have been undone. We shall never get a better Constellation of Powers for eradicating the Prussian War God....[148]

In the Foreign Office, Lancelot Oliphant, a close friend of Sykes and admirer of Fitzmaurice, had to deal with this question. From the first lukewarm about the Morgenthau mission and soon openly hostile to it, he actually suggested that Fitzmaurice should be the expert adviser to

---

in his "Balfour Declaration—Secret Facts revealed", that Sokolow's interviews were obtained "thanks to the introductions of Fitzmaurice", as well as to the help of the Italian foreign minister—and does not mention Mark Sykes at all.

[145] According to the same source, he also met Fitzmaurice on 8 August 1917 and twice (afternoon and dinner) on 6 December, HUA, DDSY(2), 2/8.

[146] Sykes, *Two Studies in Virtue*, pp. 205–6.

[147] HUA, Ormsby-Gore to Lord Robert Cecil, 10 June 1917, DDSY (2), 12/8.

[148] HUA, Fitzmaurice to Sykes, nd [though '1918' suggested by the archivist], DDSY (2), 4/168.

the "emissary of authority" who it had been agreed would meet Morgenthau at Gibraltar en route to the Near East. Oliphant's motive for this suggestion is not difficult to infer, which is probably why Hardinge, who was once more permanent under-secretary at the Foreign Office and was initially more sympathetic to separate peace negotiations, did not take it up.[149] This was, therefore, another mission on which Fitzmaurice did not go—but it did not matter. The Sykes-Fitzmaurice-Zionist axis, with help from the Armenians, won the argument.[150]

No return to Constantinople

On 30 October 1918, following negotiations at Mudros Bay between Vice-Admiral Calthorpe, British Commander-in-Chief, and a Turkish delegation in which Raouf Bey, Minister of Marine, played the most prominent role, an armistice was signed between Britain and Turkey. The ceremony took place on HMS *Agamemnon*, the same warship that had carried Fitzmaurice to the same destination over four years earlier, at a time when he was thought the most suitable person to stand by the side of the British admiral on the occasion of the anticipated victory. But he was not at Mudros Bay on 30 October 1918. Moreover, on 1 November, in a telegram to the Admiralty about the "immense importance" of the kind of representation Britain should have in Constantinople, Calthorpe said that he had received a hint from Raouf Bey, whose good English and straightforwardness had impressed him, that the Nationalist government that had just replaced that of the CUP "would regard it as unfortunate if Mr Fitzmaurice the late Dragoman were to return".[151] Raouf Bey had been with Shevket Pasha at the

---

[149] TNA, mins. of Oliphant and Hardinge, 31 May and 1 June 1917, FO371/3057; cf. Friedman, *The Question of Palestine*, p. 212.

[150] In the event, the British government sent Weizmann to Gibraltar, together with an intelligence officer called Kennerley Rumford. The Zionist leader did not need Fitzmaurice to scupper Morgenthau's mission. On this fiasco, see Weizmann, *Trial and Error*, ch. 17; William A. Yale, "Ambassador Henry Morgenthau's Special Mission of 1917", *World Politics*, 1 (3), Apr. 1919; Jehuda Reinharz, "His Majesty's Zionist emissary: Chaim Weizmann's mission to Gibraltar in 1917", *Journal of Contemporary History*, 27 (2), April 1992. On the sequel, see Friedman, *The Question of Palestine*, pp. 218–26.

[151] TNA, Calthorpe to Admiralty, 1 Nov. 1918, ADM116/1823. On the armistice negotiations generally, see Patrick Kinross, *Atatürk: The Rebirth of a Nation* (Phoenix: London, 1996), ch. 16.

time of the counter-revolution in April 1909 and obviously had a long memory.[152]

Though it was probably already a foregone conclusion, therefore, Fitzmaurice was not at the side of Calthorpe when his flagship, HMS *Superb*, led the Allied fleet through the Dardanelles to Constantinople on 12 November.[153] If he knew about it, it would at least have been some consolation that Sir Adam Block was also rejected for the role of conducting initial negotiations with the Turks, though for the opposite reason: he was considered by the Foreign Office to be "completely identified with the C.U.P.".[154]

Thus spurned, it could have come as no surprise to Fitzmaurice when he was denied the resumption of his position as chief dragoman when a *de facto* British embassy was re-opened in Constantinople immediately following the Armistice. The final blow, this was delivered despite the acknowledged need for someone with his kind of expertise to pilot the British representatives through the political minefield awaiting them in Constantinople; despite the fact that it proved extremely difficult to obtain suitable staff for the British mission and that there were fears in the Foreign Office, in consequence, that the French would run rings round it;[155] and despite awareness of the vital importance of obtaining reliable information on conditions in Armenia, where killings during the war had reached genocidal proportions. Perhaps an unspoken consideration was that the Foreign Office, which regarded the new Turkish government as but a facade for the CUP, was apprehensive that Fitzmaurice would be unable to resist the temptation to help unseat it, which was not at all what was wanted in the immediate future. The foreign secretary, Arthur Balfour, did not wish to be under moral pressure to be gentle on the Turks in the peace negotiations as a result of being faced with Ententist ministers across the table; he also wished the CUP to take the blame for a harsh settlement.[156]

---

[152] Kinross, *Atatürk*, pp. 36–7.

[153] TNA, Calthorpe to Secretary of the Admiralty, 10 Dec. 1918, ADM116/1823 [Calthorpe's report on the armistice negotiations and his reception in Constantinople].

[154] TNA, min. on Charles Staniforth to Lloyd George [recommending Block], 22 Oct. 1918, FO371/3414.

[155] TNA, mins. of Kidston, Cecil and Tilley on Webb (Constantinople) to Balfour, 5 Dec. 1918, FO371/3415.

[156] TNA, Balfour to Calthorpe [private instructions], 9 Nov. 1918, FO371/3415; see also Lord Robert Cecil's remarks at the War Cabinet on 29 Oct. 1918, mins., CAB23/8.

Since Turkey was still technically an enemy state, the forms of ordinary diplomatic relations could not be established. As a result, during the lengthy transition to peace, British representation was given the anodyne title of 'High Commission' rather than 'Embassy'. Calthorpe was appointed 'High Commissioner' (while remaining Commander-in-Chief of the Mediterranean Fleet), Rear-Admiral Richard Webb 'Assistant High Commissioner', and Thomas Hohler 'Chief Political Officer'.[157] In his memoirs, Ryan wrote: "I became Second Political Officer, but was to all intents and purposes Chief Dragoman, as there was less question than ever of the return of Fitzmaurice, though he continued to hold the post in theory".[158] For the time being, Fitzmaurice remained in the Admiralty.

Throwing in the towel

By this time Fitzmaurice seems to have drifted apart from George Lloyd, so it was probably a matter of no great moment to him that his former protégée—now Sir George Lloyd—had departed for India to take up the post of Governor of Bombay in November 1918, only days after the Allied fleet arrived at Constantinople.[159] It must have been a much more severe blow to Fitzmaurice when he learned of the death in Paris in February 1919, while attending the peace conference, of Sir Mark Sykes, who had succumbed to the influenza then sweeping Europe.

With the war over and economies needed at NID, Fitzmaurice left the Admiralty in May but had to take sick leave and did not return to the Foreign Office until late November.[160] He then joined the recently merged News and Political Intelligence Department, superintended by his long-time patron Sir William Tyrrell.[161] According to the assistant director of the hitherto separate Political Intelligence Department (PID), J. W. Headlam-Morley, it required persons with "a very peculiar

---

[157] TNA, Instructions to Admiral Sir S. Caltorpe; and Balfour to Calthorpe, 9 Nov. 1918, FO371/3415. See also Ryan, *The Last of the Dragomans*, pp. 118–73; and Waugh, *Turkey*, ch. 9.

[158] *The Last of the Dragomans*, p. 121.

[159] Among the great many letters of congratulation to Lloyd that came in on news of this appointment there was none from Fitzmaurice; see CAC Cam., GLLD 10/2.

[160] MECA Oxford, Tilley to Ryan, 23 July 1919, Ryan Papers, V/2.

[161] *FO List* 1920, p. 8.

and exceptional combination of qualities".[162] Among other things, this
department evaluated the reports received three times a day from the
Secret Service. At the beginning of 1920 it was also asked by the rabidly
anti-semitic editor of the *Morning Post*, H. A. Gwynne, to advise on the
authenticity of the so-called 'Protocols of the Elders of Zion', which
he was anxious to serialise in order to push up his newspaper's flagging
circulation figures. Tyrrell, who was a long-time intimate of Gwynne's,
was happy to oblige. Whether Fitzmaurice was among the members of
his staff whom he consulted we do not know, and the memorandum
on the subject was written by his colleague, George Saunders, the
former Berlin and Paris correspondent of *The Times*. However, it is
likely that, in view of his well known interest in the politics of world
Jewry, Fitzmaurice would have been asked for his opinion as well.
Saunders maintained, correctly, that the 'Protocols' were spurious and
Tyrrell more or less endorsed this view.[163] It was probably supported
by Fitzmaurice, who by this time was of course on good terms with
leading Jews and, as a political warfare specialist himself, was likely to
have been able to spot a forgery of this nature when he saw one.

Arnold Toynbee had until recently been the leading light of PID and
in the newly merged department Fitzmaurice worked with others who
were to make their names as major historians, namely, Lewis Namier
and Harold Temperley.[164] However, once more he found himself in
a department that seemed bloated if not out of place in peacetime
and was thus being run down prior to being broken up.[165] In fact, like
Namier (who had returned to Balliol College in April), by the time that
Tyrrell was advised on the manner of its retrenchment in August 1920

---

[162] TNA, Headlam-Morley to Howarth (Treasury), 15 Oct. 1919, T1/12333.

[163] University of Leeds, Brotherton Library, Tyrrell to Gwynne, 4 Feb. 1920, Gle-
nesk-Bathurst Papers, 1990/1/5123; Keith Wilson, *A Study in the History and Politics of the
Morning Post, 1905–1926* (Edwin Mellen: Lewiston, New York, 1990), ch. 6 (the Saunders
Memorandum of 19 January 1920 is reproduced as an appendix to this chapter).

[164] Namier came from a family of "Polonized Jews, who had embraced Catholicism"; he was also a supporter of Zionism, John Cannon, "Namier, Sir Lewis Bernstein
(1888–1960)", *ODNB* [35183, accessed 20 Jan. 2007].

[165] TNA, Tyrrell to Koppel, 23 Aug. 1920; Montgomery (Chief Clerk) to Secretary to
Treasury, 16 Nov. 1920, FO366/790. The Political Intelligence section was closed down
altogether at the end of 1920, though a slimmed down News section survived, Philip M.
Taylor, *The Projection of Britain: British Overseas Publicity and Propaganda 1919–1939* (Cam-
bridge University Press: Cambridge, 1981), p. 15. See also Sir John Tilley and Stephen
Gaselee, *The Foreign Office* (Putnam: London and New York, 1933), pp. 190–1.

his name had already disappeared from the staff list.[166] So once more there was the problem of what to do with Fitzmaurice.

According to a letter that he wrote to Andrew Ryan in early 1921, first he was offered the position of consul-general in Beirout, one of the other top posts in the Levant Service. However, he had to turn this down for fear that its climate would not suit his health. A second suggestion was that he should become a paid servant of the Bulgarian government on the Reparations Commission. The idea of having money transferred to him by the government in Sofia rather than the other way round must have amused him but he had to reject this suggestion on the grounds that he lacked the necessary financial experience. At this point, though still only 55 years old but with his health impaired and anxious not to obstruct the confirmation as his successor of Andrew Ryan, he decided to throw in the towel.[167] Though still doing "work of sorts" in early 1921, he was retired by the Foreign Office as from 1 January of that year—"A tragedy, I think", another former colleague wrote to Ryan, "and you will agree".[168] Ryan was thus formally appointed chief dragoman, with a local diplomatic rank never given to Fitzmaurice, namely, counsellor.[169] But at least the distinction was given to a man whom he regarded as a friend.

---

[166] TNA, Koppel [head of NPID] to Tyrrell, 20 Aug., FO366/790. Temperley was transferred to the Central European Department in a temporary capacity, Note of Montgomery, 28 July 1921, FO366/795.

[167] MECA Oxf., Edmunds to Ryan, 22 Dec. 1920 and 7 Feb. 1921, Ryan Papers V/5.

[168] MECA Oxf., Edmunds to Ryan, 22 Dec. 1920, Ryan Papers V/5. His retirement was granted for medical reasons rather than on grounds of redundancy, though Fitzmaurice had argued for the latter because it would have given him a somewhat larger pension, MECA Oxf., Fitzmaurice to Ryan, 28 Feb. 1921, Ryan Papers V/6.

[169] *The Last of the Dragomans*, p. 152.

EPILOGUE

Having spent most of the final seven years of his career in London, Fitzmaurice had broadened his acquaintance and ensured that at least among those who new the East his reputation remained intact—even enhanced. 'Mr Fitzmaurice' had become 'Fitzmaurice of Constantinople'.[1] Nevertheless, he had not had a good war. He was sent on hopeless missions in 1915 first to bribe Turkey out of the war and then to bribe Bulgaria into it. Thereafter, one interesting mission after another was trailed past him and then, for one reason or another, fell away. These included what seemed the near certainty that he was to join the Arab Bureau at the time of the Arab Revolt in 1916. At the last moment this decision was reversed and the 'Sheikh', as he was known to a small circle of friends, had to witness T. E. Lawrence stealing the limelight. Finally, he was denied a triumphant return to Constantinople in November 1918 and condemned instead to finish his days in the obscurity of News and Political Intelligence Department in the Foreign Office. It was only the Balfour Declaration of 1917 on which he could look back with some real pride of war-time workmanship.

Since his return from the Yemen frontier in 1905, no more honours had come Fitzmaurice's way either, though those who had been on a formal par with him in the Levant Service had either been knighted already or would be before long. These included his successor, Andrew Ryan, who freely admitted that he could not hold a candle to him. "It irks me still, as I think it did some others who had served with Fitzmaurice," wrote another, "that we were given honours that did not come to him."[2]

What are we now to make of this man? Throughout his career Gerald Fitzmaurice remained formally a consular officer, only being given *local* diplomatic rank in order to lend him more standing in the eyes of the natives once he became chief dragoman in 1907. But this makes him even more of a classic example of what Wicquefort, the first great writer on what diplomats actually did, as opposed to what they were supposed

---

[1] Thomas Hohler to the Editor of *The Times*, 9 May 1941.
[2] Bullard, *The Camels Must Go*, p. 64.

to do, called a 'Minister of the Second Order', as mentioned in the Prologue to this work.[3] Such a man, of which Wicquefort himself was an outstanding example, did much of the real business of diplomacy, in particular that which involved risks. This included gathering intelligence, purchasing influence, and—above all—establishing contact with, and if necessary encouraging, opposition elements active in the countries where he found himself posted. He could do this precisely because, unlike the ambassador, he did not enjoy 'the full representative character' and thus could not to the same extent compromise his sovereign if caught out.

Fitzmaurice had no fear of getting his hands dirty and took plenty of risks. The result was that the British Embassy in Turkey, weakly led for most of his time and used too much as a training school for the diplomatic aristocracy, had good reason to be grateful to him. So, too, did many British companies, not to mention, of course, thousands of Armenians. Naturally he was guilty of misjudgements, notably in underestimating the strength of the CUP at the time of the counter-revolution in April 1909 and in predicting the over-running of Constantinople by the Bulgarians in the winter of 1912. He also seems to have come to believe too much in his own propaganda about the conspiracy of Jewish Freemasons behind the Young Turks. Nevertheless, he remained, as was often said of him, a remarkable man: clear-headed, ruthless, persuasive, and full of energy—a Lenin of diplomacy.

Fitzmaurice's enemies were as quick as his friends to acknowledge his huge ability and influence. T. E. Lawrence, for example, who was among the former, admitted frankly that he had "an eagle-mind and personality of iron vigour... knew everything and was feared from end to end of Turkey". His prestige, he said, "was enormous and our Ambassadors and the F.O. staff went down before him like ninepins".[4] As for Marmaduke Pickthall, he thought that Fitzmaurice should actually have been British Ambassador had "the reactionary Turkish party" been in power, "for no man living would have had such influence with a Turkish Government of that colour".[5]

---

[3] See the extract on this subject from Digby's translation: Abraham de Wicquefort, *The Embassador and His Functions* (London, 1716), in my *Diplomatic Classics: Selected texts from Commynes to Vattel* (Palgrave Macmillan: Basingstoke, 2004), p. 125.

[4] T. E. Lawrence, *To His Biographers Robert Graves and Liddell Hart: Information about himself, in the form of letters, notes, answers to questions and conversations* (Cassell: London, 1963), pp. 87–8.

[5] "In Defence of British Diplomacy".

The main controversy about Fitzmaurice has always centred on the decision of Turkey to side with Germany in November 1914. His admirers said he would have preserved Turkey as a friendly neutral had he remained in Constantinople, or—having been ejected—been allowed to return in the summer. His detractors said that if he had been permitted to return it would either have made no difference or just made matters worse because—thanks to his hostility to the Young Turks—Turkey had already been driven too deeply into the arms of Germany. Of course, we shall never know the answer to this question, though I like to think that his admirers were nearer the mark. The problem really was how Fitzmaurice was used. In view of his anti-CUP reputation, he should probably either have been granted his own wish for an important provincial consular post on returning from the Aden hinterland in 1905 or given a freer rein as chief dragoman to get rid of the CUP when its true character became obvious. By keeping him in Constantinople but on a tight leash, it seems to me that the Foreign Office succeeded merely in angering the Young Turks without seriously harming them.

In private letters written at the time of his retirement to Andrew Ryan, who was uncomfortable at stepping so prematurely into his shoes, Fitzmaurice concealed any bitterness about his treatment by the Foreign Office. What he revealed instead was just sadness and deep weariness. He was also keen to reassure his successor that he had made no sacrifice to make way for him. Ryan had undertaken to sell or arrange shipment of his personal effects—all of which he had left behind in Constantinople in February 1914—and he was anxious to thank him. His collection of rugs, valued at about £5000 and "some of which", he thought "may one day grace a Dublin museum", was of particular concern to him and he toyed with the idea of returning to collect them himself: "One is reluctant to revisit haunts with which one has severed official connection but a sea voyage would do me good", he told Ryan. As for current events in Turkey, he said: "I take but a meagre and waning interest in the N. East where Palestine seems 'the one bright spot'".[6] In 1922 he had such a serious bout of illness that he had to go to a nursing home in Surrey to recover, and his rugs must have had

---

[6] MECA Oxf., Fitzmaurice to Ryan, 25 Oct. 1920 and 28 Feb. 1921, Ryan Papers V/6.

to make their own way back.[7] There were, however, compensations in his life in retirement after the war.

Andrew Ryan and his wife invited Fitzmaurice to be godfather to their son, and he gladly accepted, saying "I'm a bit old to be an effective godfather but, mayhap, I shall live long enough to be helpful. As you so kindly put it, it is a link to replace the one severed".[8] And then there was Ireland.

In April 1908 Fitzmaurice had told George Lloyd that Ireland was "the Bull's Eye" at the centre of the concentric circles that represented the map of his own politics. This had not changed. Indeed, with the Irish question hotting up immediately before and during the war, it is likely that he began to feel its pull more strongly. While he seems not to have spent much time in the country of his birth, he launched himself into charitable activities with the large London Irish community. He worked for boys' clubs and seamen's homes in the East End,[9] and had a close connection with Campion House, the Jesuit-run pre-seminary college in West London which flourished after the war when many young men who had seen its horrors offered themselves for the priesthood.[10]

Fitzmaurice also gravitated into the circle of John Pius Boland, a lawyer by training who had been the Irish Nationalist MP for South Kerry since 1900 and was a party whip.[11] Described by his daughter Bridget as a "gentle fanatic", Boland disapproved deeply of the violent tactics of Sinn Fein and had a particularly strong interest in Irish education.[12] In 1918 he lost his seat to a Sinn Fein candidate, and the subsequent partition of Ireland caused him to despair. He retired from politics, settled permanently in London, refused to return to Ireland until the 1930s, and devoted most of his energies to the Catholic Truth Society, for which he served as secretary from 1926 until 1947. His

---

[7] MECA Oxf., Fitzmaurice to Ryan, 24 May 1922, Ryan Papers V/6.

[8] MECA Oxf., Fitzmaurice to Ryan, 28 Feb. 1921, Ryan Papers V/6.

[9] Bullard, *The Camels Must Go*, p. 64.

[10] His will, written in 1933, stipulated that in the event that he should be pre-deceased by his sister, Alice, his entire estate (bar £2,100) should go to this institution. See also Ann Smith, *The Story of Campion* House (James House: London, 2004).

[11] When the Tories were in power the Irish Party had applied pressure for home rule by ingenious methods of obstructing government business in the House of Commons. Under the more sympathetic Liberals, however, it had generally been more restrained and had also supported the war effort, Boland, *At My Mother's Knee*, pp. 42–4; John Boland, *Irishman's Day: A Day in the Life of an Irish M.P.* (MacDonald: London, n.d. but circa 1944), p. 123.

[12] Boland, *At My Mother's Knee*, pp. 35–42.

wife Eileen, who had a cosmopolitan upbringing and never returned to Ireland at all, was also deeply religious.[13]

The Bolands had numerous children and kept a large and welcoming house at 40 St. George's Square in Pimlico, close to the houses of parliament.[14] This became a focal point in the life of Fitzmaurice, and not just because he shared his close friend's view of the Irish question.[15] He might have been long on acquaintances but he was short on friends, and lived not so far away from the Bolands, at Earls Court, in what seems to have been a succession of "cheerless private hotels, all sad widows and doilies". Sick of being pestered for his views, he had also been obliged to give up the St. James's Club.[16] According to Bridget Boland, who was born in 1913, he loved her mother dearly and was a regular visitor for tea on Sundays for many years. "Fitzie was short and broad, but wiry, with a hooked nose and a big drooping moustache," she says, "and one could see how easily he could pass, as he often had, for a Turk."[17]

In an obituary notice on Fitzmaurice, Harold Temperley, his former colleague in the News and Political Intelligence Department, regretted that "In retirement he maintained an exceptional discretion about his career and refused to write his memoirs".[18] What a pity that Temperley could not have hidden, pencil and notepaper in hand, behind the curtains at 40 St. George's Square on Sunday afternoons. For the Boland children were able to sit and listen agog to "the most fascinating conversation in the world". Claiming plausibly (but wrongly) that he was the original of Sandy Arbuthnot in John Buchan's novel *Greenmantle*, Bridget exclaims:

---

[13] Boland, *At My Mother's Knee*, p. 50.

[14] Bridget gives a detailed description of "Forty" and its inhabitants in *At My Mother's Knee*, pp. 53–81. Fitzmaurice became godfather to the Bolands' youngest daughter, Anne, born in 1923.

[15] MECA Oxf., Fitzmaurice to Ryan, 28 Aug. 1922[?], Ryan Papers V/6.

[16] Bullard, *The Camels Must Go*, p. 64. Fitzmaurice lived in Pimlico, SW1, in the last years of the war but then moved to SW5.

[17] Boland, *At My Mother's Knee*, p. 70.

[18] *The Times*, 30 Mar. 1939, Obituary Notice on Mr. G. H. Fitzmaurice by Harold Temperley. However, this is not entirely consistent with what Fitzmaurice told Temperley in 1927, following the latter's request that he might pick his brains. "I'm afraid you may find me a broken reed in matters of historical research", Fitzmaurice said, but nevertheless agreed to meet him, on a regular basis if necessary, 28 Sept. 1927, Temperley Mss. I am grateful to Dr. Thomas Otte for this evidence.

And his own, true stories! As a young man, for instance, he had gone, disguised as a Turk, to stay in remote villages, taking a room if possible overlooking the graveyard, and counting, as they were buried at night, the victims of a cholera epidemic whose proportions it was suspected that the Sultan's government was concealing.[19]

Questions occurred to the children—and many more would no doubt have occurred to Temperley—but "Fitzie" was not to be interrupted in full spate. "As I said to Mark Sykes", he would invariably begin, and then regale the family with another story from one of the more exciting episodes in his life, including his career as "a very early Zionist" and the Aden frontier. The last topic would provoke him to sound off about Lawrence of Arabia, whom he regarded as a "tiresome poseur", according to Bridget. "'The fellow couldn't even speak Arabic,' he said, 'except to give orders.'"[20]

Fitzmaurice died in a London nursing home on 23 March 1939. *The Times* gave him a long and flattering obituary, to which Harold Temperley added an even more flattering postscript: "His power of inspiring awe was most remarkable", he wrote.[21] John Boland was the executor of Fitzmaurice's estate,[22] and it was he who arranged for his burial in St. Mary's Roman Catholic Cemetery at Kensal Green in north-west London. The simple gravestone can still be seen, though the lettering is badly eroded. Across the road is a public house called *The Masons' Arms*.

---

[19] Boland, *At My Mother's Knee*, p. 71.

[20] Boland, *At My Mother's Knee*, pp. 71–2. Fitzmaurice was not, of course, the only person to be irritated by Lawrence's behaviour and reputation as an Arabist. However, he went too far in saying that he could barely speak Arabic, Wilson, *Lawrence of Arabia*, p. 198.

[21] *The Times*, 30 Mar. 1939, Obituary Notice on Mr. G. H. Fitzmaurice by Harold Temperley.

[22] Fitzmaurice bequeathed his entire estate to his sister, Alice, except for £2000 which was to be given "towards the completion of the decoration of St. Patrick's Chapel in the Catholic Cathedral of Westminster as a memorial to the Irish Regiments". (Three battalions of the 'Dublins', the arrival of men from which had so cheered Fitzmaurice on the Yemen frontier, had served in the disastrous Dardanelles campaign in 1915, the 1st Battalion having been virtually obliterated during the landing at Cape Helles in April.) The Cathedral was a recent construction (1895–1903), and the decoration of the Chapel of St. Patrick and the Saints of Ireland remained incomplete a century later.

LIST OF PUBLISHED WORKS CITED

Adam, C. F., *Life of Lord Lloyd* (Macmillan: London, 1948).

Adelson, Roger, *Mark Sykes: Portrait of an Amateur* (Cape: London, 1975).

Ahmad, Feroz, "Great Britain's relations with the Young Turks, 1908–1914", *Middle Eastern Studies*, 2 (4), July 1966.

——, *The Young Turks: The Committee of Union and Progress in Turkish Politics, 1908–1914* (Clarendon Press: Oxford, 1969).

——, "The Late Ottoman Empire", in Marian Kent (ed.), *The Great Powers and the End of the Ottoman Empire* (Allen & Unwin: London, 1984).

Allen, Cptn. G. R. G., "A Ghost from Gallipoli", *Journal of the Royal United Service Institute*, 108 (630), May 1963.

Anderson, M. S., *The Eastern Question, 1774–1923: A study in international relations* (Macmillan: London, 1966).

Askew, William C., *Europe and Italy's Acquisition of Libya 1911–1912* (Duke University Press: Durham, N.C., 1942).

Beesly, Patrick, *Room 40: British Naval Intelligence 1914–18* (Hamish Hamilton: London, 1982).

Beckett, Ian F. W., "Macdonogh, Sir George Mark Watson (1865–1942)", *ODNB* [38446, accessed 30 Nov. 2006].

Berridge, G. R., *Diplomatic Classics: Selected texts from Commynes to Vattel* (Palgrave Macmillan: Basingstoke, 2004).

——, "Nation, Class, and Diplomacy: The Diminishing of the Dragomanate of the British Embassy in Constantinople, 1810–1914", in Markus Mösslang and Torsten Riotte (eds.), *Outsiders in the Diplomats' World* (Oxford University Press for the German Historical Institute: London, forthcoming).

Bidwell, R., *The Two Yemens* (Longman: Harlow, 1983).

Boland, Bridget, *At My Mother's Knee* (The Bodley Head: London, 1978).

Boland, John, *Irishman's Day: A Day in the Life of an Irish M.P.* (MacDonald: London, n.d. but circa 1944).

Bosworth, R. J. B., *Italy, the Least of the Great Powers: Italian foreign policy before the First World War* (Cambridge University Press: Cambridge, 1979).

——, "Italy and the End of the Ottoman Empire", in Marian Kent (ed.), *The Great Powers and the End of the Ottoman Empire*, 2nd ed. (Cass: London, 1996).

Brailsford, H. N., *Macedonia: Its races and their future* (Methuen: London, 1906).

British and Foreign State Papers 1905–1906, vol. XCIV (HMSO: London, 1910).

Buchan, John, *Memory Hold-the-Door* (Hodder and Stoughton: London, 1940).

Bullard, Sir Reader, *The Camels Must Go: An autobiography* (Faber and Faber: London, 1961).

Buxton, Noel, "Young Turkey after Two Years", *The Nineteenth Century and After*, vol. LXIX, Mar. 1911.

Cannon, John, "Namier, Sir Lewis Bernstein (1888–1960)", *ODNB* [35183, accessed 20 Jan. 2007].

Cecil, Hugh, *Lord Lansdowne* (FCO: London, 2004).

Chamberlain, Muriel E., "Bulwer, (William) Henry Lytton Earle, Baron Dalling and Bulwer (1801–1872)", *ODNB* [3935, accessed 3 May 2006].

Charmley, John, *Lord Lloyd and the Decline of the British Empire* (Weidenfeld and Nicolson: London, 1987).

Chirol, Valentine, *Fifty Years in a Changing World* (Cape: London, 1927).

Churchill, Winston S., *The World Crisis, 1911–1918*, vol. I (Odhams Press: London, 1938).

Crowe, Sibyl and Corp, Edward, *Our Ablest Public Servant: Sir Eyre Crowe, 1864–1925* (Merlin: Braunton, Devon, 1993).

Cunningham, Allan, *Eastern Questions in the Nineteenth Century: Collected Essays*, vol. 2, ed. E. Ingram (Cass: London, 1993).

Daly, Mary E., *Dublin: The Deposed Capital—A social and economic history, 1860–1914* (Cork University Press: Cork, 1985).

Dilks, David, *Curzon in India*, vol. 1 (Rupert Hart-Davis: London, 1969).

Djemal Pasha, *Memories of a Turkish Statesman, 1913–1919* (Hutchinson: London, 1922).

Dugdale, Edgar T. S., *Maurice de Bunsen: Diplomat and friend* (John Murray: London, 1934).

Encyclopedia Britannica, 11th ed. (Cambridge University Press: Cambridge, 1910–11).

Farragher, Seán P. CSSp and Annraoi Wyer, *Blackrock College, 1860–1995* (Paraclete Press: Blackrock, co. Dublin, Ireland, 1995).

Farragher, Seán P. CSSp, *Père Leman (1826–1880): Educator and Missionary, Founder of Blackrock College* (Paraclete Press: Dublin and London, 1988).

FitzHerbert, M., *The Man Who Was Greenmantle: A biography of Aubrey Herbert* (John Murray: London, 1983).

Foreign Office. 1893. Annual Series. No. 1242. *Diplomatic and Consular Reports on Trade and Finance. Turkey. Report for the Year 1892 on the Trade of the Consular District of Erzeroum.* Presented to Parliament June 1893.

Friedman, Isaiah, *The Question of Palestine: British-Jewish-Arab Relations: 1914–1918*, 2nd expanded ed. (Transaction: New Brunswick and London, 1992).

——, *Germany, Turkey, and Zionism, 1897–1918* (Clarendon Press: Oxford, 1977).

Garraty, John A. (ed.), *Dictionary of American Biography*, Supplement Six, 1956–1960 (Scribner's: New York, 1980).

Gavin, R. J., *Aden Under British Rule, 1839–1967* (Hurst: London, 1975).

Gilmour, D., *Curzon* (Macmillan: London, 1995).

Goldstein, Erik, "Tyrrell, William George, Baron Tyrrell (1866–1947)", *ODNB* [36608, accessed 20 Jan. 2007].

Gould, R. F., *The History of Freemasonry*, vol. VI (Caxton: London, circa 1886).

Graves, Philip P., *Briton and Turk* (Hutchinson: London, 1941).

Graves, Sir Robert, *Storm Centres of the Near East: Personal memoirs, 1879–1929* (Hutchinson: London, 1933).

Gregory, J. D., *On the Edge of Diplomacy: Rambles and Reflections* (Hutchinson: London, 1928).

Grey, Viscount Fallodon, *Twenty-Five Years, 1892–1916*, vols. I and II (Hodder & Stoughton: London, 1925).

Griscom, Lloyd C., *Diplomatically Speaking* (The Literary Guild of America: New York, 1940).

Hanioğlu, M. Sükrü, *The Young Turks in Opposition* (Oxford University Press: London, 1995).

Hardinge, Sir Arthur H., *A Diplomatist in the East* (Cape: London, 1928).

Hardinge of Penshurst, Lord [Charles], *Old Diplomacy* (John Murray: London, 1947).

Healy, Laurence, *History of Blackrock College 1860–1910*, unpublished mss.

Heffernan, Michael, "Geography, cartography and military intelligence: the Royal Geographical Society and the First World War", *Transactions of the Institute of British Geographers*, New Series, 21 (3), 1996.

Heller, Joseph, *British Policy towards the Ottoman Empire, 1908–1914* (Frank Cass: London, 1983).

Herbert, Aubrey, *Ben Kendim: A Record of Eastern Travel*, ed. D. MacCarthy (Hutchinson: London, 1924).

Hohler, Sir Thomas, *Diplomatic Petrel* (John Murray: London, 1942).

House of Commons Blue Books: *Turkey.* No. 5 (1896), vol. XCVI. Correspondence relating to the Asiatic Provinces of Turkey. Reports by Vice-Consul Fitzmaurice from Birejik, Urfa, Adiaman, and Behesni (June 1986).

Hulme-Beaman, A. G., *Twenty Years in the Near East* (Methuen: London, 1898).

James, Adm. Sir William, *The Eyes of the Navy: A Biographical Study of Admiral Sir Reginald Hall* (Methuen: London, 1955).

Jeffery, Keith, "Wilson, Sir Henry Hughes, baronet (1864–1922)", *ODNB* [36955, accessed 30 Nov. 2006].

Johnston, Sir Harry, "The final solution of the Eastern question", *The Nineteenth Century and After*, 73 (433), Mar. 1913.

Jones, Ray, *The Nineteenth Century Foreign Office: An administrative history* (Weidenfeld and Nicolson: London, 1971).

Judd, Alan, *The Quest for C: Sir Mansfield Cumming and the Founding of the British Secret Service* (HarperCollins: London, 1999).

Katz, J., *Jews and Freemasons in Europe, 1723–1939*, translated from the Hebrew by L. Oschry (Harvard University Press: Cambridge, Mass., 1970).

Kedourie, Elie, "Young Turks, Freemasons and Jews", *Middle Eastern Studies*, 7 (1), Jan. 1971.

Kennedy, Paul, "James, Sir William Milbourne (1881–1973)", rev., *ODNB*; online ed., Jan. 2007 [31283, accessed 20 Jan. 2007].

Kent, Marian, "Great Britain and the end of the Ottoman Empire, 1900–23", in Marian Kent (ed.), *The Great Powers and the End of the Ottoman Empire*, 2nd ed. (Cass: London, 1996).

Kinross, Patrick, *Atatürk: The Rebirth of a Nation* (Phoenix: London, 1996).

Landman, Samuel, "Balfour Declaration—Secret Facts Revealed", *World Jewry*, 2 (42–3), 11 Feb., 1 Mar. 1935.

——, *Great Britain, the Jews and Palestine* (New Zionist Press: London, 1936).

Langer, William L., *The Diplomacy of Imperialism, 1890–1902*, 2nd ed. (Knopf: New York, 1951).

Lawrence, T. E., *To His Biographers Robert Graves and Liddell Hart: Information about himself, in the form of letters, notes, answers to questions and conversations* (Cassell: London, 1963).

Lees-Milne, James, *Harold Nicolson: A biography, 1886–1929* (Hamish Hamilton: London, 1987).

Lewis, Bernard, *The Emergence of Modern Turkey*, 2nd ed. (Oxford University Press: London, 1968).

Lister, Charles, *Letters and Recollections, with a Memoir by His Father Lord Ribblesdale* (Fisher Unwin: London, 1917).

Lloyd, G., "Some Aspects of the Reform Movement in Turkey", *National Review*, Nov. 1908.

Lockhart, R. H. Bruce, *Memoirs of a British Agent* (Putnam: London and New York, 1932).

Lowe, C. J., "The failure of British diplomacy in the Balkans, 1914–1916", *Canadian Journal of History*, 4 (1), 1969.

——, "Grey and the Tripoli War, 1911–1912", in F. H. Hinsley (ed.), *British Foreign Policy under Sir Edward Grey* (Cambridge University Press: Cambridge, 1977).

Lynch, H. F. B., *Armenia: Travels and Studies*, in 2 volumes (Longmans, Green: London, 1901).

McCullagh, F., "The Constantinople Mutiny of April 13th", *The Fortnightly Review*, 1 July 1909.

Mackenzie, Compton, *First Athenian Memories* (Cassell: London, 1931).

Marsh, Peter, "Lord Salisbury and the Ottoman massacres", *The Journal of British Studies*, 11 (2), May 1972.

Medlicott, W. N., *The Congress of Berlin and After* (Methuen: London, 1938).

Miller, Geoffrey, *Straits: British Policy towards the Ottoman Empire and the Origins of the Dardanelles Campaign* (Hull University Press: Hull, 1997).

Moreman, T. R., "McMahon, Sir (Arthur) Henry (1862–1949)", *ODNB* [34794, accessed 20 Jan. 2007].

Morgenthau, Ambassador Henry, *Secrets of the Bosphorus*, 3rd ed. (Hutchinson: London, 1918).

Morray, David, "The selection, instruction and examination of the student interpreters of the Levant consular service 1877–1916", in John F. Healey and Venetia Porter (eds.), *Studies on Arabia in Honour of G. Rex Smith* (Oxford University Press: Oxford and New York, 2002).

Mulligan, William, "'We Can't be more Russian than the Russians': British policy during the Liman von Sanders crisis", *Diplomacy & Statecraft*, 17 (2), June 2006.

Napier, Lt. Col. H. D., *The Experiences of a Military Attaché in the Balkans* (Drane's: London, 1924).

Neave, Dorina Lady, *Romance of the Bosphorus* (Hutchinson: London, 1949).

Neilson, Keith, *Britain and the Last Tsar: British Policy and Russia, 1894–1917* (Clarendon Press: Oxford, 1995).

Newton, Lord, *Lord Lansdowne: A Biography* (Macmillan: London, 1929).

Nicolson, Harold, *Portrait of a Diplomatist: Being the life of Sir Arthur Nicolson First Lord Carnock, and a study of the origins of the Great War* (Houghton Mifflin: Boston and New York, 1930).

O'Halpin, Eunan, "Hall, Sir (William) Reginald (1870–1943)", *ODNB* [33657, accessed 20 Jan. 2007].

Oliphant, Sir Lancelot, *An Ambassador in Bonds* (Putnam: London, 1946).

Oppenheimer, Sir Francis, *Stranger Within: Autobiographical pages* (Faber and Faber: London, 1960).

Pears, Sir Edwin, *Forty Years in Constantinople: The recollections of Sir Edwin Pears 1873–1915* (Herbert Jenkins: London, 1916).

——, *Life of Abdul Hamid* (Henry Holt: New York, 1917).

Pickthall, Marmaduke, "In Defence of British Diplomacy", *The New Age*, 21 Oct. 1915, p. 590.

Platt, D. C. M., *The Cinderella Service: British Consuls since 1825* (Longman: London, 1971).

Reay Committee, Minutes of Evidence [short title; for full reference, see '*Treasury Committee…*' below].

Reinharz, Jehuda, "His Majesty's Zionist emissary: Chaim Weizmann's mission to Gibraltar in 1917", *Journal of Contemporary History*, 27 (2), Apr. 1992.

Rhodes James, Robert, *Gallipoli* (Pimlico: London, 1999).

Robbins, Keith, *Sir Edward Grey: A biography of Lord Grey of Fallodon* (Cassell: London, 1971).

Roberts, Andrew, *Salisbury: Victorian Titan* (Weidenfeld and Nicolson: London, 1999).

Romer, Major C. F., and Mainwaring, Major A. E., *The Second Battalion Royal Dublin Fusiliers in the South African War: With a Description of Operations in the Aden Hinterland* (A. L. Humphries: London, 1908).

Ronaldshay, Lord, *The Life of Lord Curzon: being the authorized biography*, vol. 2 (Ernest Benn: London, 1928).

Roskill, Stephen, *Hankey: Man of Secrets, vol. I, 1877–1918* (Collins: London, 1970).

Ryan, Sir Andrew, *The Last of the Dragomans* (Bles: London, 1951).

Salt, Jeremy, *Imperialism, Evangelism and the Ottoman Armenians, 1878–1896* (Cass: London, 1993).

Sanderson, T. H., "O'Conor, Sir Nicholas Roderick (1843–1908)", rev. H. C. G. Matthew, *ODNB* [35288, accessed 20 Jan. 2007].

Shaw, Stanford J. and Shaw, Ezel Kural, *History of the Ottoman Empire and Modern Turkey, Vol. II: Reform, Revolution, and Republic: The Rise of Modern Turkey, 1808–1975* (Cambridge University Press: Cambridge, 1977).

Shepherd, Naomi, *Ploughing Sand: British Rule in Palestine, 1917–1948* (John Murray: London, 1999).

Silberstein, Gerard E., "The Serbian campaign of 1915: its diplomatic background", *The American Historical Review*, 73 (1), Oct. 1967.

Smith, Ann, *The Story of Campion House* (James House: London, 2004).

Smith, Colin L., *The Embassy of Sir William White at Constantinople, 1886–1891* (Oxford University Press: Oxford, 1957).

Staley, Eugene, *War and the Private Investor* (Doubleday: New York, 1935).

Stein, Leonard, *The Balfour Declaration* (Vallentine-Mitchell: London, 1961).

Steiner, Zara S., *The Foreign Office and Foreign Policy, 1898–1914* (The Ashfield Press: London, 1986).

Story, Sommerville (ed.), *The Memoirs of Ismail Kemal Bey* (Constable: London, 1920).

Sonyel, Salahi Ramsdan, *The Ottoman Armenians: Victims of Great Power Diplomacy* (Rustem: London, 1987).

Sykes, Christopher, *Two Studies in Virtue* (Collins: London, 1953).

Taylor, Philip M., *The Projection of Britain: British Overseas Publicity and Propaganda 1919– 1939* (Cambridge University Press: Cambridge, 1981).

Temperley, Harold, "British policy towards parliamentary rule and constitutionalism in Turkey (1830–1914)", *Cambridge Historical Journal*, 4 (2), 1933.

Tilley, Sir John, *London to Tokyo* (Hutchinson: London, n.d.).

Tilley, Sir John and Gaselee, Stephen, *The Foreign Office* (Putnam: London and New York, 1933).

Tomes, Jason, "Lloyd, George Ambrose, first Baron Lloyd (1879–1941)", *ODNB* [34567, accessed 1 Feb. 2007].

Treasury Committee on the Organisation of Oriental Studies in London. Minutes of Evidence taken by the Committee, Cd. 4561 (HMSO: London, 1909).

Turkey No. 5 [short title; for full reference, see 'House of Commons Blue Books: *Turkey.* No. 5...' above].

Ullman, Richard H., *Anglo-Soviet Relations, 1917–1921: Intervention and the War* (Princeton University Press: Princeton, N.J., 1961).

Unal, Hasan, "Britain and Ottoman domestic politics: from the Young Turk Revolution to the Counter-Revolution, 1908–9", *Middle Eastern Studies*, 37 (2), Apr. 2001.

Vansittart, Lord, *The Mist Procession* (Hutchinson: London, 1958).

Walker, Christopher J., *Armenia: The Survival of a Nation* (Croom Helm: London, 1980).

Waterfield, Gordon, *Layard of Nineveh* (John Murray: London, 1963).

——, *Professional Diplomat: Sir Percy Loraine of Kirkharle Bt.* (Murray: London, 1973).

Waugh, Sir [Alexander] Telford, *Turkey: Yesterday, Today and Tomorrow* (Chapman & Hall's: London, 1930).

Weizmann, Chaim, *Trial and Error: The Autobiography of Chaim Weizmann* (Harper: New York, 1949).

Westrate, Bruce, *The Arab Bureau: British Policy in the Middle East, 1916–1920* (The Pennsylvania State University Press: Pennsylvania, 1992).

Wilkinson, John C., *Arabia's Frontiers: The Story of Britain's Boundary Drawing in the Desert* (I. B. Tauris: London, 1991).

Wilson, Jeremy, *Lawrence of Arabia: The Authorised Biography of T. E. Lawrence* (Minerva: London, 1990).

Wilson, Keith, *A Study in the History and Politics of the Morning Post, 1905–1926* (Edwin Mellen: Lewiston, New York, 1990).

Winstone, H. V. F., *Gertrude Bell* (Cape: London, 1978).
———, *The Illicit Adventure: The Story of Political and Military Intelligence in the Middle East from 1898 to 1926* (Cape: London, 1982).
Winterton, Earl, *Pre-War* (Macmillan: London, 1932).
Wratislaw, A. C., *A Consul in the East* (Blackwood: Edinburgh and London, 1924).
Yale, William A., "Ambassador Henry Morgenthau's Special Mission of 1917", *World Politics*, 1 (3), Apr. 1919.
Yasamee, F. A. K., *Ottoman Diplomacy: Abdülhamid II and the Great Powers 1878–1888* (The Isis Press: Istanbul, 1996).

INDEX

LIST OF PREVIOUS PUBLICATIONS BY G. R. BERRIDGE

A DICTIONARY OF DIPLOMACY (*second edition; with Alan James*)

DIPLOMACY AT THE UN (*co-editor with A. Jennings*)

DIPLOMACY: Theory and Practice (*third edition*)

DIPLOMATIC CLASSICS: Selected Texts from Commynes to Vattel

DIPLOMATIC THEORY FROM MACHIAVELLI TO KISSINGER
  (*with Maurice Keens-Soper and T. G. Otte*)

ECONOMIC POWER IN ANGLO-SOUTH AFRICAN DIPLOMACY:
  Simonstown, Sharpeville and After

INTERNATIONAL POLITICS: States, Power and Conflict since 1945 (*third edition*)

AN INTRODUCTION TO INTERNATIONAL RELATIONS (*with D. Heater*)

THE POLITICS OF THE SOUTH AFRICA RUN: European Shipping and Pretoria

RETURN TO THE UN: UN diplomacy in regional conflicts

SOUTH AFRICA, THE COLONIAL POWERS AND 'AFRICAN DEFENCE':
  The Rise and Fall of the White Entente, 1948–60

TALKING TO THE ENEMY: How States without 'Diplomatic Relations'
  Communicate